NOVELS

OF

SIR EDWARD BULWER LYTTON

Library Edition

ROMANCES.

VOL. XLI.

A STRANGE STORY

AND THE

HAUNTED AND THE HAUNTERS

BY

SIR EDWARD BULWER LYTTON, BART.

"To doubt and to be astonished is to recognize our ignorance. Hence it is that the lover of wisdom is in a certain sort a lover of mythi (φιλόμυθός πως), for the subject of mythi is the astonishing and marvellous." — SIR W. HAMILTON (after Aristotle), *Lectures on Metaphysics*, vol. i. p. 78.

LIBRARY EDITION—IN TWO VOLUMES

VOL. I.

PHILADELPHIA:
J. B. LIPPINCOTT & CO.
1865.

PREFACE.

Of the many illustrious thinkers whom the schools of France have contributed to the intellectual philosophy of our age, Victor Cousin, the most accomplished, assigns to Maine de Biran the rank of the most original.

In the successive developments of his own mind, Maine de Biran may, indeed, be said to represent the change that has been silently at work throughout the general mind of Europe since the close of the last century. He begins his career of philosopher with blind faith in Condillac and Materialism. As an intellect severely conscientious in the pursuit of truth expands amidst the perplexities it revolves, phenomena which cannot be accounted for by Condillac's sensuous theories open to his eye. To the first rudimentary life of man, the animal life, "characterized by impressions, appetites, movements, organic in their origin and ruled by the Law of Necessity," * he is compelled to add "the second or human life, from which Free-will and Self-consciousness emerge." He thus arrives at the union of mind and matter; but still a something is wanted — some key to the marvels which neither of these conditions of vital being suffices to explain. And at last the grand self-completing Thinker attains to the Third Life of Man in Man's Soul.

"There are not," says this philosopher, towards the close of his last and loftiest work — "There are not only two principles opposed to each other in Man, there are three. For there are, in him, three lives and three orders of faculties. Though all should be in accord and in harmony between the sensitive and the active faculties which constitute Man, there would still be a nature superior, a third life which would not be satisfied; which would make felt (*ferait sentir*) the truth that there is another happiness, another wisdom, another perfection, at once above the greatest human happiness, above the highest wisdom, or intellectual and moral perfection of which the human being is susceptible." †

Now, as Philosophy and Romance both take their origin in the Principle of Wonder, so in the Strange Story submitted to the Public, it will be seen that

* Œuvres inédites de Maine de Biran, vol. i. See Introduction.

† Œuvres inédites de Maine de Biran, vol. iii. p. 546 (Anthropologie).

Romance, through the freest exercise of its wildest vagaries, conducts its bewildered hero towards the same goal to which Philosophy leads its luminous Student, through far grander portents of Nature, far higher visions of Supernatural Power than Fable can yield to Fancy. That goal is defined in these noble words: "The relations (*rapports*) which exist between the elements and the products of the three lives of Man are the subjects of meditation, the fairest and finest, but also the most difficult. The Stoic Philosophy shows us all which can be most elevated in active life; but it makes abstraction of the animal nature, and absolutely fails to recognize all which belongs to the life of the spirit. Its practical morality is beyond the forces of humanity. Christianity alone embraces the whole Man. It dissimulates none of the sides of his nature, and avails itself of his miseries and his weakness in order to conduct him to his end in showing him all the want that he has of a succor more exalted." *

In the passages thus quoted I imply one of the objects for which this tale has been written; and I cite them, with a wish to acknowledge one of those priceless obligations which writings the lightest and most fantastic often incur to reasoners the most serious and profound.

* Œuvres inédites de Maine de Biran, vol. iii. p. 524.

But I here construct a romance which should have, as a romance, some interest for the general reader. I do not elaborate a treatise submitted to the logic of sages. And it is only when "in fairy fiction drest" that Romance gives admission to "truths severe."

I venture to assume that none will question my privilege to avail myself of the marvellous agencies which have ever been at the legitimate command of the fabulist.

To the highest form of romantic narrative, the Epic, critics, indeed, have declared that a supernatural machinery is indispensable. That the Drama has availed itself of the same license as the Epic, it would be unnecessary to say to the countrymen of Shakespeare, or to the generation that is yet studying the enigmas of Goethe's Faust. Prose Romance has immemorially asserted, no less than the Epic or the Drama, its heritage in the Realm of the Marvellous. The interest which attaches to the supernatural is sought in the earliest Prose Romance which modern times take from the ancient, and which, perhaps, had its origin in the lost Novels of Miletus; * and the right to invoke such interest has, ever since, been maintained by Romance through all varieties of form and fancy — from the majestic epopee of

* The Golden Ass of Apuleius.

Télémaque to the graceful phantasies of Undine, or the mighty mockeries of Gulliver's Travels, down to such comparatively commonplace elements of wonder as yet preserve from oblivion the Castle of Otranto and the old English Baron.

Now, to my mind, the true reason why a supernatural agency is indispensable to the conception of the Epic, is that the Epic is the highest and the completest form in which Art can express either Man or Nature, and that without some gleams of the supernatural, Man is not man, nor Nature, nature.

It is said, by a writer to whom an eminent philosophical critic justly applies the epithets of "pious and profound:" * — "Is it unreasonable to confess that we believe in God, not by reason of the Nature which conceals Him, but by reason of the Supernatural in Man, which alone reveals and proves Him to exist? * * * Man reveals God; for Man, by his intelligence, rises above Nature; and in virtue of this intelligence is conscious of himself as a power not only independent of, but opposed to, Nature, and capable of resisting, conquering, and controlling her." †

If the meaning involved in the argument of which

* Sir William Hamilton. Lectures on Metaphysics, p. 40.

† Jacobi — *Von der Göttlichen Dingen; Werke*, pp. 424–6.

I have here made but scanty extracts be carefully studied, I think that we shall find deeper reasons than the critics who dictated canons of taste to the last century discovered — why the supernatural is indispensable to the Epic, and why it is allowable to all works of imagination, in which Art looks on Nature with Man's inner sense of a something beyond and above her.

But the Writer who, whether in verse or prose, would avail himself of such sources of pity or terror as flow from the Marvellous, can only attain his object in proportion as the wonders he narrates are of a kind to excite the curiosity of the age he addresses.

In the brains of our time, the faculty of *Causation* is very markedly developed. People, nowadays, do not delight in the Marvellous according to the old childlike spirit. They say in one breath, "Very extraordinary!" and in the next breath, ask, "How do you account for it?" If the Author of this work has presumed to borrow from science some elements of interest for Romance, he ventures to hope that no thoughtful reader — and certainly no true son of science — will be disposed to reproach him. In fact, such illustrations from the masters of Thought were essential to the completion of the purpose which pervades the work.

That purpose, I trust, will develop itself in proportion as the story approaches the close; and whatever may appear violent or melodramatic in the catastrophe, will perhaps be found, by a reader capable of perceiving the various symbolical meanings conveyed in the story, essential to the end in which those meanings converge, and towards which the incidents that give them the character and interest of fiction have been planned and directed from the commencement.

Of course, according to the most obvious principles of art, the narrator of a fiction must be as thoroughly in earnest as if he were the narrator of facts. One could not tell the most extravagant fairy-tale so as to rouse and sustain the attention of the most infantine listener, if the tale were told as if the tale-teller did not believe in it. But when the reader lays down this Strange Story, perhaps he will detect, through all the haze of Romance, the outlines of these images suggested to his reason: Firstly, the image of sensuous, soulless Nature, such as the Materialist had conceived it. Secondly, the image of Intellect, obstinately separating all its inquiries from the belief in the spiritual essence and destiny of man, and incurring all kinds of perplexity, and resorting to all kinds of visionary speculation before it settles at last into the simple faith which unites the philosopher and the infant. And, Thirdly, the image of the erring but pure-thoughted visionary, seeking overmuch on this earth to separate soul from mind, till innocence itself is led astray by a phantom, and reason is lost in the space between earth and the stars. Whether in these pictures there be any truth worth the implying, every reader must judge for himself; and if he doubt or deny that there be any such truth, still, in that process of thought which the doubt or denial enforces, he may chance on a truth which it pleases himself to discover.

"Most of the Fables of Æsop"—thus says Montaigne in his charming essay "Of Books" *—"have several senses and meanings, of which the Mythologists choose some one that tallies with the fable. But for the most part 'tis only what presents itself at the first view, and is superficial; there being others more lively, essential, and internal, into which they have not been able to penetrate; and"—adds Montaigne —"the case is the very same with me."

* Translation 1776, vol. ii. p. 103.

A STRANGE STORY.

CHAPTER I.

In the year 18— I settled as a physician at one of the wealthiest of our great English towns, which I will designate by the initial L——. I was yet young, but I had acquired some reputation by a professional work, which is, I believe, still amongst the received authorities on the subject of which it treats. I had studied at Edinburgh and at Paris, and had borne away from both those illustrious schools of medicine whatever guarantees for future distinction the praise of professors may concede to the ambition of students. On becoming a member of the College of Physicians, I made a tour of the principal cities of Europe, taking letters of introduction to eminent medical men; and gathering, from many theories and modes of treatment, hints to enlarge the foundations of unprejudiced and comprehensive practice. I had resolved to fix my ultimate residence in London. But before this preparatory tour was completed, my resolve was changed by one of those unexpected events which determine the fate man in vain would work out for himself. In passing through the Tyrol, on my way into the north of Italy, I found in a small inn, remote from medical attendance, an English traveller, seized with acute inflammation of the lungs, and in a state of imminent danger. I devoted myself to him night and day; and, perhaps, more through careful nursing than active remedies, I had the happiness to effect his complete recovery. The traveller proved to be Julius Faber, a physician of great distinction, contented to reside, where he was born, in the provincial city of L——, but whose reputation as a profound and original pathologist was widely spread; and whose writings had formed no unimportant part of my special studies. It was during a short holiday excursion, from which he was about to return with renovated vigor, that he had been thus stricken down. The patient so accidentally met with became the founder of my professional fortunes. He conceived a warm attachment for me; perhaps the more affectionate because he was a childless bachelor, and the nephew who would succeed to his wealth evinced no desire to succeed to the toils by which the wealth had been acquired. Thus, having an heir for the one, he had long looked about for an heir to the other, and now resolved on finding that heir in me. So when we parted, Dr. Faber made me promise to correspond with him regularly, and it was not long before he disclosed by letter the plans he had formed in my favor. He said that he was growing old; his practice was beyond his strength; he needed a partner; he was not disposed to put up to sale the health of patients whom he had learned to regard as his children; money was no object to him, but it was an object close at his heart that the humanity he had served, and the reputation he had acquired, should suffer no loss in his choice of a successor. In fine, he proposed that I should at once come to L—— as his partner, with the view of succeeding to his entire practice at the end of two years, when it was his intention to retire.

The opening into fortune thus afforded to me was one that rarely presents itself to a young man entering upon an overcrowded profession. And to an aspirant less allured by the desire of fortune than the hope of distinction, the fame of the physician who thus generously offered to me the inestimable benefits of his long experience and his cordial introduction, was in itself an assurance that a metropolitan practice is not essential to a national renown.

I went then to L——, and before the two years of my partnership had expired, my success justified my kind friend's selection, and far more than realized my own expectations. I was fortunate in effecting some notable cures in the earliest cases submitted to me, and it is everything in the career of a physician when good luck wins betimes for him that confidence which patients rarely accord except to lengthened experience. To the rapid facility with which my way was made, some circumstances apart from professional skill probably contributed. I was saved from the suspicion of a medical adventurer by the accidents of birth and fortune. I belonged to an ancient family (a branch of the once powerful border clan of the Fenwicks) that had for many generations held a fair estate in the neighborhood of Windermere. As an only son I had succeeded to that estate on attaining my majority, and had sold it to pay off the debts which had been made by my father, who had the costly tastes of an antiquary and collector. The residue on the sale insured me a modest independence apart from the profits of a profession; and as I had not been legally bound to defray my father's debts, so I obtained that character for disinterestedness and integrity which always in England tends to propitiate the public to the successes achieved by industry or talent. Perhaps, too, any professional ability I might possess was the more readily conceded, because I had cultivated with assiduity the sciences and the scholarship which are collaterally connected with the study of medicine. Thus, in a word, I established a social position which came in aid of my professional repute, and silenced much of that envy which usually embitters and sometimes impedes success.

Dr. Faber retired at the end of the two years agreed upon. He went abroad; and being, though advanced in years, of a frame still robust, and habits of mind still inquiring and eager, he commenced a lengthened course of foreign travel, during which our correspondence, at first frequent, gradually languished, and finally died away.

I succeeded at once to the larger part of the practice which the labors of thirty years had secured to my predecessor. My chief rival was a Dr. Lloyd, a benevolent, fervid man, not without genius — if genius be present where judgment is absent; not without science, if that may be science which fails in precision. One of those clever, desultory men who, in adopting a profession, do not give up to it the whole force and heat of their minds. Men of that kind habitually accept a mechanical routine, because, in the exercise of their ostensible calling, their imaginative faculties are drawn away to pursuits more alluring. Therefore, in their proper vocation they are seldom bold or inventive — out of it they are sometimes both to excess. And when they do take up a novelty in their own profession, they cherish it with an obstinate tenacity and an extravagant passion unknown to those quiet philosophers who take up novelties every day, examine them with the sobriety of practised eyes, to lay down altogether, modify in part, or accept in whole, according as inductive experiment supports or destroys conjecture.

Dr. Lloyd had been esteemed a learned naturalist long before he was admitted to be a tolerable physician. Amidst the privations of his youth he had contrived to form, and with each succeeding year he had perseveringly increased, a zoological collection of creatures not alive, but, happily for the beholder, stuffed or embalmed. From what I have said, it will be truly inferred that Dr. Lloyd's earlier career as a physician had not been brilliant; but of late years he had gradually rather *aged*, than worked himself, into that professional authority and station which time confers on a thoroughly respectable man, whom no one is disposed to envy, and all are disposed to like.

Now in L—— there were two distinct social circles. That of the wealthy merchants and traders, and that of a few privileged families inhabiting a part of the town aloof from the marts of commerce, and called the Abbey Hill. These superb Areopagites exercised over the wives and daughters of the inferior citizens to whom all of L——, except the Abbey Hill, owed its prosperity, the same kind of mysterious influence which the fine ladies of May Fair and Belgravia are reported to hold over the female denizens of Bloomsbury and Marylebone.

Abbey Hill was not opulent; but it was powerful by a concentration of its resources in all matters of patronage. Abbey Hill had its own milliner and its own draper, its own confectioner, butcher, baker, and tea-dealer; and the patronage of Abbey Hill was like the patronage of royalty, less lucrative in itself than as a solemn certificate of general merit. The shops on which Abbey Hill conferred its custom were certainly not the cheapest, possibly not the best. But they were undeniably the most imposing. The proprietors were decorously pompous—the shopmen superciliously polite. They could not be more so if they had belonged to the State, and been paid by a public which they benefited and despised. The ladies of Low Town (as the city subjacent to the Hill had been styled from a date remote in the feudal ages) entered those shops with a certain awe, and left them with a certain pride. There they had learned what the Hill approved. There they had bought what the Hill had purchased. It is much in this life to be quite sure that we are in the right, whatever that conviction may cost us. Abbey Hill had been in the habit of appointing, amongst other objects of patronage, its own physician. But that habit had fallen into disuse during the latter years of my predecessor's practice. His superiority over all other medical men in the town had become so incontestable, that, though he was emphatically the doctor of Low Town, the head of its hospitals and infirmaries, and by birth related to its principal traders, still as Abbey Hill was occasionally subject to the physical infirmities of meaner mortals, so on those occasions it deemed it best not to push the point of honor to the wanton sacrifice of life. Since Low Town possessed one of the most famous physicians in England, Abbey Hill magnanimously resolved not to crush him by a rival. Abbey Hill let him feel its pulse.

When my predecessor retired, I had presumptuously expected that the Hill would have continued to suspend its normal right to a special physician, and shown to me the same generous favor it had shown to him who had declared me worthy to succeed to his honors. I had the more excuse for this presumption because the Hill had already allowed me to visit a fair proportion of its invalids, had said some very gracious things to me about the great respectability of the Fenwick family, and sent me some invitations to dinner, and a great many invitations to tea.

But my self-conceit received a notable check. Abbey Hill declared that the time had come to reassert its dormant privilege — it must have a doctor of its own choosing—a doctor who might, indeed, be permitted to visit Low Town from motives of humanity or gain, but who must emphatically assert his special allegiance to Abbey Hill by fixing his home on that venerable promontory. Miss Brabazon, a spinster of uncertain age, but undoubted pedigree, with small fortune, but high nose, which she would pleasantly observe was a proof of her descent from Humphrey Duke of Gloucester (with whom, indeed, I have no doubt, in spite of chronology, that she very often dined), was commissioned to inquire of me diplomatically, and without committing Abbey Hill too much by the overture, whether I would take a large and antiquated mansion, in which abbots were said to have lived many centuries ago, and which was still popularly styled Abbots' House, situated on the verge of the Hill, as in that case the "Hill," would think of me.

"It is a large house for a single man, I allow," said

Miss Brabazon, candidly; and then added, with a side-long glance of alarming sweetness, "But when Dr. Fenwick has taken his true position (so old a family!) amongst us, he need not long remain single, unless he prefer it."

I replied, with more asperity than the occasion called for, that I had no thought of changing my residence at present. And if the Hill wanted me, the Hill must send for me.

Two days afterwards Dr. Lloyd took Abbots' House, and in less than a week was proclaimed medical adviser to the Hill. The election had been decided by the fiat of a great lady, who reigned supreme on the sacred eminence, under the name and title of Mrs. Colonel Poyntz.

"Dr. Fenwick," said this lady, "is a clever young man and a gentleman, but he gives himself airs — the Hill does not allow any airs but its own. Besides, he is a new comer; resistance to new comers, and, indeed, to all things new, except caps and novels, is one of the bonds that keep old established societies together. Accordingly, it is by my advice that Dr. Lloyd has taken Abbots' House; the rent would be too high for his means if the Hill did not feel bound in honor to justify the trust he has placed in its patronage. I told him that all my friends, when they were in want of a doctor, would send for him; those who are my friends will do so. What the Hill does, plenty of common people down *there* will do also: — so that question is settled!"

And it was settled.

Dr. Lloyd, thus taken by the hand, soon extended the range of his visits beyond the Hill, which was not precisely a mountain of gold to doctors, and shared with myself, though in a comparatively small degree, the much more lucrative practice of Low Town.

I had no cause to grudge his success, nor did I. But to my theories of medicine his diagnosis was shallow, and his prescriptions obsolete. When we were summoned to a joint consultation, our views as to the proper course of treatment seldom agreed. Doubtless he thought I ought to have deferred to his seniority in years; but I held the doctrine which youth deems a truth and age a paradox, namely, that in science the young men are the practical elders, inasmuch as they are schooled in the latest experiences science has gathered up, while their seniors are cramped by the dogmas they were schooled to believe when the world was some decades the younger.

Meanwhile my reputation continued rapidly to advance; it became more than local; my advice was sought even by patients from the metropolis. That ambition which, conceived in early youth, had decided my career and sweetened all its labors — the ambition to take a rank and leave a name as one of the great pathologists, to whom humanity accords a grateful, if calm, renown — saw before it a level field and a certain goal.

I know not whether a success far beyond that usually

attained at the age I had reached served to increase, but it seemed to myself to justify, the main characteristic of my moral organization — intellectual pride.

Though mild and gentle to the sufferers under my care, as a necessary element of professional duty, I was intolerant of contradiction from those who belonged to my calling, or even from those who, in general opinion, opposed my favorite theories.

I had espoused a school of medical philosophy severely rigid in its inductive logic. My creed was that of stern materialism. I had a contempt for the understanding of men who accepted with credulity what they could not explain by reason. My favorite phrase was "common sense." At the same time I had no prejudice against bold discovery, and discovery necessitates conjecture, but I dismissed as idle all conjecture that could not be brought to a practical test.

As in medicine I had been the pupil of Broussais, so in metaphysics I was the disciple of Condillac. I believed with that philosopher that "all our knowledge we owe to Nature, that in the beginning we can only instruct through her lessons, and that the whole art of reasoning consists in continuing as she has compelled us to commence." Keeping natural philosophy apart from the doctrines of revelation, I never assailed the last, but I contended that by the first no accurate reasoner could arrive at the existence of the soul as a third principle of being equally distinct from mind and body. That by a miracle man might live again, was a question of faith and not of understanding. I left faith to religion, and banished it from philosophy. How define, with a precision to satisfy the logic of philosophy, what was to live again? The body? We know that the body rests in its grave till by the process of decomposition its elemental parts enter into other forms of matter. The mind? But the mind was as clearly the result of the bodily organization as the music of the harpsichord is the result of the instrumental mechanism. The mind shared the decrepitude of the body in extreme old age, and in the full vigor of youth a sudden injury to the brain might forever destroy the intellect of a Plato or a Shakspeare. But the third principle — the soul — the something lodged within the body, which yet was to survive it? Where was that soul hidden out of the ken of the anatomist? When philosophers attempted to define it, were they not compelled to confound its nature and its actions with those of the mind? Could they reduce it to the mere moral sense, varying according to education, circumstances, and physical constitution? But even the moral sense in the most virtuous of men may be swept away by a fever. Such at the time I now speak of were the views I held. Views certainly not original or pleasing; but I cherished them with as fond a tenacity as if they had been consolatory truths of which I was the first discoverer. I was intolerant to those who maintained opposite doctrines —despised them as irrational, or disliked them as insincere. Certainly if I had fulfilled the career which my ambition predicted—become the founder of a new school in pathology, and summed up my theories in academical lectures, I should have added another authority, however feeble, to the sects which circumscribe the interest of man to the life that has its close in his grave.

Possibly that which I have called my intellectual pride was more nourished than I should have been willing to grant by the self-reliance which an unusual degree of physical power is apt to bestow. Nature had blessed me with the thews of an athlete. Among the hardy youths of the Northern Athens I had been pre-eminently distinguished for feats of activity and strength. My mental labors, and the anxiety which is inseparable from the conscientious responsibilities of the medical profession, kept my health below the par of keen enjoyment, but had in no way diminished my rare muscular force. I walked through the crowd with the firm step and lofty crest of the mailed knight of old, who felt himself, in his casement of iron, a match against numbers. Thus the sense of a robust individuality, strong alike in disciplined reason and animal vigor—habituated to aid others, needing no aid for itself—contributed to render me imperious in will and arrogant in opinion. Nor were such defects injurious to me in my profession; on the contrary, aided as they were by a calm manner, and a presence not without that kind of dignity which is the livery of self-esteem, they served to impose respect and to inspire trust.

CHAPTER II.

I HAD been about six years at L—— when I became suddenly involved in a controversy with Dr. Lloyd. Just as this ill-fated man appeared at the culminating point of his professional fortunes, he had the imprudence to proclaim himself not only an enthusiastic advocate of mesmerism, as a curative process, but an ardent believer of the reality of somnambular clairvoyance as an invaluable gift of certain privileged organizations. To these doctrines I sternly opposed myself —the more sternly, perhaps, because on these doctrines Dr. Lloyd founded an argument for the existence of soul, independent of mind as of matter, and built thereon a superstructure of physiological phantasies, which, could it be substantiated, would replace every system of metaphysics on which recognized philosophy condescends to dispute.

About two years before he became a disciple rather of Puysegur than Mesmer (for Mesmer had little faith in that gift of clairvoyance of which Puysegur was, I believe, at least in modern times, the first audacious asserter), Dr. Lloyd had been afflicted with the loss of a wife many years younger than himself, and to whom he had been tenderly attached. And this bereavement, in directing the hopes that consoled him to a world beyond the grave, had served perhaps to render him more credulous of the phenomena in which he greeted additional proofs of purely spiritual existence. Certainly, if, in controverting the notions of another physiologist, I had restricted myself to that fair antagonism which belongs to scientific disputants, anxious only for the truth, I should need no apology for sincere conviction and honest argument; but when, with condescending good nature, as if to a man much younger than himself, who was ignorant of the phenomena which he nevertheless denied, Dr. Lloyd invited me to attend his *séances* and witness his cures, my *amour propre* became roused and nettled, and it seemed to me necessary to put down what I asserted to be too gross an outrage on common sense to justify the ceremony of examination. I wrote, therefore, a small pamphlet on the subject, in which I exhausted all the weapons that irony can lend to contempt. Dr. Lloyd replied, and as he was no very skilful arguer, his reply injured him perhaps more than my assault. Meanwhile, I had made some inquiries as to the moral character of his favorite clairvoyants. I imagined that I had learned enough to justify me in treating them as flagrant cheats — and himself as their egregious dupe.

Low Town soon ranged itself, with very few exceptions, on my side. The Hill at first seemed disposed to rally round its insulted physician, and to make the dispute a party question, in which the Hill would have been signally worsted, when suddenly the same lady paramount, who had secured to Dr. Lloyd the smile of the Eminence, spoke forth against him, and the Eminence frowned.

"Dr. Lloyd," said the Queen of the Hill, "is an amiable creature, but on this subject decidedly cracked. Cracked poets may be all the better for being cracked —cracked doctors are dangerous. Besides, in deserting that old-fashioned routine, his adherence to which made his claim to the Hill's approbation, and unsettling the mind of the Hill with wild revolutionary theories, Dr. Lloyd has betrayed the principles on which the Hill itself rests its social foundations. Of those principles Dr. Fenwick has made himself champion; and the Hill is bound to support him. There, the question is settled!"

And it was settled.

From the moment Mrs. Colonel Poyntz thus issued the word of command, Dr. Lloyd was demolished. His practice was gone, as well as his repute. Mortification or anger brought on a stroke of paralysis which, disabling my opponent, put an end to our controversy. An obscure Dr. Jones, who had been the special pupil and *protégé* of Dr. Lloyd, offered himself as a candidate for the Hill's tongues and pulses. The Hill gave him little encouragement. It once more suspended its electoral privileges, and, without insisting on calling me up to it, the Hill quietly called me in whenever its health needed other advice than that of its visiting apothecary. Again, it invited me, sometimes to dinner, often to tea. And again, Miss Brabazon assured me by a sidelong glance that it was no fault of hers if I was still single.

I had almost forgotten the dispute which had obtained for me so conspicuous a triumph, when one winter's night I was roused from sleep by a summons to attend Dr. Lloyd, who, attacked by a second stroke a few hours previously, had, on recovering, expressed a vehement desire to consult the rival by whom he had suffered so severely. I dressed myself in haste and hurried to his house.

A February night, sharp and bitter. An iron-grey frost below — a spectral melancholy moon above. I had to ascend the Abbey Hill by a steep, blind lane between high walls. I passed through stately gates, which stood wide open, into the garden ground that surrounded the old Abbots' House. At the end of a short carriage-drive, the dark and gloomy building cleared itself from leafless, skeleton trees; the moon resting keen and cold on its abrupt gables and lofty chimney-stacks. An old woman-servant received me at the door, and, without saying a word, led me through a long low hall, and up dreary oak stairs, to a broad landing, at which she paused for a momeut, listening. Round and about hall, staircase, and landing were ranged the dead specimens of the savage world which it had been the pride of the naturalist's life to collect. Close where I stood yawned the open jaws of the fell anaconda — its lower coils hidden, as they rested on the floor below, by the winding of the massive stairs. Against the dull wainscot walls were pendent cases stored with grotesque unfamiliar mummies, seen imperfectly by the moon that shot through the window-panes, and the candle in the old woman's hand. And as now she turned towards me, nodding her signal to follow, and went on up the shadowy passage, rows of gigantic birds—ibis and vulture, and huge sea-glaucus—glared at me in the false light of their hungry eyes.

So I entered the sick-room, and the first glance told me that my art was powerless there.

The children of the stricken widower were grouped round his bed, the eldest apparently about fifteen, the youngest four; one little girl—the only female child—was clinging to her father's neck, her face pressed to his bosom, and in that room her sobs alone were loud.

As I passed the threshold, Dr. Lloyd lifted his face, which had been bent over the weeping child, and gazed on me with an aspect of strange glee, which I failed to interpret. Then, as I stole towards him softly and slowly, he pressed his lips on the long fair tresses that streamed wild over his breast, motioned to a nurse who stood beside his pillow to take the child away, and, in a voice clearer than I could have expected in one on whose brow lay the unmistakable hand of death, he bade the nurse and the children quit the room. All went sorrowfully, but silently, save the little girl, who, borne off in the nurse's arms, continued to sob as if her heart were breaking.

I was not prepared for a scene so affecting; it moved me to the quick. My eyes wistfully followed the children so soon to be orphans, as one after one went out into the dark, chill shadow, and amidst the bloodless forms of the dumb brute nature, ranged in grisly vista beyond the death-room of man. And when the last infant shape had vanished, and the door closed with a jarring click, my sight wandered loiteringly around the chamber before I could bring myself to fix it on the broken form, beside which I now stood in all that glorious vigor of frame which had fostered the pride of my mind.

In the moment consumed by my mournful survey, the whole aspect of the place impressed itself ineffaceably on life-long remembrance. Through the high, deep-sunken casement, across which the thin, faded curtain was but half drawn, the moonlight rushed, and then settled on the floor in one shroud of white glimmer, lost under the gloom of the death-bed. The roof was low, and seemed lower still by heavy, intersecting beams, which I might have touched with my lifted hand. And the tall, guttering candle by the bedside, and the flicker from the fire struggling out through the fuel but newly heaped on it, threw their reflection on the ceiling just over my head in a reek of quivering blackness, like an angry cloud.

Suddenly I felt my arm grasped: with his left hand (the right side was already lifeless) the dying man drew me towards him nearer and nearer, till his lips almost touched my ear. And, in a voice now firm, now splitting into gasp and hiss, thus he said:

"I have summoned you to gaze on your own work!

You have stricken down my life at the moment when it was most needed by my children, and most serviceable to mankind. Had I lived a few years longer, my children would have entered on manhood, safe from the temptations of want and undejected by the charity of strangers. Thanks to you, they will be penniless orphans. Fellow-creatures afflicted by maladies your pharmacopœia had failed to reach, came to me for relief, and they found it. 'The effect of imagination,' you say. What matters, if I directed the imagination to cure? Now you have mocked the unhappy ones out of their last chance of life. They will suffer and perish. Did you believe me in error? Still you knew that my object was research into truth. You employed against your brother in art venomous drugs and a poisoned probe. Look at me! Are you satisfied with your work?"

I sought to draw back and pluck my arm from the dying man's grasp. I could not do so without using a force that would have been inhuman. His lips drew nearer still to my ear:

"Vain pretender, do not boast that you brought a genius for epigram to the service of science. Science is lenient to all who offer experiment as the test of conjecture. You are of the stuff of which inquisitors are made. You cry that truth is profaned when your dogmas are questioned. In your shallow presumption you have meted the dominions of nature, and where your eye halts its vision, you say, 'There, nature must close;'

in the bigotry which adds crime to presumption, you would stone the discoverer who, in annexing new realms to her chart, unsettles your arbitrary landmarks. Verily, retribution shall await you. In those spaces which your sight has disdained to explore you shall yourself be a lost and bewildered straggler. Hist! I see them already! The gibbering phantoms are gathering round you!"

The man's voice stopped abruptly; his eye fixed in a glazing stare; his hand relaxed its hold; he fell back on his pillow. I stole from the room; on the landing-place I met the nurse and the old woman-servant. Happily the children were not there. But I heard the wail of the female child from some room not far distant.

I whispered hurriedly to the nurse, "All is over!"—passed again under the jaws of the vast anaconda, and, on through the blind lane between the dead walls, on through the ghastly streets, under the ghastly moon, went back to my solitary home.

CHAPTER III.

It was some time before I could shake off the impression made on me by the words and the look of that dying man.

It was not that my conscience upbraided me. What had I done? Denounced that which I held, in common with most men of sense in or out of my profession, to be one of those illusions by which quackery draws profit from the wonder of ignorance. Was I to blame if I refused to treat with the grave respect due to asserted discovery in legitimate science pretensions to powers akin to the fables of wizards? was I to descend from the Academe of decorous science to examine whether a slumbering sibyl could read from a book placed at her back, or tell me at L—— what at that moment was being done by my friend at the Antipodes?

And what though Dr. Lloyd himself might be a worthy and honest man, and a sincere believer in the extravagances for which he demanded an equal credulity in others, do not honest men every day incur the penalty of ridicule if, from a defect of good sense, they make themselves ridiculous? Could I have foreseen that a satire so justly provoked would inflict so deadly a wound? Was I inhumanly barbarous because the antagonist destroyed was morbidly sensitive? My conscience, therefore, made no reproach, and the public was as little severe as my conscience. The public had been with me in our contest — the public knew nothing of my opponent's death-bed accusations — the public knew only that I attended him in his last moments — it saw me walk beside the bier that bore him to his grave — it admired the respect to his memory which I evinced in the simple tomb that I placed over his remains, inscribed with an epitaph that did justice to his unquestionable benevolence and integrity; — above all, it praised the energy with which I set on foot a subscription for his orphan children, and the generosity with which I headed that subscription by a sum that was large in proportion to my means.

To that sum I did not, indeed, limit my contribution. The sobs of the poor female child rang still on my heart. As her grief had been keener than that of her brothers, so she might be subjected to sharper trials than they, when the time came for her to fight her own way through the world; therefore I secured to her, but with such precautions that the gift could not be traced to my hand, a sum to accumulate till she was of marriageable age, and which then might suffice for a small wedding-portion; or if she remained single, for an income that would place her beyond the temptation of want, or the bitterness of a servile dependence.

That Dr. Lloyd should have died in poverty was a matter of surprise at first, for his profits during the last few years had been considerable, and his mode of life far from extravagant. But just before the date of our controversy he had been induced to assist the brother of his lost wife, who was a junior partner in a London bank, with the loan of his accumulated savings. This man proved dishonest; he embezzled that and other sums intrusted to him, and fled the country. The same sentiment of conjugal affection which had cost Dr. Lloyd his fortune kept him silent as to the cause of the loss. It was reserved for his executors to discover the treachery of the brother-in-law, whom he, poor man, would have generously screened from additional disgrace.

The Mayor of L——, a wealthy and public-spirited merchant, purchased the museum which Dr. Lloyd's passion for natural history had induced him to form; and the sum thus obtained, together with that raised by subscription, sufficed, not only to discharge all debts due by the deceased, but to insure to the orphans the benefits of an education that might fit at least the boys to enter fairly armed into that game, more of skill than of chance, in which Fortune is really so little blinded that we see, in each turn of her wheel, wealth and its honors pass away from the lax fingers of ignorance and sloth, to the resolute grasp of labor and knowledge.

Meanwhile, a relation in a distant county undertook the charge of the orphans; they disappeared from the scene, and the tides of life in a commercial community soon flowed over the place which the dead man had occupied in the thoughts of his bustling townsfolk.

One person at L——, and only one, appeared to share and inherit the rancor with which the poor physician had denounced me on his death-bed. It was a gentleman named Vigors, distantly related to the deceased, and who had been, in point of station, the most eminent of Dr. Lloyd's partisans in the controversy with myself; a man of no great scholastic acquirements, but of respectable abilities. He had that kind of power which the world concedes to respectable abilities when accompanied with a temper more than usually stern, and a moral character more than usually austere. His ruling passion was to sit in judgment upon others; and, being a magistrate, he was the most active and the most rigid of all the magistrates L—— had ever known.

Mr. Vigors at first spoke of me with great bitterness, as having ruined, and in fact killed, his friend, by the uncharitable and unfair acerbity which he declared I had brought into what ought to have been an unprejudiced examination of simple matter of fact. But finding no sympathy in these charges, he had the discretion to cease from making them, contenting himself with a solemn shake of his head if he heard my name mentioned in terms of praise, and an oracular sentence or two, such as "Time will show;" "All's well that ends well," &c. Mr. Vigors, however, mixed very little in the more convivial intercourse of the townspeople. He called himself domestic; but, in truth, he was ungenial. A stiff man, starched with self-esteem. He thought that his dignity of station was not sufficiently acknowledged by the merchants of Low Town, and his superiority of intellect not sufficiently recognized by the exclusives of the Hill. His visits were, therefore, chiefly confined to the houses of neighboring squires, to whom his reputation as a magistrate, conjoined with his solemn exterior, made him one of those oracles by which men consent to be awed on condition that the awe is not often inflicted. And though he opened his house three times a week, it was only to a select few, whom he first fed and then biologized. Electro-biology was very naturally the special entertainment of a man whom no intercourse ever pleased in which his will was not imposed upon others. Therefore he only invited to his table persons whom he could stare into the abnegation of their senses, willing to say that beef was lamb, or brandy was coffee, according as he willed them to say. And, no doubt, the persons asked would have said anything he willed, so long as they had, in substance, as well as in idea, the beef and the brandy, the lamb and the coffee. I did not, then, often meet Mr. Vigors at the houses in which I occasionally spent my evenings. I heard of his enmity as a man safe in his home hears the sough of a wind on a common without. If now and then we chanced to pass in the streets, he looked up at me (he was a small man walking on tiptoe) with the sullen scowl of dislike. And, from the height of my stature, I dropped upon the small man and sullen scowl the affable smile of supreme indifference.

CHAPTER IV.

I HAD now arrived at that age when an ambitious man, satisfied with his progress in the world without, begins to feel, in the cravings of unsatisfied affection, the void of a solitary hearth. I resolved to marry, and looked out for a wife. I had never hitherto admitted into my life the passion of love. In fact, I had regarded that passion, even in my earlier youth, with a certain superb contempt — as a malady engendered by an effeminate idleness, and fostered by a sickly imagination.

I wished to find in a wife a rational companion, an affectionate and trustworthy friend. No views of matrimony could be less romantic, more soberly sensible, than those which I conceived. Nor were my requirements mercenary or presumptuous. I cared not for fortune; I asked nothing from connections. My ambition was exclusively professional; it could be served by no titled kindred, accelerated by no wealthy dower. I was no slave to beauty. I did not seek in a wife the accomplishments of a finishing school-teacher.

Having decided that the time had come to select my helpmate, I imagined that I should find no difficulty in a choice that my reason would approve. But day upon day, week upon week, passed away, and though among the families I visited there were many young ladies who possessed more than the qualifications with which I conceived that I should be amply contented, and by whom I might flatter myself that my proposals would not be disdained, I saw not one to whose life-long companionship I should not infinitely have preferred the solitude I found so irksome.

One evening, in returning home from visiting a poor female patient whom I attended gratuitously, and whose case demanded more thought than that of any other in my list — for though it had been considered hopeless in the hospital, and she had come home to die, I felt certain that I could save her, and she seemed recovering under my care — one evening, it was the fifteenth of May, I found myself just before the gates of the house that had been inhabited by Dr. Lloyd. Since his death the house had been unoccupied; the rent asked for it by the proprietor was considered high; and from the sacred Hill on which it was situated, shyness or pride banished the wealthier traders. The garden gates stood wide open, as they had stood in the winter night on which I had passed through them to the chamber of death. The remembrance of that death-bed came vividly before me, and the dying man's fantastic threat rang again in my startled ears. An irresistible impulse, which I could not then account for, and which I cannot account for now — an impulse the reverse of that which usually makes us turn away with quickened step from a spot that recalls associations of pain — urged me on through the open gates up the neglected, grass-grown road, urged me to look, under the westering sun of the joyous spring, at that house which I had never seen but in the gloom of a winter night, under the melancholy moon. As the building came in sight, with dark-red bricks, partially overgrown with ivy, I perceived that it was no longer unoccupied. I saw forms passing athwart the open windows; a van laden with articles of furniture stood before the door; a servant in livery was beside it giving directions to the men who were unloading. Evidently some family was just entering into possession. I felt somewhat ashamed of my trespass, and turned round quickly to retrace my steps. I had retreated but a few yards, when I saw before me at the entrance gates Mr. Vigors, walking beside a lady apparently of middle age; while, just at hand, a path cut through the shrubs gave view of a small wicket-gate at the end of the grounds. I felt unwilling not only to meet the lady, whom I guessed to be the new occupier, and to whom I should have to make a somewhat awkward apology for intrusion, but still more to encounter the scornful look of Mr. Vigors, in what appeared to my pride a false or undignified position. Involuntarily, therefore, I turned down the path which would favor my escape unobserved. When about half way between the house and the wicket-gate, the shrubs that had clothed the path on either side suddenly opened to the left, bringing into view a circle of sward, surrounded by irregular fragments of old brickwork partially covered with ferns, creepers, or rock-plants, weeds, or wild flowers; and, in the centre of the circle, a fountain, or rather well, over which was built a Gothic, monastic dome or canopy, resting on small Norman columns, time-worn, dilapidated. A large willow overhung this unmistakable relic of the ancient abbey. There was an air of antiquity, romance, legend about this spot, so abruptly disclosed amidst the delicate green of the young shrubberies. But it was not the ruined wall nor the Gothic well that chained my footstep and charmed my eye.

It was a solitary human form, seated amidst the mournful ruins.

The form was so slight, the face so young, that at the first glance I murmured to myself, "What a lovely child!" But as my eye lingered, it recognized in the upturned, thoughtful brow, in the sweet, serious aspect, in the rounded outlines of that slender shape, the inexpressible dignity of virgin woman.

A book was on her lap, at her feet a little basket, half filled with violets and blossoms culled from the rock-plants that nestled amidst the ruins. Behind her the willow, like an emerald waterfall, showered down its arching abundant green, bough after bough, from the tree-top to the sward, descending in wavy verdure, bright towards the summit, in the smile of the setting sun, and darkening into shadow as it neared the earth.

She did not notice, she did not see me; her eyes were fixed upon the horizon, where it sloped farthest into space, above the tree-tops and the ruins; fixed so intently that mechanically I turned my own gaze to follow the flight of hers. It was as if she watched for some expected, familiar sign to grow out from the depths of heaven; perhaps to greet, before other eyes beheld it, the ray of the earliest star.

The birds dropped from the boughs on the turf around her, so fearlessly that one alighted amidst the flowers in the little basket at her feet. There is a famous German poem, which I had read in my youth, called the Maiden from Abroad, variously supposed to be an allegory of Spring or of Poetry, according to the choice of commentators; it seemed to me as if the poem had been made for her. Verily, indeed, in her, poet or painter might have seen an image equally true to either of those adorners of the earth; both outwardly a delight to sense, yet both wakening up thoughts within us, not sad, but akin to sadness.

I heard now a step behind me, and a voice which I recognized to be that of Mr. Vigors. I broke from the charm by which I had been so lingeringly spell-bound, hurried on confusedly, gained the wicket-gate, from which a short flight of stairs descended into the common thoroughfare. And there the every-day life lay again before me. On the opposite side, houses, shops, church spires; a few steps more, and the bustling streets! How immeasurably far from, yet how familiarly near to, the world in which we move and have being is that fairy land of romance which opens out from the hard earth before us, when Love steals at first to our side; fading back into the hard earth again as Love smiles or sighs its farewell!

CHAPTER V.

AND before that evening I had looked on Mr. Vigors with supreme indifference! — what importance he now assumed in my eyes! The lady with whom I had seen him was doubtless the new tenant of that house in which the young creature by whom my heart was so strangely moved evidently had her home. Most probably the relation between the two ladies was that of mother and daughter. Mr. Vigors, the friend of one, might himself be related to both—might prejudice them against me — might — here, starting up, I snapped the thread of conjecture, for right before my eyes, on the table beside which I had seated myself on entering my room, lay a card of invitation :

MRS. POYNTZ,
At Home,
Wednesday, May 15th.
Early.

Mrs. Poyntz — Mrs. Colonel Poyntz? the Queen of the Hill. There, at her house, I could not fail to learn all about the new comers, who could never without her sanction have settled on her domain.

I hastily changed my dress, and, with beating heart, wound my way up the venerable eminence.

I did not pass through the lane which led direct to Abbots' House (for that old building stood solitary amidst its grounds, a little apart from the spacious platform on which the society of the Hill was concentrated), but up the broad causeway, with vistaed gas-lamps; the gayer shops still unclosed, the tide of busy life only slowly ebbing from the still animated street, on to a square, in which the four main thoroughfares of the city converged, and which formed the boundary of Low Town. A huge dark archway, popularly called Monk's Gate, at the angle of this square, made the entrance to Abbey Hill. When the arch was passed, one felt at once that one was in the town of a former day. The pavement was narrow, and rugged; the shops small, their upper stories projecting, with, here and there, plastered fronts, quaintly arabesqued. An ascent, short, but steep and tortuous, conducted at once to the old Abbey Church, nobly situated in a vast quadrangle, round which were the genteel and gloomy dwellings of the Areopagites of the Hill. More genteel and less gloomy than the rest—lights at the windows and flowers on the balcony — stood forth, flanked by a garden wall at either side, the mansion of Mrs. Colonel Poyntz.

As I entered the drawing-room, I heard the voice of the hostess; it was a voice clear, decided, metallic, bell-like, uttering these words: "Taken Abbots' House? I will tell you."

CHAPTER VI.

Mrs. Poyntz was seated on the sofa; at her right sat fat Mrs. Bruce, who was a Scotch lord's granddaughter; at her left thin Miss Brabazon, who was an Irish baronet's neice. Around her—a few seated, many standing — had grouped all the guests, save two old gentlemen, who remained aloof with Colonel Poyntz near the whist-table, waiting for the fourth old gentleman, who was to make up the rubber, but who was at that moment spell-bound in the magic circle, which curiosity, that strongest of social demons, had attracted round the hostess.

"Taken Abbots' House? I will tell you —— Ah, Dr. Fenwick, charmed to see you. You know Abbots' House is let at last? Well, Miss Brabazon, dear, you ask who has taken it. I will inform you — a particular friend of mine."

"Indeed! Dear me!" said Miss Brabazon, looking confused. "I hope I did not say anything to ——"

"Wound my feelings. Not in the least. You said your uncle, Sir Phelim, employed a coachmaker named Ashleigh, that Ashleigh was an uncommon name, though Ashley was a common one; you intimated an appalling suspicion that the Mrs. Ashleigh who had come to the Hill was the coachmaker's widow. I relieve your mind — she is not; she is the widow of Gilbert Ashleigh, of Kirby Hall."

"Gilbert Ashleigh," said one of the guests, a bachelor, whose parents had reared him for the Church, but who, like poor Goldsmith, did not think himself good enough for it — a mistake of over-modesty, for he matured into a very harmless creature: "Gilbert Ashleigh. I was at Oxford with him — a gentleman commoner of Christ Church. Good-looking man — very; *sapped*——"

"Sapped! what's that? — Oh, studied. That he did all his life. He married young — Anne Chaloner; she and I were girls together; married the same year. They settled at Kirby Hall — nice place, but dull. Poyntz and I spent a Christmas there. Ashleigh when he talked was charming, but he talked very little. Anne, when she talked, was commonplace, and she talked very much. Naturally, poor thing, she was so happy. Poyntz and I did not spend another Christmas there. Friendship is long, but life is short. Gilbert Ashleigh's life was short, indeed; he died in the seventh year of his marriage, leaving only one child, a girl. Since then, though I never spent another Christmas at Kirby Hall, I have frequently spent a day there, doing my best to cheer up Anne. She was no longer talkative, poor dear. Wrapt up in her child, who has now grown into a beautiful girl of eighteen — such eyes, her father's — the real dark-blue — rare; sweet creature, but delicate; not, I hope, consumptive, but delicate; quiet — wants life. My girl Jane adores her. Jane has life enough for two."

"Is Miss Ashleigh the heiress to Kirby Hall?" asked Mrs. Bruce, who had an unmarried son.

"No. Kirby Hall passed to Ashleigh Sumner, the male heir, a cousin. And the luckiest of cousins! Gilbert's sister, showy woman (indeed all show), had contrived to marry her kinsman, Sir Walter Ashleigh Haughton, the head of the Ashleigh family — just the man made to be the reflector of a showy woman! He died years ago, leaving an only son, Sir James, who was killed last winter, by a fall from his horse. And here, again, Ashleigh Sumner proved to be the male heir-at-law. During the minority of this fortunate youth, Mrs. Ashleigh had rented Kirby Hall of his guardian. He is now just coming of age, and that is why she leaves. Lilian Ashleigh will have, however, a very good fortune — is what we genteel paupers call an heiress. Is there anything more you want to know?"

Said thin Miss Brabazon, who took advantage of her thinness to wedge herself into every one's affairs, "A most interesting account. What a nice place Abbots' House could be made with a little taste! So aristocratic! Just what I should like if I could afford it! The drawing-room should be done up in the Moorish style, with geranium-colored silk curtains like dear Lady L——'s boudoir at Twickenham. And Mrs. Ashleigh has taken the house! on lease, too, I suppose!" Here Miss Brabazon fluttered her fan angrily, and then exclaimed, "But what on earth brings Mrs. Ashleigh here?"

Answered Mrs. Colonel Poyntz, with the military

frankness by which she kept her company in good humor, as well as awe:

"Why do any of us come here? Can any one tell me?"

There was a blank silence, which the hostess herself was first to break.

"None of us present can say why we came here. I can tell you why Mrs. Ashleigh came. Our neighbor, Mr. Vigors, is a distant connection of the late Gilbert Ashleigh, one of the executors to his will, and the guardian to the heir-at-law. About ten days ago Mr. Vigors called on me, for the first time since I felt it my duty to express my disapprobation of the strange vagaries so unhappily conceived by our poor dear friend Dr. Lloyd. And when he had taken the chair, just where you now sit, Dr. Fenwick, he said, in a sepulchral voice, stretching out two fingers, so—as if I was one of the what-do-you-call-'ems who go to sleep when he bids them: 'Marm, you know Mrs. Ashleigh? You correspond with her.' 'Yes, Mr. Vigors; is there any crime in that? You look as if there were.' 'No crime, marm,' said the man, quite seriously. 'Mrs. Ashleigh is a lady of amiable temper, and you are a woman of masculine understanding.'"

Here there was a general titter. Mrs. Colonel Poyntz hushed it with a look of severe surprise: "What is there to laugh at? All women would be men if they could. If my understanding is masculine, so much the better for me. I thanked Mr. Vigors for his very handsome compliment, and he then went on to say, 'that though Mrs. Ashleigh would now have to leave Kirby Hall in a very few weeks, she seemed quite unable to make up her mind where to go; that it had occurred to him that, as Miss Ashleigh was of an age to see a little of the world, she ought not to remain buried in the country; while, being of a quiet mind, she recoiled from the dissipations of London. Between the seclusion of the one and the turmoil of the other, the society of L—— was a happy medium. He should be glad of my opinion. He had put off asking for it, because he owned his belief that I had behaved unkindly to his lamented friend, Dr. Lloyd; but he now found himself in rather an awkward position. His ward, young Sumner, had prudently resolved on fixing his country residence at Kirby Hall, rather than at Haughton Park, the much larger seat, which had so suddenly passed to his inheritance, and which he could not occupy without a vast establishment, that to a single man, so young, would be but a cumbersome and costly trouble. Mr. Vigors was pledged to his ward to obtain him possession of Kirby Hall the precise day agreed upon, but Mrs. Ashleigh did not seem disposed to stir—could not decide where else to go. Mr. Vigors was loth to press hard on his old friend's widow and child. It was a thousand pities Mrs. Ashleigh could not make up her mind; she had had ample time for preparation. A word from me at this moment, would be an effective kindness. Abbots' House was vacant, with a garden so extensive that the ladies would not miss the country. Another party was after it, but—' 'Say no more,' I cried; 'no party but my dear old friend Anne Ashleigh shall have Abbots' House. So that question is settled.' I dismissed Mr. Vigors, sent for my carriage—that is, for Mr. Barker's yellow fly and his best horses—and drove that very day to Kirby Hall, which, though not in this county, is only twenty-five miles distant. I slept there that night. By nine o'clock the next morning I had secured Mrs. Ashleigh's consent, on the promise to save her all trouble; came back, sent for the landlord, settled the rent, lease, agreement; engaged Forbes' vans to remove the furniture from Kirby Hall; told Forbes to begin with the beds. When her own bed came, which was last night, Anne Ashleigh came too. I have seen her this morning. She likes the place, so does Lilian. I asked them to meet you all here to-night; but Mrs. Ashleigh was tired. The last of the furniture was to arrive to-day; and though dear Mrs. Ashleigh is an undecided character, she is not inactive. But it is not only the planning where to put tables and chairs that would have tired her to-day; she has had Mr. Vigors on her hands all the afternoon, and he has been—here's her little note—what are the words? no doubt, 'most overpowering and oppressive'—no, 'most kind and attentive'—different words, but, as applied to Mr. Vigors, they mean the same thing.

"And now, next Monday—we must leave them in

peace till then — you will all call on the Ashleighs. The Hill knows what is due to itself; it cannot delegate to Mr. Vigors, a respectable man indeed, but who does not belong to its set, its own proper course of action towards those who would shelter themselves on its bosom. The Hill cannot be kind and attentive, overpowering or oppressive, by proxy. To those new-born into its family circle it cannot be an indifferent godmother; it has towards them all the feelings of a mother, or of a stepmother, as the case may be. Where it says, 'This can be no child of mine,' it is a stepmother, indeed; but, in all those whom I have presented to its arms, it has hitherto, I am proud to say, recognized desirable acquaintances, and to them the Hill has been a mother. And now, my dear Mr. Sloman, go to your rubber; Poyntz is impatient, though he don't show it. Miss Brabazon, love, we all long to see you seated at the piano — you play so divinely! Something gay, if you please; something gay, but not very noisy — Mr. Leopold Smythe will turn the leaves for you. Mrs. Bruce, your own favorite set at vingt-un, with four new recruits. Dr. Fenwick, you are like me, don't play cards, and don't care for music; sit here, and talk or not, as you please, while I knit."

The other guests thus disposed of, some at the card-tables, some round the piano, I placed myself at Mrs. Poyntz's side, on a seat niched in the recess of a window which an evening unusually warm for the month of May permitted to be left open. I was next to one who had known Lilian as a child, one from whom I had learned by what sweet name to call the image which my thoughts had already shrined. How much that I still longed to know she could tell me! But in what form of question could I lead to the subject, yet not betray my absorbing interest in it? Longing to speak, I felt as if stricken dumb; stealing an unquiet glance towards the face beside me, and deeply impressed with that truth which the Hill had long ago reverently acknowledged, viz., that Mrs. Colonel Poyntz was a very superior woman — a very powerful creature.

And there she sat knitting — rapidly, firmly; a woman somewhat on the other side of forty, complexion a bronzed paleness, hair a bronzed brown, in strong ringlets cropped short behind — handsome hair for a man; lips that, when closed, showed inflexible decision, when speaking, became supple and flexile with an easy humor and a vigilant finesse; eyes of a red hazel, quick but steady; observant, piercing, dauntless eyes; altogether a fine countenance — would have been a very fine countenance in a man; profile sharp, straight, clear-cut, with an expression, when in repose, like that of a sphinx; a frame robust, not corpulent, of middle height, but with an air and carriage that made her appear tall; peculiarly white firm, hands, indicative of vigorous health, not a vein visible on the surface.

There she sat knitting, knitting, and I by her side,

gazing now on herself, now on her work, with a vague idea that the threads in the skein of my own web of love or of life were passing quick through those noiseless fingers. And, indeed, in every web of romance, the fondest one of the Parcæ is sure to be some matter-of-fact She, Social Destiny, as little akin to romance herself—as was this worldly Queen of the Hill.

CHAPTER VII.

I HAVE given a sketch of the outward woman of Mrs. Colonel Poyntz. The inner woman was a recondite mystery, deep as that of the sphinx, whose features her own resembled. But between the outward and the inward woman there is ever a third woman — the conventional woman — such as the whole human being appears to the world — always mantled, sometimes masked.

I am told that the fine people of London do not recognize the title of "Mrs. Colonel." If that be true, the fine people of London must be clearly in the wrong, for no people in the universe could be finer than the fine people of Abbey Hill; and they considered their sovereign had as good a right to the title of Mrs. Colonel as the Queen of England has to that of "our Gracious Lady." But Mrs. Poyntz, herself, never assumed the title of Mrs. Colonel; it never appeared on her cards any more than the title of "Gracious Lady" appears on the cards which convey the invitation that a Lord Steward or Lord Chamberlain is commanded by her Majesty to issue. To titles, indeed, Mrs. Poyntz evinced no superstitious reverence. Two peeresses, related to her, not distantly, were in the habit of paying her a yearly visit, which lasted two or three days. The Hill considered these visits an honor to its eminence. Mrs. Poyntz never seemed to esteem them an honor to herself; never boasted of them; never sought to show off her grand relations, nor put herself the least out of the way to receive them. Her mode of life was free from ostentation. She had the advantage of being a few hundreds a year richer than any other inhabitant of the Hill; but she did not devote her superior resources to the invidious exhibition of superior splendor. Like a wise sovereign the revenues of her exchequer were applied to the benefit of her subjects, and not to the vanity of egotistical parade. As no one else on the Hill kept a carriage, she declined to keep one. Her entertainments were simple, but numerous. Twice a week she received the Hill, and was genuinely at home to it. She contrived to make her parties proverbially agreeable. The refreshments were of the same kind as those which the poorest of her old maids of honor might proffer; but they were better of their kind, the best of their kind—the best tea, the best lemonade, the best cakes. Her rooms had an air of comfort, which was peculiar to them. They looked like rooms accustomed to receive, and receive in a friendly way; well warmed, well lighted, card-tables and piano each in the place that made cards and music inviting. On the walls a few old family portraits, and three or four other pictures said to be valuable and certainly pleasing, two Watteaus, a Canaletti, a Weenix—plenty of easy-chairs and settees covered with a cheerful chintz. In the arrangement of the furniture generally, an indescribable careless elegance. She herself was studiously plain in dress, more conspicuously free from jewellery and trinkets than any married lady on the Hill. But I have heard from those who were authorities on such a subject, that she was never seen in a dress of the last year's fashion. She adopted the mode as it came out, just enough to show that she was aware it was out; but with a sober reserve, as much as to say, "I adopt the fashion as far as it suits myself; I do not permit the fashion to adopt me." In short, Mrs. Colonel Poyntz was sometimes rough, sometimes coarse, always masculine, and yet somehow or other masculine in a womanly way; but she was never vulgar because never affected. It was impossible not to allow that she was a thorough gentlewoman, and she could do things that lower other gentlewomen, without any loss of dignity. Thus she was an admirable mimic, certainly in itself the least ladylike condescension of humor. But when she mimicked, it was with so tranquil a gravity, or so royal a good humor, that one could only say, "What talents for society dear Mrs. Colonel has!" As she was a gentlewoman emphatically, so the other colonel, the he-colonel, was emphatically a gentleman; rather shy, but not cold; hating trouble of every kind, pleased to seem a cipher in his own house. If the sole study of Mrs. Colonel had been to make her husband comfortable, she could not have succeeded better than by bringing friends about him and then taking them off his hands. Colonel Poyntz, the he-colonel, had seen, in his youth, actual service; but had retired from his profession many years ago, shortly after his marriage. He was a younger brother of one of the principal squires in the county; inherited the house he lived in, with some other valuable property in and about L——, from an uncle; was considered a good landlord; and popular in Low Town, though he never interfered in its affairs. He was punctiliously neat in his dress; a thin, youthful figure, crowned with a thick, youthful wig. He never seemed to read anything but the newspapers and the Meteorological Journal; was supposed to be the most weather-wise man in all L——. He had another intellectual predilection—whist. But in that he had less reputation for wisdom. Perhaps it requires a rarer combination of mental faculties to win an odd trick than to divine a fall in the glass. For the rest, the he-colonel, many years older than his wife, despite the thin, youthful figure, was an admirable aide-de-camp to the general in command, Mrs. Colonel; and she could not have found one more obedient, more devoted, or more proud of a distinguished chief.

In giving to Mrs. Colonel Poyntz the appellation of Queen of the Hill, let there be no mistake. She was not a constitutional sovereign; her monarchy was absolute. All her proclamations had the force of laws.

Such ascendancy could not have been attained without considerable talents for acquiring and keeping it. Amidst all her off-hand, brisk, imperious frankness, she had the ineffable discrimination of tact. Whether civil or rude, she was never civil or rude but what she carried public opinion along with her. Her knowledge of general society must have been limited, as must be that of all female sovereigns. But she seemed gifted with an intuitive knowledge of human nature, which she applied to her special ambition of ruling it. I have not a doubt that if she had been suddenly transferred, a perfect stranger, to the world of London, she would have soon forced her way to its selectest circles, and, when once there, held her own against a duchess.

I have said that she was not affected; this might be one cause of her sway over a set in which nearly every other woman was trying rather to seem, than to be, a somebody.

But if Mrs. Colonel Poyntz was not artificial, she was artful, or perhaps I might more justly say, artistic. In all she said and did there were conduct, system, plan. She could be a most serviceable friend, a most damaging enemy; yet I believe she seldom indulged in strong likings or strong hatreds. All was policy — a policy akin to that of a grand party chief, determined to raise up those whom, for any reason of state, it was prudent to favor, and to put down those whom, for any reason of state, it was expedient to humble or to crush.

Ever since the controversy with Dr. Lloyd, this lady had honored me with her benignest countenance. And nothing could be more adroit than the manner in which, while imposing me on others as an oracular authority, she sought to subject to her will the oracle itself.

She was in the habit of addressing me in a sort of motherly way, as if she had the deepest interest in my welfare, happiness, and reputation. And thus, in every compliment, in every seeming mark of respect, she maintained the superior dignity of one who takes from responsible station the duty to encourage rising merit; so that, somehow or other, despite all that pride which made me believe that I needed no helping hand to advance or to clear my way through the world, I could not shake off from my mind the impression that I was mysteriously patronized by Mrs. Colonel Poyntz.

We might have sat together five minutes, side by side — in silence as complete as if in the cave of Tro phonius — when, without looking up from her work, Mrs. Poyntz said, abruptly :

"I am thinking about you, Dr. Fenwick. And you — are thinking about some other woman. Ungrateful man!"

"Unjust accusation! My very silence should prove

how intently my thoughts were fixed on you, and on the weird web which springs under your hand in meshes that bewilder the gaze and snare the attention."

Mrs. Poyntz looked up at me for a moment — one rapid glance of the bright red hazel eye — and said:

"Was I really in your thoughts? Answer truly."

"Truly, I answer, you were."

"That is strange! Who can it be?"

"Who can it be? What do you mean?"

"If you were thinking of me, it was in connection with some other person — some other person of my own sex. It is certainly not poor dear Miss Brabazon. Who else can it be?"

Again the red eye shot over me, and I felt my cheek redden beneath it.

"Hush!" she said, lowering her voice; "you are in love!"

"In love! — I! Permit me to ask you why you think so?"

"The signs are unmistakable; you are altered in your manner, even in the expression of your face, since I last saw you; your manner is generally quiet and observant, it is now restless and distracted; your expression of face is generally proud and serene, it is now humbled and troubled. You have something on your mind! It is not anxiety for your reputation, that is established; nor for your fortune, that is made; it is not anxiety for a patient, or you would scarcely be here. But anxiety it is, an anxiety that is remote from your profession, that touches your heart and is new to it!"

I was startled, almost awed. But I tried to cover my confusion with a forced laugh.

"Profound observer! Subtle analyst! You have convinced me that I must be in love, though I did not suspect it before. But when I strive to conjecture the object, I am as much perplexed as yourself; and with you, I ask, who can it be?"

"Whoever it be," said Mrs. Poyntz, who had paused, while I spoke, from her knitting, and now resumed it very slowly and very carefully, as if her mind and her knitting worked in unison together; "whoever it be, love in you would be serious; and, with or without love, marriage is a serious thing to us all. It is not every pretty girl that would suit Allen Fenwick."

"Alas! is there any pretty girl whom Allen Fenwick would suit?"

"Tut! You should be above the fretful vanity that lays traps for a compliment. Yes; the time has come in your life and your career when you would do well to marry. I give my consent to that," she added, with a smile as if in jest, and a slight nod as if in earnest. The knitting here went on more decidedly, more quickly. "But I do not yet see the person. No! 'Tis a pity, Allen Fenwick" (whenever Mrs. Poyntz called me by my Christian name, she always assumed her majestic, motherly manner) — "a pity that, with your birth, energies, perseverance, talents, and, let me add, your advantages of manner and person — a pity that you did not choose a career that might achieve higher fortunes and louder fame than the most brilliant success can give to a provincial physician. But in that very choice you interest me. My choice has been much the same. A small circle, but the first in it. Yet, had I been a man, or had my dear colonel been a man whom it was in the power of a woman's art to raise one step higher in that metaphorical ladder which is not the ladder of the angels, why, then — what then? No matter! I am contented. I transfer my ambition to Jane. Do you not think her handsome?"

"There can be no doubt of that," said I, carelessly and naturally.

"I have settled Jane's lot in my own mind," resumed Mrs. Poyntz, striking firm into another row of knitting. "She will marry a country gentleman of large estate. He will go into parliament. She will study his advancement as I study Poyntz's comfort. If he be clever, she will help to make him a minister; if he be not clever, his wealth will make her a personage, and lift him into a personage's husband. And, now that you see I have no matrimonial designs on you, Allen Fenwick, think if it will be worth while to confide in me. Possibly I may be useful ——"

"I know not how to thank you. But as yet, I have nothing to confide."

While thus saying, I turned my eyes towards the open window beside which I sat. It was a beautiful soft night. The May moon in all her splendor. The town stretched, far and wide, below with all its numberless lights; below — but somewhat distant; an intervening space was covered, here, by the broad quadrangle (in the midst of which stood, massive and lonely, the grand old church); and, there by the gardens and scattered cottages or mansions that clothed the sides of the hill.

"Is not that house," I said, after a short pause, "yonder, with the three gables, the one in which — in which poor Dr. Lloyd lived — Abbots' House?"

I spoke abruptly, as if to intimate my desire to change the subject of conversation. My hostess stopped her knitting, half rose, looked forth.

"Yes. But what a lovely night! How is it that the moon blends into harmony things of which the sun only marks the contrast? That stately, old church-tower, grey with its thousand years — those vulgar tile-roofs and chimney-pots raw in the freshness of yesterday; now, under the moonlight, all melt into one indivisible charm!"

As my hostess thus spoke, she had left her seat, taking her work with her, and passed from the window into the balcony. It was not often that Mrs. Poyntz condescended to admit what is called "sentiment" into the range of her sharp, practical, worldly talk, but she did so at times; always when she did, giving me the notion of an intellect much too comprehensive not to allow that sentiment has a place in this life, but keeping it in its proper place, by that mixture of affability and indifference with which some high-born beauty allows the genius, but checks the presumption, of a charming and penniless poet. For a few minutes her eyes roved over the scene in evident enjoyment; then, as they slowly settled upon the three gables of Abbots' House, her face regained that something of hardness which belonged to its decided character; her fingers again mechanically resumed her knitting, and she said, in her clear, unsoftened, metallic chime of voice, "Can you guess why I took so much trouble to oblige Mr. Vigors and locate Mrs. Ashleigh yonder?"

"You favored us with a full explanation of your reasons."

"Some of my reasons; not the main one. People who undertake the task of governing others, as I do, be their rule a kingdom or a hamlet, must adopt a principle of government and adhere to it. The principle that suits best with the Hill is respect for the Proprieties. We have not much money, *entre nous*; we have no great rank. Our policy is, then, to set up the Proprieties as an influence which money must court and rank is afraid of. I had learned just before Mr. Vigors called on me that Lady Sarah Bellasis entertained the idea of hiring Abbots' House. London has set its face against her; a provincial town would be more charitable. An earl's daughter, with a good income and an awfully bad name, of the best manners and of the worst morals, would have made sad havoc among the Proprieties. How many of our primmest old maids would have deserted tea and Mrs. Poyntz for champagne and her ladyship? The Hill was never in so imminent a danger. Rather than Lady Sarah Bellasis should have taken that house, I would have taken it myself, and stocked it with owls.

"Mrs. Ashleigh turned up just in the critical moment. Lady Sarah is foiled, the Proprieties safe, and so that question is settled."

"And it will be pleasant to have your early friend so near you."

Mrs. Poyntz lifted her eyes full upon me:

"Do you know Mrs. Ashleigh?"

"Not in the least."

"She has many virtues and few ideas. She is commonplace weak, as I am commonplace strong. But commonplace weak can be very lovable. Her husband, a man of genius and learning, gave her his whole heart—a heart worth having, but he was not ambitious, and he despised the world."

"I think you said your daughter was very much attached to Miss Ashleigh? Does her character resemble her mother's?"

I was afraid while I spoke that I should again meet Mrs. Poyntz's searching gaze, but she did not this time look up from her work.

"No; Lilian is anything but commonplace."

"You described her as having delicate health; you implied a hope that she was not consumptive. I trust that there is no serious reason for apprehending a constitutional tendency which at her age would require the most careful watching!"

"I trust not. If she were to die—Dr. Fenwick, what is the matter?"

So terrible had been the picture which this woman's words had brought before me, that I started as if my own life had received a shock.

"I beg pardon," I said, falteringly, pressing my hand to my heart; "a sudden spasm here—it is over now. You were saying that—that—"

"I was about to say—" and here Mrs. Poyntz laid her hand lightly on mine. "I was about to say, that if Lilian Ashleigh were to die, I should mourn for her less than I might for one who valued the things of the earth more. But I believe there is no cause for the alarm my words so inconsiderately excited in you. Her mother is watchful and devoted; and if the least thing ailed Lilian, she would call in medical advice. Mr. Vigors would, I know, recommend Dr. Jones."

Closing our conference with those stinging words, Mrs. Poyntz here turned back into the drawing-room.

I remained some minutes on the balcony, disconcerted, enraged. With what consummate art had this practised diplomatist wound herself into my secret. That she had read my heart better than myself was evident from that Parthian shaft, barbed with Dr. Jones, which she had shot over her shoulder in retreat. That, from the first moment in which she had decoyed me to her side, she had detected "the something" on my mind was, perhaps, but the ordinary quickness of female penetration. But it was with no ordinary craft that her whole conversation afterwards had been so shaped as to learn the something, and lead me to reveal the some one to whom the something was linked. For what purpose? What was it to her? What motive could she have beyond the mere gratification of curiosity? Perhaps, at first, she thought I had been caught by her daughter's showy beauty, and hence the half-friendly, half-cynical frankness with which she had avowed her ambitious projects for that young lady's matrimonial advancement. Satisfied by my manner that I cherished no presumptuous hopes in that quarter, her scrutiny was doubtless continued from that pleasure in the exercise of a wily intellect which impels schemers and politicians to an activity for which, without that pleasure itself, there would seem no adequate inducement; and, besides, the ruling passion of this petty sovereign was power. And if knowledge be power, there is no better instrument of power over a contumacious subject than that hold on his heart which is gained in the knowledge of its secret.

But "secret!" Had it really come to this? Was it possible that the mere sight of a human face, never beheld before, could disturb the whole tenor of my life — a stranger of whose mind and character I knew nothing, whose very voice I had never heard? It was only by the intolerable pang of anguish that had rent my heart in the words, carelessly, abruptly spoken, "if she were to die," that I had felt how the world would be changed to me, if indeed that face were seen in it no more! Yes, secret it was no longer to myself—I loved! And like all on whom love descends, sometimes softly, slowly, with the gradual wing of the cushat settling down into its nest, sometimes with the swoop of the eagle on his unsuspecting quarry, I believed that none ever before loved as I loved—that such love was an abnormal wonder, made solely for me, and I for it. Then my mind insensibly hushed its angrier and more turbulent thoughts, as my gaze rested upon the roof-tops of Lilian's home, and the shimmering silver of the moonlit willow, under which I had seen her gazing into the roseate heavens.

CHAPTER VIII.

WHEN I returned to the drawing-room, the party was evidently about to break up. Those who had grouped round the piano were now assembled round the refreshment table. The card players had risen, and were settling or discussing gains and losses. While I was searching for my hat, which I had somewhere mislaid, a poor gentleman, tormented by tic-douloreux, crept timidly up to me—the proudest and the poorest of all the hidalgoes settled on the Hill. He could not afford a fee for a physician's advice, but pain had humbled his pride, and I saw at a glance that he was considering how to take a surreptitious advantage of social intercourse, and obtain the advice without paying the fee. The old man discovered the hat before I did, stooped, took it up, extended it to me with the profound bow of the old school, while the other hand, clenched and quivering, was pressed into the hollow of his cheek, and his eyes met mine with wistful, mute entreaty. The instinct of my profession seized me at once. I could never behold suffering without forgetting all else in the desire to relieve it.

"You are in pain," said I, softly. "Sit down and describe the symptoms. Here, it is true, I am no professional doctor, but I am a friend who is fond of doctoring, and knows something about it."

So we sat down a little apart from the other guests, and after a few questions and answers, I was pleased to find that his "tic" did not belong to the less curable kind of that agonizing neuralgia. I was especially successful in my treatment of similar sufferings, for which I had discovered an anodyne that was almost specific. I wrote on a leaf of my pocket-book a prescription which I felt sure would be efficacious, and as I tore it out and placed it in his hand, I chanced to look up, and saw the hazel eyes of my hostess fixed upon me with a kinder and softer expression than they often condescended to admit into their cold and penetrating lustre. At that moment, however, her attention was drawn from me to a servant, who entered with a note, and I heard him say, though in an undertone, "From Mrs. Ashleigh."

She opened the note, read it hastily, ordered the servant to wait without the door, retired to her writing table, which stood near the place at which I still lingered, rested her face on her hand, and seemed musing. Her meditation was very soon over. She turned her head, and, to my surprise, beckoned to me. I approached.

"Sit here," she whispered; "turn your back towards those people, who are no doubt watching us. Read this."

She placed in my hand the note she had just received. It contained but a few words to this effect:

"DEAR MARGARET:—I am so distressed. Since I wrote to you, a few hours ago, Lilian is taken suddenly ill, and I fear seriously. What medical man should I send for? Let my servant have his name and address. A. A."

I sprang from my seat.

"Stay," said Mrs. Poyntz. "Would you much care if I sent the servant to Dr. Jones?"

"Ah, madam, you are cruel! What have I done that you should become my enemy?"

"Enemy! No. You have just befriended one of my friends. In this world of fools intellect should ally itself with intellect. No; I am not your enemy! But you have not yet asked me to be your friend."

Here she put into my hands a note she had written while thus speaking: "Receive your credentials. If there be any cause for alarm, or if I can be of use, send for me." Resuming the work she had suspended, but with lingering, uncertain fingers, she added, "So far, then, this is settled. Nay, no thanks! it is but little that is settled as yet."

CHAPTER IX.

In a very few minutes I was once more in the grounds of that old gable house; the servant, who went before me, entered them by the stairs and the wicket-gate of the private entrance; that way was the shortest. So again I passed by the circling glade and the monastic well — sward, trees, and ruins, all suffused in the limpid moonlight.

And now I was in the house; the servant took upstairs the note with which I was charged, and a minute or two afterwards returned and conducted me to the corridor above, in which Mrs. Ashleigh received me. I was the first to speak: "Your daughter — is — is — not seriously ill, I hope. What is it?"

"Hush!" she said, under her breath. "Will you step this way for a moment?" She passed through a doorway to the right. I followed her, and as she placed on the table the light she had been holding, I looked round with a chill at the heart — it was the room in which Dr. Lloyd had died. Impossible to mistake. The furniture, indeed, was changed — there was no bed in the chamber; but the shape of the room, the position of the high casement, which was now wide open, and through which the moonlight streamed more softly than on that drear winter night, the great square beams intersecting the low ceiling — all were impressed vividly on my memory. The chair to which Mrs. Ashleigh beckoned me was placed just on the spot where I had stood by the bed-head of the dying man.

I shrank back — I could not have seated myself there. So, I remained leaning against the chimney-piece, while Mrs. Ashleigh told her story.

She said that on their arrival the day before, Lilian had been in more than usually good health and spirits, delighted with the old house, the grounds, and especially the nook by the Monk's Well, at which Mrs. Ashleigh had left her that evening in order to make some purchases in the town, in company with Mr. Vigors. When Mrs. Ashleigh returned, she and Mr. Vigors had sought Lilian in that nook, and Mrs. Ashleigh then detected, with a mother's eye, some change in Lilian, which alarmed her. She seemed listless and dejected, and was very pale; but she denied that she felt unwell. On regaining the house she had sat down in the room in which we then were — "which," said Mrs. Ashleigh, "as it is not required for a sleeping-room, my daughter, who is fond of reading, wished to fit up as her own morning-room, or study. I left her here and went into the drawing-room below with Mr. Vigors. When he quitted me, which he did very soon, I remained for nearly an hour giving directions about the placing of furniture, which had just arrived from our late residence. I then went upstairs to join my daughter, and to my terror found her apparently lifeless in her chair. She had fainted away."

I interrupted Mrs. Ashleigh here: "Has Miss Ashleigh been subject to fainting fits?"

"No, never. When she recovered she seemed bewildered — disinclined to speak. I got her to bed, and as she then fell quietly to sleep, my mind was relieved. I thought it only a passing effect of excitement, in a change of abode; or caused by something like malaria in the atmosphere of that part of the grounds in which I had found her seated."

"Very likely. The hour of sunset at this time of year is trying to delicate constitutions. Go on."

"About three-quarters of an hour ago she woke up with a loud cry, and has been ever since in a state of great agitation, weeping violently, and answering none of my questions. Yet she does not seem light-headed, but rather what we call hysterical."

"You will permit me now to see her. Take comfort — in all you tell me I see nothing to warrant serious alarm."

CHAPTER X.

To the true physician there is an inexpressible sanctity in the sick-chamber. At its threshold the more human passions quit their hold on his heart. Love there would be profanation. Even the grief permitted to others he must put aside. He must enter that room — a calm intelligence. He is disabled for his mission if he suffer aught to obscure the keen, quiet glance of his science. Age or youth, beauty or deformity, innocence or guilt, merge their distinctions in one common attribute — human suffering appealing to human skill.

Woe to the households in which the trusted Healer feels not on his conscience the solemn obligations of his glorious art. Reverently, as in a temple, I stood in the virgin's chamber. When her mother placed her hand in mine, and I felt the throb of its pulse, I was aware of no quicker beat of my own heart. I looked with a steady eye on the face, more beautiful from the flush that deepened the delicate hues of the young cheek, and the lustre that brightened the dark blue of the wandering eyes. She did not at first heed me; did not seem aware of my presence; but kept murmuring to herself words which I could not distinguish.

At length, when I spoke to her, in that low, soothing tone which we learn at the sick-bed, the expression of her face altered suddenly; she passed the hand I did not hold over her forehead, turned round, looked at me full and long, with unmistakable surprise, yet not as if the surprise displeased her; less the surprise which recoils from the sight of a stranger than that which seems doubtfully to recognize an unexpected friend. Yet on the surprise there seemed to creep something of apprehension — of fear — her hand trembled, her voice quivered, as she said:

"Can it be, can it be? Am I awake? Mother, who is this!"

"Only a kind visitor, Dr. Fenwick, sent by Mrs. Poyntz, for I was uneasy about you, darling. How are you now?"

"Better. Strangely better."

She removed her hand gently from mine, and with an involuntary, modest shrinking, turned towards Mrs. Ashleigh, drawing her mother towards herself, so that she became at once hidden from me.

Satisfied that there was here no delirium, nor even more than the slight and temporary fever which often accompanies a sudden nervous attack in constitutions peculiarly sensitive, I retired noiselessly from the room, and went, not into that which had been occupied by the ill-fated Naturalist, but down stairs into the drawing-room, to write my prescription. I had already sent the servant off with it to the chemist's before Mrs. Ashleigh joined me.

"She seems recovering surprisingly; her forehead is

cooler; she is perfectly self-possessed, only she cannot account for her own seizure, cannot account either for the fainting or the agitation with which she awoke from sleep."

"I think I can account for both. The first room in which she entered — that in which she fainted — had its window open; the sides of the window are overgrown with rank creeping-plants in full blossom. Miss Ashleigh had already predisposed herself to injurious effects from the effluvia, by fatigue, excitement, imprudence in sitting out at the fall of a heavy dew. The sleep after the fainting fit was the more disturbed, because Nature, always alert and active in subjects so young, was making its own effort to right itself from an injury. Nature has nearly succeeded. What I have prescribed will a little aid and accelerate that which Nature has yet to do, and in a day or two I do not doubt that your daughter will be perfectly restored. Only let me recommend care to avoid exposure to the open air during the close of day. Let her avoid also the room in which she was first seized, for it is a strange phenomenon in nervous temperaments that a nervous attack may, without visible cause, be repeated in the same place where it was first experienced. You had better shut up the chamber for at least some weeks, burn fires in it, repaint and paper it, sprinkle chloroform. You are not, perhaps, aware that Dr. Lloyd died in that room after a prolonged illness. Suffer me to wait till your servant returns with the medicine, and let me employ the interval in asking you a few questions. Miss Ashleigh, you say, never had a fainting fit before. I should presume that she is not what we call strong. But has she ever had any illness that alarmed you?"

"Never."

"No great liability to cold and cough, to attacks of the chest or lungs?"

"Certainly not. Still I have feared that she may have a tendency to consumption. Do you think so? Your questions alarm me!"

"I do not think so; but before I pronounce a positive opinion, one question more. You say you have feared a tendency to consumption. Is that disease in her family? She certainly did not inherit it from you. But on her father's side?"

"Her father," said Mrs. Ashleigh, with tears in her eyes, "died young, but of brain fever, which the medical men said was brought on by over-study."

"Enough, my dear madam. What you say confirms my belief that your daughter's constitution is the very opposite to that in which the seeds of consumption lurk. It is rather that far nobler constitution, which the keenness of the nervous susceptibility renders delicate but elastic — as quick to recover as it is to suffer."

"Thank you, thank you, Dr. Fenwick, for what you say. You take a load from my heart. For Mr. Vigors, I know, thinks Lilian consumptive, and Mrs. Poyntz has rather frightened me at times by hints to the same effect. But when you speak of nervous susceptibility, I do not quite understand you. My daughter is not what is commonly called nervous. Her temper is singularly even."

"But if not excitable, should you also say that she is not impressionable? The things which do not disturb her temper, may, perhaps, deject her spirits. Do I make myself understood?"

"Yes, I think I understand your distinction. But I am not quite sure it applies. To most things that affect the spirits she is not more sensitive than other girls, perhaps less so. But she is certainly very impressionable in some things."

"In what?"

"She is more moved than any one I ever knew by objects in external nature, rural scenery, rural sounds, by music, by the books that she reads — even books that are not works of imagination. Perhaps in all this she takes after her poor father, but in a more marked degree—at least, I observe it more in her. For he was very silent and reserved. And perhaps also her peculiarities have been fostered by the seclusion in which she has been brought up. It was with a view to make her a little more like girls of her own age that our friend, Mrs. Poyntz, induced me to come here. Lilian was reconciled to this change; but she shrank from the thoughts of London, which I should have preferred. Her poor father could not endure London."

"Miss Ashleigh is fond of reading?"

"Yes, she is fond of reading, but more fond of musing. She will sit by herself for hours without book or work, and seem as abstracted as if in a dream. She was so even in her earliest childhood. Then she would tell me what she had been conjuring up to herself. She would say that she had seen—positively seen—beautiful lands far away from earth; flowers and trees not like ours. As she grew older this visionary talk displeased me, and I scolded her, and said that if others heard her, they would think that she was not only silly but very untruthful. So of late years she never ventures to tell me what, in such dreamy moments, she suffers herself to imagine; but the habit of musing continues still. Do you not agree with Mrs. Poyntz, that the best cure would be a little cheerful society amongst other young people?"

"Certainly," said I, honestly, though with a jealous pang. "But here comes the medicine. Will you take it up to her, and then sit with her half an hour or so? By that time I expect she will be asleep. I will wait here till you return. Oh, I can amuse myself with the newspapers and books on the table. Stay! one caution: be sure there are no flowers in Miss Ashleigh's sleeping-room. I think I saw a treacherous rose-tree in a stand by the window. If so, banish it."

Left alone, I examined the room in which, oh thought of joy! I had surely now won the claim to become a privileged guest. I touched the books Lilian must have touched; in the articles of furniture, as yet so hastily disposed that the settled look of home was not about them, I still knew that I was gazing on things which her mind must associate with the history of her young life. That lute-harp — must be surely hers, and the scarf, with a girl's favorite colors, pure white and pale blue, and the bird-cage, and the childish ivory work-case, with implements too pretty for use — all spoke of her.

It was a blissful, intoxicating reverie, which Mrs. Ashleigh's entrance disturbed.

Lilian was sleeping calmly. I had no excuse to linger there any longer.

"I leave you, I trust, with your mind quite at ease," said I. "You will allow me to call to-morrow, in the afternoon?"

"Oh yes, gratefully."

Mrs. Ashleigh held out her hand as I made towards the door.

Is there a physician who has not felt at times how that ceremonious fee throws him back from the garden-land of humanity into the market-place of money — seems to put him out of the pale of equal friendship, and say, "True, you have given health and life. Adieu! there, you are paid for it." With a poor person there would have been no dilemma, but Mrs. Ashleigh was affluent; to depart from custom here was almost impertinence. But had the penalty of my refusal been the doom of never again beholding Lilian, I could not have taken her mother's gold. So I did not appear to notice the hand held out to me, and passed by with a quickened step.

"But, Dr. Fenwick, stop!"

"No, ma'am, no! Miss Ashleigh would have recovered as soon without me. Whenever my aid is really wanted, then—but heaven grant that time may never come! We will talk again about her to-morrow."

I was gone. Now in the garden ground, odorous with blossoms; now in the lane, enclosed by the narrow walls; now in the deserted streets, over which the moon shone full as in that winter night when I hurried from the chamber of death. But the streets were not ghastly now, and the moon was no longer Hecate, that dreary goddess of awe and spectres, but the sweet, simple Lady of the Stars, on whose gentle face lovers have gazed ever since (if that guess of astronomers be true) she was parted from earth to rule the tides of its deeps from afar, even as love, from love divided, rules the heart that yearns towards it with mysterious law!

CHAPTER XI.

WITH what increased benignity I listened to the patients who visited me the next morning. The whole human race seemed to be worthier of love, and I longed to diffuse amongst all some rays of the glorious hope that had dawned upon my heart. My first call, when I went forth, was on the poor young woman from whom I had been returning the day before, when an impulse, which seemed like a fate, had lured me into the grounds where I had first seen Lilian. I felt grateful to this poor patient; without her, Lilian herself might be yet unknown to me.

The girl's brother, a young man employed in the police, and whose pay supported a widowed mother and the suffering sister, received me at the threshold of the cottage.

"Oh, sir! she is so much better to-day; almost free from pain. Will she live now? can she live?"

"If my treatment has really done the good you say; if she be really better under it, I think her recovery may be pronounced. But I must first see her."

The girl was indeed wonderfully better. I felt that my skill was achieving a signal triumph; but that day even my intellectual pride was forgotten in the luxurious unfolding of that sense of heart which had so newly waked into blossom.

As I recrossed the threshold, I smiled on the brother, who was still lingering there:

"Your sister is saved, Waby. She needs now chiefly wine, and good though light nourishment; these you will find at my house; call there for them every day."

"God bless you, sir! If ever I can serve you ——" His tongue faltered — he could say no more.

Serve me — Allen Fenwick — that poor policeman!

Me, whom a king could not serve! What did I ask from earth but Fame and Lilian's heart? Thrones and bread man wins from the aid of others. Fame and woman's heart he can only gain through himself.

So I strode gaily up the hill, through the iron gates into the fairy ground, and stood before Lilian's home.

The man-servant, on opening the door, seemed somewhat confused, and said hastily, before I spoke:

"Not at home, sir; a note for you."

I turned the note mechanically in my hand; I felt stunned.

"Not at home! Miss Ashleigh cannot be out. How is she?"

"Better, sir, thank you."

I still could not open the note; my eyes turned wistfully towards the windows of the house, and there—at the drawing-room window—I encountered the scowl of Mr. Vigors. I colored with resentment, divined that I was dismissed, and walked away with a proud crest and a firm step.

When I was out of the gates, in the blind lane, I opened the note. It began formally: "Mrs. Ashleigh presents her compliments," and went on to thank me, civilly enough, for my attendance the night before; would not give me the trouble to repeat my visit, and enclosed a fee, double the amount of the fee prescribed by custom. I flung the money, as an asp that had stung me, over the high wall, and tore the note into shreds. Having thus idly vented my rage, a dull gnawing sorrow came heavily down upon all other emotions, stifling and replacing them. At the mouth of the lane I halted. I shrank from the thought of the crowded streets beyond. I shrank yet more from the routine of duties, which stretched before me in the desert into which daily life was so suddenly smitten. I sat down by the roadside, shading my dejected face with a nerveless hand. I looked up as the sound of steps reached my ear, and saw Dr. Jones coming briskly along the lane, evidently from Abbots' House. He must have been there at the very time I had called. I was not only dismissed, but supplanted. I rose before he reached the spot on which I had seated myself, and went my way into the town, went through my allotted round of professional visits; but my attentions were not so tenderly devoted, my skill so genially quickened by the glow of benevolence, as my poorer patients had found them in the morning. I have said how the physician should enter the sick-room. "A Calm Intelligence!" But if you strike a blow on the heart, the intellect suffers. Little worth, I suspect, was my "calm intelligence" that day. Bichat, in his famous book upon Life and Death, divides life into two classes — animal and organic. Man's intellect, with the brain for its centre, belongs to life animal; his passions to life organic, centred in the heart, in the viscera. Alas! if the noblest passions through which alone we lift ourselves into the moral realm of the sublime and beautiful really have their centre in the life which the very vegetable, that lives organically, shares with us! And, alas! if it be that life which we share with the vegetable, that can cloud, obstruct, suspend, annul that life centred in the brain, which we share with every being howsoever angelic, in every star howsoever remote, on whom the Creator bestows the faculty of thought!

CHAPTER XII.

BUT suddenly I remembered Mrs. Poyntz. I ought to call on her. So I closed my round of visits at her door. The day was then far advanced, and the servant politely informed me that Mrs. Poyntz was at dinner. I could only leave my card, with a message that I would pay my respects to her the next day. That evening I received from her this note:

"DEAR DR. FENWICK:—I regret much that I cannot have the pleasure of seeing you to-morrow. Poyntz and I are going to visit his brother, at the other end of the county, and we start early. We shall be away some days. Sorry to hear from Mrs. Ashleigh that she has been persuaded by Mr. Vigors to consult Dr. Jones about Lilian. Vigors and Jones both frighten the poor mother, and insist upon consumptive tendencies. Unluckily, you seemed to have said there was little the matter. Some doctors gain their practice, as some preachers fill their churches, by adroit use of the appeals to terror. You do not want patients, Dr. Jones does. And, after all, better perhaps as it is.

Yours, &c. M. POYNTZ."

To my more selfish grief anxiety for Lilian was now added. I had seen many more patients die from being mistreated for consumption than from consumption itself. And Dr. Jones was a mercenary, cunning, needy man, with much crafty knowledge of human foibles, but very little skill in the treatment of human maladies. My fears were soon confirmed. A few days after I heard from Miss Brabazon that Miss Ashleigh was seriously ill; kept her room. Mrs. Ashleigh made this excuse for not immediately returning the visits which the Hill had showered upon her. Miss Brabazon had seen Dr. Jones, who had shaken his head, said it was a serious case; but that time and care (his time and his care!) might effect wonders.

How stealthily at the dead of the night I would climb the Hill, and look toward the windows of the old sombre house — one window, in which a light burnt dim and mournful, the light of a sick-room — of hers!

At length Mrs. Poyntz came back, and I entered her house, having fully resolved beforehand on the line of policy to be adopted towards the potentate whom I hoped to secure as an ally. It was clear that neither disguise nor half-confidence would baffle the penetration of so keen an intellect, nor propitiate the good will of so imperious and resolute a temper. Perfect frankness here was the wisest prudence; and, after all, it was most agreeable to my own nature, and most worthy of my own honor.

Luckily, I found Mrs. Poyntz alone, and taking in both mine the hand she somewhat coldly extended to me, I said, with the earnestness of suppressed emotion:

"You observed when I last saw you, that I had not yet asked you to be my friend. I ask it now! Listen to me with all the indulgence you can vouchsafe, and let me at least profit by your counsel, if you refuse to give me your aid."

Rapidly, briefly, I went on to say how I had first seen Lilian, and how sudden, how strange to myself, had been the impression which that first sight of her had produced.

"You remarked the change that had come over me," said I; "you divined the cause before I divined it myself; divined it as I sat there beside you, thinking that through you I might see, in the freedom of social intercourse, the face that was then haunting me. You know what has since passed. Miss Ashleigh is ill; her case is, I am convinced, wholly misunderstood. All other feelings are merged in one sense of anxiety — of alarm. But it has become due to me, due to all, to incur the risk of your ridicule even more than of your reproof, by stating to you thus candidly, plainly, bluntly, the sentiment which renders alarm so poignant, and which, if scarcely admissible to the romance of some wild dreamy boy, may seem an unpardonable folly in a man of my years and my sober calling; due to me, to you, to Mrs. Ashleigh; because still the dearest thing in life to me is honor. And if you who know Mrs. Ashleigh so intimately, who must be more or less aware of her plans or wishes for her daughter's future; if you believe that those plans or wishes lead to a lot far more ambitious than an alliance with me could offer to Miss Ashleigh, then aid Mr. Vigors in excluding me from the house; aid me in suppressing a presumptuous, visionary passion. I cannot enter that house without love and hope at my heart. And the threshold of that house I must not cross if such love and such hope be a sin and a treachery in the eyes of its owner. I might restore Miss Ashleigh to health; her gratitude might—I cannot continue. This danger must not be to me nor to her, if her mother has views far above such a son-in-law. And I am the more bound to consider all this while it is yet time, because I heard you state that Miss Ashleigh had a fortune — was what would be here termed an heiress. And the full consciousness that whatever fame one in my profession may live to acquire, does not open those vistas of social power and grandeur which are opened by professions to my eyes less noble in themselves — that full consciousness, I say, was forced upon me by certain words of your own. For the rest, you know my descent is sufficiently recognized as that amidst well-born gentry to have rendered me no mésalliance to families the most proud of their ancestry, if I had kept my hereditary estate and avoided the career that makes me useful to man. But I acknowledge that on entering a profession such as mine — entering any profession except that of arms or the senate — all leave their pedigree at its door, an erased or dead letter. All must come as equals, high-born or low-born, into that arena in which men ask aid from a man as he makes himself; to them his dead forefathers are idle dust. Therefore, to the advantage of birth I cease to have a claim. I am but a provincial physician, whose station would be the same had he been a cobbler's son. But gold retains its grand privilege in all ranks. He who has gold is removed from the suspicion that attaches to the greedy fortune-hunter. My private fortune, swelled by my savings, is sufficient to secure to any one I marry a larger settlement than many a wealthy squire can make. I need no fortune with a wife; if she have one, it would be settled on herself. Pardon these vulgar details. Now, have I made myself understood?"

"Fully," answered the Queen of the Hill, who had listened to me quietly, watchfully, and without one interruption. "Fully. And you have done well to confide in me with so generous an unreserve. But before I say further, let me ask, what would be your advice for Lilian, supposing that you ought not to attend her? You have no trust in Dr. Jones; neither have I. And Anne Ashleigh's note received to-day, begging me to call, justifies your alarm. Still you think there is no tendency to consumption?"

"Of that I am certain, so far as my slight glimpse of a case that to me, however, seems a simple and not uncommon one, will permit. But in the alternative you put—that my own skill, whatever its worth, is forbidden — my earnest advice is, that Mrs. Ashleigh should take her daughter at once to London, and consult there those great authorities to whom I cannot compare my own opinion or experience; and by their counsel abide."

Mrs. Poyntz shaded her eyes with her hand for a few moments, and seemed in deliberation with herself. Then she said, with her peculiar smile, half grave, half ironical:

"In matters more ordinary you would have won me to your side long ago. That Mr. Vigors should have presumed to cancel my recommendation to a settler on the Hill, was an act of rebellion, and involved the honor of my prerogative. But I suppressed my indignation at an affront so unusual, partly out of pique against yourself, but much more, I think, out of regard for you."

"I understand. You detected the secret of my heart; you knew that Mrs. Ashleigh would not wish to see her daughter the wife of a provincial physician."

"Am I sure, or are you sure, that the daughter herself would accept that fate; or if she accepted it, would not repent?"

"Do not think me the vainest of men when I say

this — that I cannot believe I should be so enthralled by a feeling at war with my reason, unfavored by anything I can detect in my habits of mind, or even by the dreams of a youth which exalted science and excluded love, unless I was intimately convinced that Miss Ashleigh's heart was free — that I could win, and that I could keep it! Ask me why I am convinced of this, and I can tell you no more why I think that she could love me, than I can tell you why I love her!"

"I am of the world, worldly. But I am a woman, womanly — though I may not care to be thought it. And, therefore, though what you say is, regarded in a worldly point of view, sheer nonsense, regarded in a womanly point of view, it is logically sound. But still you cannot know Lilian as I do. Your nature and hers are in strong contrast. I do not think she is a safe wife for you. The purest, the most innocent creature imaginable, certainly that, but always in the seventh heaven. And you in the seventh heaven, just at this moment, but with an irresistible gravitation to the solid earth, which will have its way again when the honeymoon is over. I do not believe you two would harmonize by intercourse. I do not believe Lilian would sympathize with you, and I am sure you could not sympathize with her throughout the long dull course of this workday life. And, therefore, for your sake as well as hers, I was not displeased to find that Dr. Jones had replaced you; and now, in return for your frankness, I say frankly — do not go again to that house.

Conquer this sentiment, fancy, passion, whatever it be. And I will advise Mrs. Ashleigh to take Lilian to town. Shall it be so settled?"

I could not speak. I buried my face in my hands — misery, misery, desolation!

I know not how long I remained thus silent, perhaps many minutes. At length I felt a cold, firm, but not ungentle, hand placed upon mine; and a clear, full, but not discouraging, voice said to me:

"Leave me to think well over this conversation, and to ponder well the value of all you have shown that you so deeply feel. The interests of life do not fill both scales of the balance. The heart which does not always go in the same scale with the interests, still has its weight in the scale opposed to them. I have heard a few wise men say, as many a silly woman says, 'Better be unhappy with one we love, than be happy with one we love not.' Do you say that, too?"

"With every thought of my brain, every beat of my pulse, I say it."

"After that answer, all my questionings cease. You shall hear from me to-morrow. By that time I shall have seen Anne and Lilian. I shall have weighed both scales of the balance, and the heart here, Allen Fenwick, seems very heavy. Go, now. I hear feet on the stairs, Poyntz bringing up some friendly gossiper; gossipers are spies."

I passed my hand over my eyes, tearless, but how tears would have relieved the anguish that burdened them! and, without a word, went down the stairs, meeting at the landing-place Colonel Poyntz and the old man whose pain my prescription had cured. The old man was whistling a merry tune, perhaps first learned on the playground. He broke from it to thank, almost to embrace me, as I slid by him. I seized his jocund blessing as a good omen, and carried it with me as I passed into the broad sunlight. Solitary—solitary! Should I be so evermore?

CHAPTER XIII.

THE next day I had just dismissed the last of my patients, and was about to enter my carriage and commence my round, when I received a twisted note containing but these words:

"Call on me to-day, as soon as you can. M. POYNTZ."

A few minutes afterwards I was in Mrs. Poyntz's drawing-room.

"Well, Allen Fenwick," said she, "I do not serve friends by halves. No thanks! I but adhere to a principle I have laid down for myself. I spent last evening with the Ashleighs. Lilian is certainly much altered—very weak, I fear very ill, and I believe very unskilfully treated by Dr. Jones. I felt that it was my duty to insist on a change of physician, but there was something else to consider before deciding who that physician should be. I was bound, as your confidante, to consult your own scruples of honor. Of course I could not say point-blank to Mrs. Ashleigh, 'Dr. Fenwick admires your daughter, would you object to him as a son-in-law?' Of course I could not touch at all on the secret with which you intrusted me; but I have not the less arrived at a conclusion, in agreement with my previous belief, that not being a woman of the world, Anne Ashleigh has none of the ambition which women of the world would conceive for a daughter who has a good fortune and considerable beauty; that her predominant anxiety is for her child's happiness, and her predominant fear is that her child will die. She would never oppose any attachment which Lilian might form; and if that attachment were for one who had preserved her daughter's life, I believe her own heart would gratefully go with her daughter's. So far, then, as honor is concerned, all scruples vanish."

I sprang from my seat, radiant with joy. Mrs. Poyntz dryly continued: "You value yourself on your common sense, and to that I address a few words of counsel which may not be welcome to your romance. I said that I did not think you and Lilian would suit each other in the long run; reflection confirms me in that supposition. Do not look at me so incredulously, and so sadly. Listen, and take heed. Ask yourself what, as a man whose days are devoted to a laborious profession, whose ambition is entwined with its success, whose mind must be absorbed in its pursuits — ask yourself what kind of a wife you would have sought to win, had not this sudden fancy for a charming face rushed over your better reason, and obliterated all previous plans and resolutions. Surely some one with whom your heart would have been quite at rest; by whom your thoughts would have been undistracted from the channels into which your calling should concentrate their flow; in short, a serene companion in the quiet holiday of a trustful home! Is it not so?"

"You interpret my own thoughts when they have turned towards marriage. But what is there in Lilian Ashleigh that should mar the picture you have drawn?"

"What is there in Lilian Ashleigh which in the least accords with the picture? In the first place, the wife of a young physician should not be his perpetual patient. The more he loves her, and the more worthy she may be of love, the more her case will haunt him wherever he goes. When he returns home, it is not to a holiday; the patient he most cares for, the anxiety that most gnaws him, awaits him there."

"But, good Heavens! why should Lilian Ashleigh be a perpetual patient? The sanitary resources of youth are incalculable. And ——"

"Let me stop you; I cannot argue against a physician in love! I will give up that point in dispute, remaining convinced that there is something in Lilian's constitution which will perplex, torment, and baffle you.

It was so with her father, whom she resembles in face and in character. He showed no symptoms of any grave malady. His outward form was, like Lilian's, a model of symmetry, except in this, that like hers it was too exquisitely delicate; but, when seemingly in the midst of perfect health, at any slight jar on the nerves he would become alarmingly ill. I was sure that he would die young, and he did."

"Ay, but Mrs. Ashleigh said that his death was from brain fever, brought on by over-study. Rarely, indeed, do women so fatigue the brain. No female patient, in the range of my practice, ever died of purely mental exertion."

"Of purely mental exertion, no; but of *heart* emotion, many female patients, perhaps? Oh, you own that! I know nothing about nerves. But I suppose that, whether they act on the brain or the heart, the result to life is much the same if the nerves be too finely strung for life's daily wear and tear. And this is what I mean, when I say you and Lilian will not suit. As yet, she is a mere child; her nature undeveloped, and her affections, therefore, untried. You might suppose that you had won her heart; she might believe that she gave it to you, and both be deceived. If fairies nowadays condescended to exchange their offspring with those of mortals, and if the popular tradition did not represent a fairy changeling as an ugly, peevish creature, with none of the grace of its parents, I should be half inclined to suspect that Lilian was one of the elfin people. She never seems at home on earth; and I do not think she will ever be contented with a prosaic earthly lot. Now I have told you why I do not think she will suit you. I must leave it to yourself to conjecture how far you would suit her. I say this in due season, while you may set a guard upon your impulse; while you may yet watch, and weigh, and meditate; and from this moment on that subject I say no more. I lend advice, but I never throw it away."

She came here to a dead pause, and began putting on her bonnet and scarf, which lay on the table beside her. I was a little chilled by her words, and yet more by the blunt, shrewd, hard look and manner which aided the effect of their delivery. But the chill melted away in the sudden glow of my heart when she again turned towards me and said:

"Of course you guess, from these preliminary cautions, that you are going into danger? Mrs. Ashleigh wishes to consult you about Lilian, and I propose to take you to her house."

"Oh, my friend, my dear friend, how can I ever repay you?" I caught her hand, the white, firm hand, and lifted it to my lips.

She drew it somewhat hastily away, and laying it gently on my shoulder, said, in a soft voice, "Poor Allen, how little the world knows either of us! But how little perhaps we know ourselves! Come, your carriage is here? That is right; we must put down Dr. Jones publicly and in all our state."

In the carriage Mrs. Poyntz told me the purport of that conversation with Mrs. Ashleigh to which I owed my re-introduction to Abbots' House. It seems that Mr. Vigors had called early the morning after my first visit; had evinced much discomposure on hearing that I had been summoned; dwelt much on my injurious treatment of Dr. Lloyd, whom, as distantly related to himself, and he (Mr. Vigors) being distantly connected with the late Gilbert Ashleigh, he endeavored to fasten upon his listener as one of her husband's family, whose quarrel she was bound in honor to take up. He spoke of me as an infidel "tainted with French doctrines," and as a practitioner rash and presumptuous; proving his own freedom frcm presumption and rashness by flatly deciding that my opinion must be wrong. Previously to Mrs. Ashleigh's migration to L——, Mr. Vigors had interested her in the pretended phenomena of mesmerism. He had consulted a clairvoyante, much esteemed by poor Dr. Lloyd, as to Lilian's health, and the clairvoyante had declared her to be constitutionally predisposed to consumption. Mr. Vigors persuaded Mrs. Ashleigh to come at once with him and see this clairvoyante herself, armed with a lock of Lilian's hair and a glove she had worn, as the media of mesmerical *rapport.*

The clairvoyante, one of those I had publicly denounced as an impostor, naturally enough denounced me in return. On being asked solemnly by Mr. Vigors to "look at Dr. Fenwick and see if his influence would be beneficial to the subject," the sibyl had become violently agitated and said that, "when she looked at us together, we were enveloped in a black cloud; that this portended affliction and sinister consequences; that our *rapport* was antagonistic." Mr. Vigors then told her to dismiss my image, and conjure up that of Dr. Jones. Therewith the somnambule became more tranquil and said: "Dr. Jones would do well if he would be guided by higher lights than his own skill, and consult herself daily as to the proper remedies. The best remedy of all would be mesmerism. But since Dr. Lloyd's death, she did not know of a mesmerist, sufficiently gifted, in affinity with the patient." In fine, she impressed and awed Mrs. Ashleigh, who returned in haste, summoned Dr. Jones, and dismissed myself.

"I could not have conceived Mrs. Ashleigh to be so utterly wanting in common sense," said I. "She talked rationally enough when I saw her."

"She has common sense in general, and plenty of the sense most common," answered Mrs. Poyntz. "But she is easily led and easily frightened wherever her affections are concerned, and, therefore, just as easily as she had been persuaded by Mr. Vigors and terrified by the somnambule, I persuaded her against the one, and terrified her against the other. I had positive experience on my side, since it was clear that Lilian had been getting rapidly worse under Dr. Jones's care. The main obstacles I had to encounter in inducing Mrs. Ashleigh to consult you again, were, first, her reluctance to disoblige Mr. Vigors, as a friend and connection of Lilian's father; and, secondly, her sentiment of shame in reinviting your opinion after having treated you with so little respect. Both these difficulties I took on myself. I bring you to her house, and, on leaving you, I shall go on to Mr. Vigors, and tell him what is done is my doing, and not to be undone by him; so that matter is settled. Indeed, if you were out of the question, I should not suffer Mr. Vigors to re-introduce all these mummeries of clairvoyance and mesmerism into the precincts of the Hill. I did not demolish a man I really liked in Dr. Lloyd, to set up a Dr. Jones, whom I despise, in his stead. Clairvoyance on Abbey Hill, indeed! I saw enough of it before."

"True; your strong intellect detected at once the absurdity of the whole pretence—the falsity of mesmerism—the impossibility of clairvoyance."

"No, my strong intellect did nothing of the kind. I do not know whether mesmerism be false or clairvoyance impossible; and I don't wish to know. All I do know is, that I saw the Hill in great danger; young ladies allowing themselves to be put to sleep by gentlemen, and pretending they had no will of their own against such fascination! Improper and shocking! And Miss Brabazon beginning to prophesy, and Mrs. Leopold Smythe questioning her maid (whom Dr. Lloyd declared to be highly gifted) as to all the secrets of her friends. When I saw this, I said, 'The Hill is becoming demoralized; the Hill is making itself ridiculous; the Hill must be saved!' I remonstrated with Dr. Lloyd, as a friend; he remained obdurate. I annihilated him as an enemy, not to me but to the State. I slew my best lover for the good of Rome. Now you know why I took your part—not because I have any opinion, one way or the other, as to the truth or falsehood of what Dr. Lloyd asserted; but I have a strong opinion that, whether they be true or false, his notions were those which are not to be allowed on the Hill. And so, Allen Fenwick, that matter was settled."

Perhaps at another time I might have felt some little humiliation to learn that I had been honored with the influence of this great potentate, not as a champion of truth, but as an instrument of policy; and I might have owned to some twinge of conscience in having assisted to sacrifice a fellow-seeker after science — misled, no doubt, but preferring his independent belief to his worldly interest — and sacrifice him to those deities with whom science is ever at war — the Prejudice of a Clique sanctified into the Proprieties of the World. But at that moment the words I heard made no perceptible impression on my mind. The gables of Abbots' House were visible above the evergreens and lilacs; another moment, and the carriage stopped at the door.

CHAPTER XIV.

Mrs. Ashleigh received us in the dining-room. Her manner to me, at first, was a little confused and shy. But my companion soon communicated something of her own happy ease to her gentler friend. After a short conversation we all three went to Lilian, who was in a little room on the ground-floor, fitted up as her study. I was glad to perceive that my interdict of the death-chamber had been respected.

She reclined on a sofa near the window, which was, however, jealously closed; the light of the bright May-day obscured by blinds and curtains; a large fire on the hearth; the air of the room that of a hot-house — the ignorant, senseless, exploded system of nursing into consumption those who are confined on suspicion of it! She did not heed us as we entered noiselessly; her eyes were drooped languidly on the floor, and with difficulty I suppressed the exclamation that rose to my lips on seeing her. She seemed within the last few days so changed, and on the aspect of the countenance there was so profound a melancholy! But as she slowly turned at the sound of our footsteps, and her eyes met mine, a quick blush came into the wan cheek, and she half rose, but sank back as if the effort exhausted her. There was a struggle for breath, and a low hollow cough. Was it possible that I had been mistaken, and that in that cough was heard the warning knell of the most insidious enemy to youthful life?

I sat down by her side; I lured her on to talk of indifferent subjects — the weather, the gardens, the bird in the cage, which was placed on the table near her. Her voice, at first low and feeble, became gradually stronger, and her face lighted up with a child's innocent, playful smile. No, I had not been mistaken! That was no lymphatic, nerveless temperament, on which consumption fastens as its lawful prey — here there was no hectic pulse, no hurried waste of the vital flame. Quietly and gently I made my observations, addressed my questions, applied my stethoscope; and when I turned my face towards her mother's anxious, eager eyes, that face told my opinion; for her mother sprang forward, clasped my hand, and said, through her struggling tears:

"You smile! You see nothing to fear?"

"Fear! No, indeed! You will soon be again yourself, Miss Ashleigh, will you not?"

"Yes," she said, with her sweet laugh, "I shall be well now, very soon. But may I not have the window open — may I not go into the garden? I so long for fresh air."

"No, no, darling!" exclaimed Mrs. Ashleigh, "not while the east winds last. Dr. Jones said on no account. On no account, Dr. Fenwick, eh?"

"Will you take my arm, Miss Ashleigh, for a few turns up and down the room?" said I. "We will then see how far we may rebel against Dr. Jones."

She rose with some little effort, but there was no

cough. At first her step was languid — it became lighter and more elastic after a few moments.

"Let her come out," said I to Mrs. Ashleigh. "The wind is not in the east, and, while we are out, pray bid your servant lower to the last bar in the grate that fire — only fit for Christmas."

"But —"

"Ah, no buts! He is a poor doctor who is not a stern despot."

So the straw hat and mantle were sent for. Lilian was wrapped with unnecessary care, and we all went forth into the garden. Involuntarily we took the way to the Monk's Well, and at every step Lilian seemed to revive under the bracing air and temperate sun. We paused by the well.

"You do not feel fatigued, Miss Ashleigh?"

"No."

"But your face seems changed. It is grown sadder."

"Not sadder."

"Sadder than when I first saw it — saw it when you were seated here!" I said this in a whisper. I felt her hand tremble as it lay on my arm.

"You saw me seated here!"

"Yes. I will tell you how some day."

Lilian lifted her eyes to mine, and there was in them that same surprise which I had noticed on my first visit — a surprise that perplexed me, blended with no displeasure, but yet with a something of vague alarm.

We soon returned to the house.

Mrs. Ashleigh made me a sign to follow her into the drawing-room, leaving Mrs Poyntz with Lilian.

"Well?" said she, tremblingly.

"Permit me to see Dr. Jones's prescriptions. Thank you. Ay, I thought so. My dear madam, the mistake here has been in depressing nature instead of strengthening; in narcotics instead of stimulants. The main stimulants which leave no reaction are air and light. Promise me that I may have my own way for a week—that all I recommend will be implicitly heeded?"

"I promise. But that cough; you noticed it?"

"Yes. The nervous system is terribly lowered, and nervous exhaustion is a strange impostor; it imitates all manner of complaints with which it has no connection. The cough will soon disappear! But pardon my question: Mrs. Poyntz tells me that you consulted a clairvoyante about your daughter—does Miss Ashleigh know that you did so?"

"No; I did not tell her."

"I am glad of that. And pray, for Heaven's sake, guard her against all that may set her thinking on such subjects. Above all, guard her against concentrating attention on any malady that your fears erroneously ascribe to her. It is amongst the phenomena of our organization that you cannot closely rivet your consciousness on any part of the frame, however healthy, but it will soon begin to exhibit morbid sensibility. Try to fix all your attention on your little finger for half an hour, and before the half-hour is over the little finger will be uneasy, probably even painful. How serious, then, is the danger to a young girl, at the age in which imagination is most active, most intense, if you force upon her a belief that she is in danger of a mortal disease; it is a peculiarity of youth to brood over the thought of early death much more resignedly, much more complacently, than we do in maturer years. Impress on a young, imaginative girl, as free from pulmonary tendencies as you and I are, the conviction that she must fade away into the grave, and though she may not actually die of consumption, you instil slow poison into her system. Hope is the natural aliment of youth. You impoverish nourishment where you discourage hope. As soon as this temporary illness is over, reject for your daughter the melancholy care which seems to her own mind to mark her out from others at her age. Rear her for the air — which is the kindest life-giver; to sleep with open windows; to be out at sunrise. Nature will do more for her than all our drugs can do. You have been hitherto fearing Nature; now trust to her."

Here Mrs. Poyntz joined us, and having, while I had been speaking, written my prescription and some general injunctions, I closed my advice with an appeal to that powerful protectress:

"This, my dear madam, is a case in which I need your aid, and I ask it. Miss Ashleigh should not be left with no other companion than her mother. A change of faces is often as salutary as a change of air.

If you could devote an hour or two this very evening to sit with Miss Ashleigh, to talk to her with your usual cheerfulness, and — "

"Anne," interrupted Mrs. Poyntz, "I will come and drink tea with you at half-past seven, and bring my knitting; and perhaps, if you ask him, Dr. Fenwick will come too! He can be tolerably entertaining when he likes it."

"It is too great a tax on his kindness, I fear," said Mrs. Ashleigh. "But," she added, cordially, "I should be grateful indeed if he would spare us an hour of his time."

I murmured an assent, which I endeavoured to make not too joyous.

"So that matter is settled," said Mrs. Poyntz; "and now I shall go to Mr. Vigors and prevent his further interference."

"Oh! but, Margaret, pray don't offend him — a connection of my poor dear Gilbert's. And so tetchy! I am sure I do not know how you'll manage to — "

"To get rid of him? Never fear. As I manage everything and everybody, said Mrs. Poyntz, bluntly. So she kissed her friend on the forehead, gave me a gracious nod, and, declining the offer of my carriage, walked with her usual brisk, decided tread down the short path towards the town.

Mrs. Ashleigh timidly approached me, and again the furtive hand bashfully insinuated the hateful fee.

"Stay," said I; "this is a case which needs the most

constant watching. I wish to call so often that I should seem the most greedy of doctors if my visits were to be computed at guineas. Let me be at ease to effect my cure; my pride of science is involved in it. And when amongst all the young ladies of the Hill you can point to none with a fresher bloom, or a fairer promise of healthful life, than the patient you intrust to my care, why, then the fee and the dismissal. Nay, nay; I must refer you to our friend Mrs. Poyntz. It was so settled with her before she brought me here to displace Dr. Jones." Therewith I escaped.

CHAPTER XV.

In less than a week Lilian was convalescent; in less than a fortnight she regained her usual health; nay, Mrs. Ashleigh declared that she had never known her daughter appear so cheerful and look so well. I had established a familiar intimacy at Abbots' House; most of my evenings were spent there. As horse exercise formed an important part of my advice, Mrs. Ashleigh had purchased a pretty and quiet horse for her daughter; and, except the weather was very unfavorable, Lilian now rode daily with Colonel Poyntz, who was a notable equestrian, and often accompanied by Miss Jane Poyntz, and other young ladies of the Hill. I was generally relieved from my duties in time to join her as she returned homewards. Thus we made innocent appointments, openly, frankly, in her mother's presence, she telling me beforehand in what direction excursions had been planned with Colonel Poyntz, and I promising to fall in with the party—if my avocations would permit. At my suggestion, Mrs. Ashleigh now opened her house almost every evening to some of the neighboring families; Lilian was thus habituated to the intercourse of young persons of her own age. Music and dancing and childlike games made the old house gay. And the Hill gratefully acknowledged to Mrs. Poyntz, "that the Ashleighs were indeed a great acquisition."

But my happiness was not unchequered. In thus unselfishly surrounding Lilian with others, I felt the anguish of that jealousy which is inseparable from those earlier stages of love, when the lover as yet has won no right to that self-confidence which can only spring from the assurance that he is loved.

In these social re-unions I remained aloof from Lilian. I saw her courted by the gay young admirers whom her beauty and her fortune drew around her; her soft face brightening in the exercise of the dance, which the gravity of my profession rather than my years forbade me to join — and her laugh, so musically subdued, ravishing my ear and fretting my heart as if the laugh were a mockery on my sombre self and my presumptuous dreams. But no, suddenly, shyly, her eyes would steal away from those about her, steal to the corner in which I sat, as if they missed me, and, meeting my own gaze, their light softened before they turned away; and the color on her cheek would deepen, and to her lip there came a smile different from the smile that it shed on others. And then — and then — all jealousy, all sadness vanished, and I felt the glory which blends with the growing belief that we are loved.

In that diviner epoch of man's mysterious passion, when ideas of perfection and purity, vague and fugitive before, start forth and concentre themselves round one virgin shape — that rises out from the sea of creation, welcomed by the Hours and adorned by the Graces — how the thought that this archetype of sweetness and beauty singles himself from the millions, singles himself for her choice, ennobles and lifts up his being! Though after-experience may rebuke the mortal's illusion, that mistook for a daughter of Heaven a creature of clay like himself, yet for a while the illusion has grandeur. Though it comes from the senses which shall later oppress and profane it, the senses at first shrink into shade, awed and hushed by the presence that charms them. All that is brightest and best in the man has soared up like long-dormant instincts of Heaven, to greet and to hallow what to him seems life's fairest dream of the heavenly! Take the wings from the image of Love, and the god disappears from the form!

Thus, if at moments jealous doubt made my torture, so the moment's relief from it sufficed for my rapture.

But I had a cause for disquiet less acute but less varying than jealousy.

Despite Lilian's recovery from the special illness which had more immediately absorbed my care, I remained perplexed as to its cause and true nature. To her mother I gave it the convenient epithet of "nervous." But the epithet did not explain to myself all the symptoms I classified by it. There was still, at times, when no cause was apparent or conjecturable, a sudden change in the expression of her countenance — in the beat of her pulse; the eye would become fixed, the bloom would vanish, the pulse would sink feebler and feebler till it could be scarcely felt; yet there was no indication of heart disease, of which such sudden lowering of life is in itself sometimes a warning indication. The change would pass away after a few minutes, during which she seemed unconscious, or, at least, never spoke — never appeared to heed what was said to her. But in the expression of her countenance there was no character of suffering or distress; on the contrary a wondrous serenity, that made her beauty more beauteous, her very youthfulness younger; and when this spurious or partial kind of syncope passed, she recovered at once without effort, without acknowledging that she had felt faint or unwell, but rather with a sense of recruited vitality, as the weary obtain from a sleep. For the rest her spirits were more generally light and joyous than I should have premised from her mother's previous description. She would enter mirthfully into the mirth of young companions around her; she had evidently quick perception of the sunny sides of life; an infantine gratitude for kindness; an infantine joy in the trifles that amuse only those who delight in tastes pure and simple. But when talk rose into graver and more contemplative topics, her attention became earnest and absorbed; and, sometimes, a rich eloquence, such as I have never before nor since heard from lips so young, would startle me first into a wondering silence, and soon into a disapproving alarm; for the thoughts she then uttered seemed to me too fantastic, too visionary, too much akin to the vagaries of a wild though beautiful imagination. And then I would seek to check, to sober, to distract fancies with which my reason had no sympathy, and the indulgence of which I regarded as injurious to the normal functions of the brain.

When thus, sometimes with a chilling sentence, sometimes with a half-sarcastic laugh, I would repress outpourings frank and musical as the songs of a forest-bird, she would look at me with a kind of plaintive sorrow — often sigh and shiver as she turned away. Only in these modes did she show displeasure; otherwise ever sweet and docile, and ever, if, seeing that I had pained her, I asked forgiveness, humbling herself rather to ask mine, and brightening our reconciliation with her angel smile. As yet I had not dared to speak of love; as yet I gazed on her as the captive gazes on the flowers and the stars through the gratings of his cell, murmuring to himself, "When shall the doors unclose?"

CHAPTER XVI

It was with a wrath suppressed in the presence of the fair ambassadress that Mr. Vigors had received from Mrs. Poyntz the intelligence that I had replaced Dr. Jones at Abbots' House, not less abruptly than Dr. Jones had previously supplanted me. As Mrs. Poyntz took upon herself the whole responsibility of this change, Mr. Vigors did not venture to condemn it to her face; for the Administrator of Laws was at heart no little in awe of the Autocrat of Proprieties; as Authority, howsoever established, is in awe of Opinion, howsoever capricious.

To the mild Mrs. Ashleigh the magistrate's anger was more decidedly manifested. He ceased his visits; and in answer to a long and deprecatory letter with which she endeavored to soften his resentment and win him back to the house, he replied by an elaborate combination of homily and satire. He began by excusing himself from accepting her invitations, on the ground that *his* time was valuable, *his* habits domestic; and though ever willing to sacrifice both time and habits where he could do good, he owed it to himself and to mankind to sacrifice neither where his advice was rejected and his opinion contemned. He glanced briefly, but not hastily, at the respect with which her late husband had deferred to his judgment, and the benefits which that deference had enabled him to bestow. He contrasted the husband's deference with the widow's contumely, and hinted at the evils which the contumely would not permit him to prevent. He could not presume to say what women of the world might think due to deceased husbands, but even women of the world generally allowed the claims of living children, and did not act with levity where their interests were concerned, still less where their lives were at stake. As to Dr. Jones, he, Mr. Vigors, had the fullest confidence in his skill. Mrs. Ashleigh must judge for herself whether Mrs. Poyntz was as good an authority upon medical science as he had no doubt she was upon shawls and ribbons. Dr. Jones was a man of caution and modesty; he did not indulge in the hollow boasts by which charlatans decoy their dupes; but Dr. Jones had privately assured him that, though the case was one that admitted of no rash experiments, he had no fear of the result if his own prudent system were persevered in. What might be the consequences of any other system, Dr. Jones would not say, because he was too high-minded to express his distrust of the rival who had made use of underhand arts to supplant him. But Mr. Vigors was convinced, from other sources of information (meaning, I presume, the oracular prescience of his clairvoyants), that the time would come when the poor young lady would herself insist on discarding Dr. Fenwick, and when "that person" would appear in a very different light to many who now so fondly admired and so reverentially trusted him. When that time arrived, he, Mr. Vigors, might again be of use; but, meanwhile, though he declined to renew his intimacy at Abbots' House, or to pay unavailing visits of mere ceremony, his interest in the daughter of his old friend remained undiminished, nay, was rather increased by compassion; that he should silently keep his eye upon her; and whenever anything to her advantage suggested itself to him, he should not be deterred by the slight with which Mrs. Ashleigh had treated his judgment, from calling on her, and placing before her conscience as a mother his ideas for her child's benefit, leaving to herself then, as now, the entire responsibility of rejecting the advice which he might say, without vanity, was deemed of some value by those who could distinguish between sterling qualities and specious pretences.

Mrs. Ashleigh's was that thoroughly womanly nature which instinctively leans upon others. She was diffident, trustful, meek, affectionate. Not quite justly had Mrs. Poyntz described her as "commonplace weak," for though she might be called weak, it was not because she was commonplace; she had a goodness of heart, a sweetness of disposition, to which that disparaging definition could not apply. She could only be called commonplace, inasmuch as in the ordinary daily affairs of life she had a great deal of ordinary daily commonplace good sense. Give her a routine to follow, and no routine could be better adhered to. In the allotted sphere of a woman's duties she never seemed in fault.

No household, not even Mrs. Poyntz's, was more happily managed. The old Abbots' House had merged its original antique gloom in the softer character of pleasing repose. All her servants adored Mrs. Ashleigh; all found it a pleasure to please her; her establishment had the harmony of clockwork; comfort diffused itself round her like quiet sunshine round a sheltered spot. To gaze on her pleasing countenance, to listen to the simple talk that lapsed from her guileless lips, in even, slow, and lulling murmur, was in itself a respite from "eating cares." She was to the mind what the color of green is to the eye. She had, therefore, excellent sense in all that relates to every-day life. There she needed not to consult another; there the wisest might have consulted her with profit. But the moment anything, however trivial in itself, jarred on the routine to which her mind had grown wedded — the moment an incident hurried her out of the beaten track of woman's daily life, then her confidence forsook her — then she needed a confidant, an adviser; and by that confidant or adviser she could be credulously lured or submissively controlled. Therefore, when she lost in Mr. Vigors the guide she had been accustomed to consult whenever she needed guidance, she turned, helplessly and piteously, first to Mrs. Poyntz, and then yet more imploringly to me, because a woman of that character is never quite satisfied without the advice of a man. And when an intimacy more familiar than that of his formal visits is once established with a physician, confidence in him grows fearless and rapid, as the natural result of sympathy concentred on an object of anxiety in common between himself and the home which opens its sacred recess to his observant but tender eye. Thus Mrs. Ashleigh had shown me Mr. Vigors's letter, and, forgetting that I might not be as amiable as herself, besought me to counsel her how to conciliate and soften her lost husband's friend and connection. That character clothed him with dignity and awe in her soft, forgiving eyes. So, smothering my own resentment, less perhaps at the tone of offensive insinuation against myself than at the arrogance with which this prejudiced intermeddler implied to a mother the necessity of his guardian-watch over a chlld under her own care, I sketched a reply which seemed to me both dignified and placatory, abstaining from all discussion, and conveying the assurance that Mrs. Ashleigh would be at all times glad to hear, and disposed to respect, whatever suggestion so esteemed a friend of her husband's would kindly submit to her for the welfare of her daughter.

There all communication had stopped for about a month since the date of my re-introduction to Abbots' House. One afternoon I unexpectedly met Mr. Vigors at the entrance of the blind lane, I on my way to Abbots' House, and my first glance at his face told me that he was coming from it, for the expression of that face was more than usually sinister; the sullen scowl was lit into significant menace by a sneer of unmistakable triumph. I felt at once that he had succeeded in some machination against me, and with ominous misgivings quickened my steps.

I found Mrs. Ashleigh seated alone in front of the house, under a large cedar-tree that formed a natural arbor in the centre of the sunny lawn. She was perceptibly embarrassed as I took my seat beside her.

"I hope," said I, forcing a smile, "that Mr. Vigors has not been telling you that I shall kill my patient, or that she looks much worse than she did under Dr. Jones's care?"

"No," she said. "He owned cheerfully that Lilian had grown quite strong, and said, without any displeasure, that he had heard how gay she had been, riding out and even dancing — which is very kind in him, for he disapproves of dancing, on principle."

"But still I can see he has said something to vex or annoy you; and, to judge by his countenance when I met him in the lane, I should conjecture that that something was intended to lower the confidence you so kindly repose in me."

"I assure you not; he did not mention your name, either to me or to Lilian. I never knew him more friendly; quite like old times. He is a good man at heart, very, and was much attached to my poor husband."

"Did Mr. Ashleigh profess a very high opinion of Mr. Vigors?"

"Well, I don't quite know that, because my dear

Gilbert never spoke to me much about him. Gilbert was naturally very silent. But he shrank from all trouble — all worldly affairs — and Mr. Vigors managed his estate, and inspected his steward's books, and protected him through a long lawsuit which he had inherited from his father. It killed his father. I don't know what we should have done without Mr. Vigors, and I am so glad he has forgiven me."

"Hem! Where is Miss Ashleigh? Indoors?"

"No; somewhere in the grounds. But, my dear Dr. Fenwick, do not leave me yet; you are so very, very kind, and somehow I have grown to look upon you quite as an old friend. Something has happened which has put me out — quite put me out."

She said this wearily and feebly, closing her eyes as if she were indeed put out in the sense of extinguished.

"The feeling of friendship you express," said I, with earnestness, "is reciprocal. On my side it is accompanied by a peculiar gratitude. I am a lonely man, by a lonely fireside — no parents, no near kindred, and in this town, since Dr. Faber left it, without cordial intimacy till I knew you. In admitting me so familiarly to your hearth, you have given me what I have never known before since I came to man's estate — a glimpse of the happy domestic life; the charm and relief to eye, heart and spirit, which is never known but in households cheered by the face of woman; thus my sentiment for you and yours is indeed that of an old friend;

and in any private confidence you show me, I feel as if I were no longer a lonely man, without kindred, without home."

Mrs. Ashleigh seemed much moved by these words, which my heart had forced from my lips, and, after replying to me with simple unaffected warmth of kindness, she rose, took my arm, and continued thus as we walked slowly to and fro the lawn:

"You know, perhaps, that my poor husband left a sister, now a widow like myself, Lady Haughton."

"I remember that Mrs. Poyntz said you had such a sister-in-law, but I never heard you mention Lady Haughton till now. Well!"

"Well, Mr. Vigors has brought me a letter from her, and it is that which has put me out. I dare say you have not heard me speak before of Lady Haughton, for I am ashamed to say I had almost forgotten her existence. She is many years older than my husband was — of a very different character. Only came once to see him after our marriage. Hurt me by ridiculing him as a bookworm. Offended him by looking a little down on me, as a nobody without spirit and fashion, which was quite true. And, except by a cold and unfeeling letter of formal condolence after I lost my dear Gilbert, I have never heard from her since I have been a widow, till to-day. But, after all, she is my poor husband's sister, and his eldest sister, and Lilian's aunt; and, as Mr. Vigors says, 'Duty is duty.'"

Had Mrs. Ashleigh said "Duty is torture," she could

not have uttered the maxim with more mournful and despondent resignation.

"And what does this lady require of you, which Mr. Vigors deems it your duty to comply with?"

"Dear me! What penetration! You have guessed the exact truth. But I think you will agree with Mr. Vigors. Certainly I have no option; yes, I must do it."

"My penetration is in fault now. Do what? Pray explain."

"Poor Lady Haughton, six months ago, lost her only son, Sir James. Mr. Vigors says he was a very fine young man, of whom any mother would have been proud. I had heard he was wild; Mr. Vigors says, however, that he was just going to reform, and marry a young lady whom his mother chose for him, when, unluckily, he would ride a steeplechase, not being quite sober at the time, and broke his neck. Lady Haughton has been, of course, in great grief. She has retired to Brighton; and she wrote to me from thence, and Mr. Vigors brought the letter. He will go back to her to-day."

"Will go back to Lady Haughton? What! Has he been to her? Is he, then, as intimate with Lady Haughton as he was with her brother?"

"No; but there has been a long and constant correspondence. She had a settlement on the Kirby Estate — a sum which was not paid off during Gilbert's life; and a very small part of the property went to Sir James, which part Mr. Ashleigh Sumner, the heir-at-law to the rest of the estate, wished Mr. Vigors, as his guardian, to buy during his minority, and as it was mixed up with Lady Haughton's settlement her consent was necessary as well as Sir James's. So there was much negotiation, and, since then, Ashleigh Sumner has come into the Haughton property, on poor Sir James's decease; so that complicated all affairs between Mr. Vigors and Lady Haughton, and he has just been to Brighton to see her. And poor Lady Haughton, in short, wants me and Lilian to go and visit her. I don't like it at all. But you said the other day you thought sea air might be good for Lilian during the heat of the summer, and she seems well enough now for the change. What do you think?"

"She is well enough, certainly. But Brighton is not the place I would recommend for the summer; it wants shade, and is much hotter than L——."

"Yes, but unluckily Lady Haughton foresaw that objection, and she has a jointure-house some miles from Brighton, and near the sea. She says the grounds are well wooded, and the place is proverbially cool and healthy, not far from St. Leonard's Forest. And, in short, I have written to say we will come. So we must, unless, indeed, you positively forbid it."

"When do you think of going?"

"Next Monday. Mr. Vigors would make me fix the day. If you knew how I dislike moving when I am once settled; and I do so dread Lady Haughton, she is so fine, and so satirical! But Mr. Vigors says she is very much altered, poor thing! I should like to show you her letter, but I had just sent it to Margaret — Mrs. Poyntz — a minute or two before you came. She knows something of Lady Haughton. Margaret knows everybody. And we shall have to go in mourning for poor Sir James, I suppose; and Margaret will choose it, for I am sure I can't guess to what extent we should be supposed to mourn. I ought to have gone in mourning before — poor Gilbert's nephew — but I am so stupid, and I had never seen him. And —— but oh, this *is* kind! Margaret herself — my dear Margaret!"

We had just turned away from the house, in our up-and-down walk; and Mrs. Poyntz stood immediately fronting us.

"So, Anne, you have actually accepted this invitation — and for Monday next?"

"Yes. Did I do wrong?"

"What does Dr. Fenwick say? Can Lilian go with safety?"

I could not honestly say she might not go with safety, but my heart sank like lead as I answered:

"Miss Ashleigh does not now need merely medical care; but more than half her cure has depended on keeping her spirits free from depression. She may miss the cheerful companionship of your daughter, and other young ladies of her own age. A very melancholy house, saddened by a recent bereavement, without other guests; a hostess to whom she is a stranger, and whom Mrs. Ashleigh herself appears to deem formidable — certainly these do not make that change of scene which a physician would recommend. When I spoke of sea air being good for Miss Ashleigh, I thought of our own northern coasts at a later time of the year, when I could escape myself for a few weeks and attend her. The journey to a northern watering-place would be also shorter and less fatiguing; the air there more invigorating."

"No doubt that would be better," said Mrs. Poyntz, dryly; "but so far as your objections to visiting Lady Haughton have been stated, they are groundless. Her house will not be melancholy; she will have other guests, and Lilian will find companions, young like herself — young ladies — and young gentlemen too!"

There was something ominous, something compassionate, in the look which Mrs. Poyntz cast upon me, in concluding her speech, which in itself was calculated to rouse the fears of a lover. Lilian away from me, in the house of a worldly-fine lady — such as I judged Lady Haughton to be — surrounded by young gentlemen, as well as young ladies — by admirers, no doubt of a higher rank and more brilliant fashion than she had yet known! I closed my eyes, and with strong effort suppressed a groan.

"My dear Anne, let me satisfy myself that Dr. Fenwick really *does* consent to this journey. He will say to me what he may not to you. Pardon me, then, if I take him aside for a few minutes. Let me find you here again under this cedar-tree."

Placing her arm in mine, and without waiting for Mrs. Ashleigh's answer, Mrs. Poyntz drew me into the more sequestered walk that belted the lawn; and, when we were out of Mrs. Ashleigh's sight and hearing, said:

"From what you have now seen of Lilian Ashleigh, do you still desire to gain her as your wife?"

"Still? Oh! with an intensity proportioned to the fear with which I now dreaded that she is about to pass away from my eyes — from my life!"

"Does your judgment confirm the choice of your heart? Reflect before you answer."

"Such selfish judgment as I had before I knew her would not confirm, but oppose it. The nobler judgment that now expands all my reasonings, approves and seconds my heart. No, no; do not smile so sarcastically. This is not the voice of a blind and egotistical passion. Let me explain myself if I can. I concede to you that Lilian's character is undeveloped. I concede to you that, amidst the childlike freshness and innocence of her nature, there is at times a strangeness, a mystery, which I have not yet traced to its cause. But I am certain that the intellect is organically as sound as the heart, and that intellect and heart will ultimately — if under happy auspices — blend in that felicitous union which constitutes the perfection of woman. But it is because she does, and may for years, may perhaps always, need a more devoted, thoughtful care than natures less tremulously sensitive, that my judgment sanctions my choice; for whatever is best for her is best for me. And who would watch over her as I should?"

"You have never yet spoken to Lilian as lovers speak?"

"Oh, no, indeed."

"And, nevertheless, you believe that your affection would not be unreturned?"

"I thought so once—I doubt now—yet, in doubting, hope. But why do you alarm me with these questions? You, too, forbode that in this visit I may lose her forever?"

"If you fear that, tell her so, and perhaps her answer may dispel your fear."

"What now, already, when she has scarcely known me a month. Might I not risk all if too premature?"

"There is no almanac for love. With many women love is born the moment they know they are beloved. All wisdom tells us that a moment once gone is irrevocable. Were I in your place, I should feel that I approached a moment that I must not lose. I have said enough; now I shall rejoin Mrs. Ashleigh."

"Stay — tell me first what Lady Haughton's letter really contains to prompt the advice with which you so transport, and yet so daunt, me when you proffer it."

"Not now—later, perhaps—not now. If you wish to see Lilian alone, she is by the Old Monk's Well; I saw her seated there as I passed that way to the house."

"One word more — only one. Answer this question frankly, for it is one of honor. Do you still believe that my suit to her daughter would not be disapproved of by Mrs. Ashleigh ? "

"At this moment, I am sure it would not; a week hence I might not give you the same answer."

So she passed on with her quick but measured tread, back through the shady walk, on to the open lawn, till the last glimpse of her pale gray robe disappeared under the boughs of the cedar-tree. Then, with a start, I broke the irresolute, tremulous suspense in which I had vainly endeavored to analyze my own mind, solve my own doubts, concentrate my own will, and went the way, skirting the circle of that haunted ground; as now, on one side its lofty terrace, the houses of the neighboring city came full and close into view, divided from my fairyland of life but by the trodden murmurous thoroughfare winding low beneath the ivied parapets; and as now, again, the world of men abruptly vanished behind the screening foliage of luxuriant June.

At last the enchanted glade opened out from the verdure, its borders fragrant with syringa, and rose, and woodbine; and there, by the grey memorial of the gone Gothic age, my eyes seemed to close their unquiet wanderings, resting spell-bound on that image which had become to me the incarnation of earth's bloom and youth.

She stood amidst the Past, backed by the fragments of walls which man had raised to seclude him from human passion, locking, under those lids so downcast, the secret of the only knowledge I asked from the boundless Future.

Ah! what mockery there is in that grand word, the world's fierce war-cry—Freedom! Who has not known one period of life, and that so solemn that its shadows may rest over all life hereafter, when one human creature has over him a sovereignty more supreme and absolute than Orient servitude adores in the symbols of diadem and sceptre? What crest so haughty that has not bowed before a hand which could exalt or humble! What heart so dauntless that has not trembled to call forth the voice at whose sound ope the gates of rapture or despair! That life alone is free which rules, and suffices for itself. That life we forfeit when we love!

CHAPTER XVII.

How did I utter it? By what words did my heart make itself known? I remember not. All was a dream that falls upon a restless, feverish night, and fades away as the eyes unclose on the peace of a cloudless heaven, on the bliss of a golden sun. A new sorrow seemed indeed upon the earth when I woke from a life-long yesterday—her dear hand in mine, her sweet face bowed upon my breast.

And then there was that melodious silence in which there is no sound audible from without; yet within us there is heard a lulling celestial music, as if our whole being, grown harmonious with the universe, joined from its happy deeps in the hymn that unites the stars.

In that silence our two hearts seemed to make each other understand, to be drawing nearer and nearer, blending by mysterious concord into the completeness of a solemn union, never henceforth to be rent asunder.

At length I said softly: "And it was here on this spot that I first saw you — here that I for the first time knew what power to change our world and to rule our future goes forth from the charm of a human face!"

Then Lilian asked me timidly, and without lifting her eyes, how I had so seen her, reminding me that I promised to tell her, and had never yet done so.

And then I told her of the strange impulse that had led me into the grounds, and by what chance my steps had been diverted down the path that wound to the glade; how suddenly her form had shone upon my eyes, gathering round itself the rose hues of the setting sun, and how wistfully those eyes had followed her own silent gaze into the distant heaven.

As I spoke, her hand pressed mine eagerly, convulsively, and, raising her face from my breast, she looked at me with an intent, anxious earnestness. That look! — twice before it had thrilled and perplexed me.

"What is there in that look, oh! my Lilian, which tells me that there is something that startles you — something you wish to confide, and yet shrink from explaining? See how, already, I study the fair book from which the seal has been lifted, but as yet you must aid me to construe its language."

"If I shrank from explaining, it is only because I fear that I cannot explain so as to be understood or believed. But you have a right to know the secrets of a life which you would link to your own. Turn your face aside from me; a reproving look, an incredulous smile, chill—oh! you cannot guess how they chill me, when I would approach that which to me is so serious and so solemnly strange."

I turned my face away, and her voice grew firmer, as after a brief pause, she resumed:

"As far back as I can remember in my infancy, there have been moments when there seems to fall a soft, hazy veil between my sight and the things around it, thickening and deepening till it has the likeness of one of those white, fleecy clouds which gather on the verge of the horizon when the air is yet still, but the winds are about to rise; and then this vapor or veil will suddenly open, as clouds open and let in the blue sky."

"Go on," I said gently, for here she came to a stop.

She continued, speaking somewhat more hurriedly:

"Then, in that opening, strange appearances present themselves to me as in a vision. In my childhood these were chiefly landscapes of wonderful beauty. I could but faintly describe them then; I could not attempt to describe them now, for they are almost gone from my memory. My dear mother chid me for telling her what I saw, so I did not impress it on my mind by repeating it. As I grew up, this kind of vision—if I may so call it—became much less frequent, or much less distinct; I still saw the soft veil fall, the pale cloud form and open, but often what may then have appeared was entirely forgotten when I recovered myself, waking as from a sleep. Sometimes, however, the recollection would be vivid and complete; sometimes I saw the face of my lost father; sometimes I heard his very voice, as I had seen and heard him in my early childhood, when he would let me rest for hours beside him as he mused or studied, happy to be so near him—for I loved him, oh, so dearly! and I remember him so distinctly, though I was only in my sixth year when he died. Much more recently—indeed, within the last few months—the images of things to come are reflected on the space that I gaze into as clearly as in a glass. Thus, for weeks before I came hither, or knew that such a place existed, I saw distinctly the old House, yon trees, this sward, this moss-grown Gothic fount, and, with the sight, an impression was conveyed to me that in the scene before me my old childlike life would pass into some solemn change. So that when I came here, and recognized the picture in my vision, I took an affection for the spot—an affection not without awe—a powerful, perplexing interest, as one who feels under the influence of a fate of which a prophetic glimpse has been vouchsafed. And in that evening, when you first saw me seated here——"

"Yes, Lilian, on that evening——?"

"I saw you also, but in my vision—yonder, far in the deeps of space—and—my heart was stirred as it had never been before; and near where your image grew out from the cloud I saw my father's face, and I heard his voice, not in my ear, but as in my heart, whispering——"

"Yes, Lilian—whispering—what?"

"These words—only these—'Ye will need one another.' But then, suddenly, between my upward eyes and the two forms they had beheld, there rose from the earth, obscuring the skies, a vague, dusky vapor, undulous, and coiling like a vast serpent, nothing, indeed, of its shape and figure definite, but of its face one abrupt glare; a flash from two dread, luminous eyes, and a young head, like the Medusa's, changing, more rapidly than I could have drawn breath, into a grinning skull. Then my terror made me bow my head, and when I raised it again, all that I had seen was vanished. But the terror still remained, even when I felt my mother's arm around me and heard her voice. And then, when I entered the house, and sat down again alone, the recollection of what I had seen—those eyes—that face—that skull—grew on me stronger and stronger till I fainted, and remember no more, until my eyes, opening, saw you by my side, and in my wonder there was not terror. No, a sense of joy, protection, hope, yet still shadowed by a kind of fear or awe, in recognizing the countenance which had gleamed on me from the skies before the dark vapor had risen, and while my father's voice had murmured, 'Ye will need one another.' And now — and now — will you love me less that you know a secret in my being which I have told to no other — cannot construe to myself? Only — only, at least, do not mock me — do not disbelieve me! Nay, turn from me no longer now — now I ask to meet your eyes. Now, before our hands can join again, tell me that you do not despise me as untruthful, do not pity me as insane."

"Hush — hush!" I said, drawing her to my breast. "Of all you tell me we will talk hereafter. The scales of our science have no weights fine enough for the gossamer threads of a maiden's pure fancies. Enough for me — for us both — if out from all such illusions starts one truth, told to you, lovely child, from the heavens; told to me, ruder man, on the earth; repeated by each pulse of this heart that woos you to hear and to trust — now and henceforth, through life unto death. 'Each has need of the other' — I of you — I of you! my Lilian — my Lilian!"

CHAPTER XVIII.

In spite of the previous assurance of Mrs. Poyntz, it was not without an uneasy apprehension that I approached the cedar-tree, under which Mrs. Ashleigh still sat, her friend beside her. I looked on the fair creature whose arm was linked in mine. So young, so singularly lovely, and with all the gifts of birth and fortune which bend avarice and ambition the more submissively to youth and beauty, I felt as if I had wronged what a parent might justly deem her natural lot.

"Oh, if your mother should disapprove!" said I, falteringly.

Lilian leant on my arm less lightly: "If I had thought so," she said, with her soft blush, "should I be thus by your side?"

So we passed under the boughs of the dark tree, and Lilian left me, and kissed Mrs. Ashleigh's cheek; then, seating herself on the turf, laid her head on her mother's lap. I looked on the Queen of the Hill, whose keen eye shot over me. I thought there was a momentary expression of pain or displeasure on her countenance; but it passed. Still there seemed to me something of irony, as well as of triumph or congratulation, in the half-smile with which she quitted her seat, and in the tone with which she whispered, as she glided by me to the open sward, "So, then, it is settled."

She walked lightly and quickly down the lawn. When she was out of sight I breathed more freely. I took the seat which she had left, by Mrs. Ashleigh's side, and said: "A little while ago I spoke of myself as a man without kindred, without home, and now I come to you and ask for both."

Mrs. Ashleigh looked at me benignly, then raised her daughter's face from her lap, and whispered, "Lilian!"

and Lilian's lips moved, but I did not hear her answer. Her mother did. She took Lilian's hand, simply placed it in mine, and said: "As she chooses, I choose; whom she loves, I love."

CHAPTER XIX

From that evening till the day Mrs. Ashleigh and Lilian went on the dreaded visit, I was always at their house, when my avocations allowed me to steal to it; and during those few days, the happiest I had ever known, it seemed to me that years could not have more deepened my intimacy with Lilian's exquisite nature — made me more reverential of its purity, or more enamored of its sweetness. I could detect in her but one fault, and I rebuked myself for believing that it was a fault. We see many who neglect the minor duties of life, who lack watchful forethought and considerate care for others, and we recognize the cause of this failing in levity or egotism. Certainly neither of those tendencies of character could be ascribed to Lilian. Yet still in daily trifles there was something of that neglect, some lack of that care and forethought. She loved her mother with fondness and devotion, yet it never occurred to her to aid in those petty household cares in which her mother centred so much of habitual interest. She was full of tenderness and pity to all want and suffering, yet many a young lady on the Hill was more actively beneficent — visiting the poor in their sickness, or instructing their children in the Infant Schools. I was persuaded that her love for me was deep and truthful; it was clearly void of all ambition; doubtless she would have borne, unflinching and contented, whatever the world considers to be sacrifice and privation; yet I should never have expected her to take her share in the troubles of ordinary life. I could never have applied to her the homely but significant name of helpmate. I reproach myself, while I write, for noticing such defect — if defect it were — in what may be called the practical routine of our positive, trivial, human existence. No doubt it was this that had caused Mrs. Poyntz's harsh judgment against the wisdom of my choice. But such chiller shade upon Lilian's charming nature was reflected from no inert, unamiable self-love. It was but the consequence of that self-absorption which the habit of reverie had fostered. I cautiously abstained from all allusion to those visionary deceptions, which she had confided to me as the truthful impressions of spirit, if not of sense. To me any approach to what I termed superstition was displeasing; any indulgence of phantasies, not within the measured and beaten tracks of healthful imagination, more than displeased me in her — it alarmed. I would not by a word encourage her in persuasions which I felt it would be at present premature to reason against, and cruel, indeed, to ridicule. I was convinced that of themselves these mists round her native intelligence, engendered by a solitary and musing childhood, would subside in the fuller daylight of wedded life. She seemed pained when she saw how resolutely I shunned a subject dear to her thoughts. She made one or two timid attempts to renew it, but my grave looks sufficed to check her. Once or twice, indeed, on such occasions, she would turn away and leave me, but she soon came back; that gentle heart could not bear one unkindlier shade between itself and what it loved. It was agreed that our engagement should be, for the present, confided only to Mrs. Poyntz. When Mrs. Ashleigh and Lilian returned, which would be in a few weeks at furthest, it should be proclaimed; and our marriage could take place in the autumn, when I should be most free for a brief holiday from professional toils.

So we parted — as lovers part. I felt none of those jealous fears which, before we were affianced, had made me tremble at the thought of separation, and had conjured up irresistible rivals. But it was with a settled heavy gloom that I saw her depart. From earth was gone a glory; from life a blessing!

CHAPTER XX.

During the busy years of my professional career, I had snatched leisure for some professional treatises, which had made more or less sensation, and one of them entitled The Vital Principle; its Waste and Supply, had gained a wide circulation among the general public. This last treatise contained the results of certain experiments, then new in chemistry, which were adduced in support of a theory I entertained as to the re-invigoration of the human system by principles similar to those which Liebig has applied to the replenishment of an exhausted soil — viz., the giving back to the frame those essentials to its nutrition, which it has lost by the action or accident of time; or supplying that special pabulum or energy in which the individual organism is constitutionally deficient; and neutralizing or counterbalancing that in which it superabounds — a theory upon which some eminent physicians have more recently improved with signal success. But on these essays, slight and suggestive, rather than dogmatic, I set no value. I had been for the last two years engaged on a work of much wider range, endeared to me by far bolder ambition — a work upon which I fondly hoped to found an enduring reputation as a severe and original physiologist. It was an Inquiry into Organic Life, similar in comprehensiveness of survey to that by which the illustrious Müller, of Berlin, has enriched the science of our age; however inferior, alas! to that august combination of thought and learning, in the judgment which checks presumption, and the genius which adorns speculation. But at that day I was carried away by the ardor of composition, and I admired my performance because I loved my labor. This work had been entirely laid aside for the last agitated month; now that Lilian was gone, I resumed it earnestly, as the sole occupation that had power and charm enough to rouse me from the aching sense of void and loss.

The very night of the day she went, I re-opened my MS. I had left off at the commencement of a chapter "Upon Knowledge as derived from our Senses." As my convictions on this head were founded on the well-known arguments of Locke and Condillac against innate ideas, and on the reasonings by which Hume has resolved the combination of sensations into a general idea to an impulse arising merely out of habit, so I set myself to oppose, as a dangerous concession to the sentimentalities or mysticism of a pseudo-philosophy, the doctrine favored by most of our recent physiologists, and of which some of the most eminent of German metaphysicians have accepted the substance, though refining into a subtlety its positive form — I mean the doctrine which Müller himself has expressed in these words:

"That innate ideas may exist, cannot in the slightest degree be denied; it is, indeed, a fact. All the ideas of animals, which are induced by instinct, are innate and immediate; something presented to the mind, a desire to attain which is at the same time given. The new-born lamb and foal have such innate ideas, which lead them to follow their mother and suck the teats. Is it not in some measure the same with the intellectual ideas of man?"*

To this question I answered with an indignant "No!" A "Yes" would have shaken my creed of materialism to the dust. I wrote on rapidly, warmly. I defined the properties and meted the limits of natural laws, which I would not admit that a Deity himself could alter. I clamped and soldered dogma to dogma in the links of my tinkered logic, till out from my page, to my own complacent eye, grew Intellectual Man, as the pure formation of his material senses; mind, or what is called soul, born from and nurtured by them alone; through them to act, and to perish with the machine they moved. Strange, that at the very time my love for Lilian might have taught me that there are mysteries in the core of the feelings which my analysis of ideas could not solve, I should so stubbornly have opposed as unreal all that could be referred to the spiritual! Strange, that, at the very time when the thought that I might lose from this life the being I had known scarce a month had just before so appalled me, I should thus complacently sit down to prove that, according to the laws of the nature which my passion

* Müller's Elements of Physiology, vol. ii., p. 134. Translated by Dr. Baley.

obeyed, I must lose for eternity the blessing I now hoped I had won to my life! But how distinctly dissimilar is man in his conduct from man in his systems! See the poet reclined under forest-boughs, conning odes to his mistress; follow him out into the world; no mistress ever lived for him there!* See the hard man of science, so austere in his passionless problems; follow him now where the brain rests from its toil, where the heart finds its Sabbath — what child is so tender, so yielding and soft?

But I had proved to my own satisfaction that poet and sage are dust, and no more, when the pulse ceases to beat. And on that consolatory conclusion my pen stopped.

Suddenly, beside me I distinctly heard a sigh — a compassionate, mournful sigh. The sound was unmistakable. I started from my seat, looked round, amazed to discover no one — no living thing! The windows were closed, the night was still. That sigh was not the wail of the wind. But there, in the darker angle of the room, what was that? A silvery whiteness — vaguely shaped as a human form — receding, fading, gone! Why, I know not — for no face was visible, no form, if form it were, more distinct than the colorless outline — why, I know not, but I cried aloud, "Lilian! Lilian!" My voice came strangely back to my own

* Cowley, who wrote so elaborate a series of amatory poems, is said "never to have been in love but once, and then he never had resolution to tell his passion." — *Johnson's Lives of the Poets:* COWLEY.

ear; I paused, then smiled and blushed at my folly. "So I, too, have learned what is superstition," I muttered to myself. "And here is an anecdote at my own expense (as Müller frankly tells us anecdotes of the illusions which would haunt his eyes, shut or open) — an anecdote I may quote when I come to my Chapter on the Cheats of the Senses and Spectral Phantasms." I went on with my book, and wrote till the lights waned in the grey of the dawn. And I said then, in the triumph of my pride, as I laid myself down to rest, "I have written that which allots with precision man's place in the region of nature; written that which will found a school — form disciples; and race after race of those who cultivate truth through pure reason shall accept my bases if they enlarge my building." And again I heard the sigh, but this time it caused no surprise. "Certainly," I murmured, "a very strange thing is the nervous system!" So I turned on my pillow, and, wearied out, fell asleep.

CHAPTER XXI.

The next day, the last of the visiting patients to whom my forenoons were devoted had just quitted me, when I was summoned in haste to attend the steward of a Sir Philip Derval, not residing at his family seat, which was about five miles from L——. It was rarely, indeed, that persons so far from the town, when of no higher rank than this applicant, asked my services. But it was my principle to go wherever I was summoned; my profession was not gain, it was healing, to which gain was the incident, not the essential. This case the messenger reported as urgent. I went on horseback, and rode fast; but swiftly as I cantered through the village that skirted the approach to Sir Philip Derval's park, the evident care bestowed on the accommodation of the cottagers forcibly struck me. I felt that I was on the lands of a rich, intelligent, and beneficent proprietor. Entering the park, and passing before the manor-house, the contrast between the neglect and decay of the absentee's stately hall and the smiling homes of his villagers was disconsolately mournful.

An imposing pile, built apparently by Vanbrugh, with decorated pilasters, pompous portico, and grand perron (or double flight of stairs to the entrance), enriched with urns and statues, but discolored, mildewed, chipped, half hidden with unpruned creepers and ivy. Most of the windows were closed with shutters, decaying for want of paint; in some of the casements the panes were broken; the peacock perched on the shattered balustrade, that fenced a garden overgrown with weeds. The sun glared hotly on the place, and made its ruinous condition still more painfully apparent. I was glad when a winding in the park road shut the house from my sight. Suddenly I emerged through a copse of ancient yew-trees, and before me there gleamed, in abrupt whiteness, a building evidently designed for the family mausoleum — classical in its outline, with the blind iron door niched into stone walls of massive thickness, and surrounded by a funereal garden of roses and evergreens, fenced with an iron rail, parti-gilt.

The suddenness with which this House of the Dead came upon me heightened almost into pain, if not into awe, the dismal impression which the aspect of the deserted home in its neighborhood had made. I spurred my horse, and soon arrived at the door of my patient, who lived in a fair brick house at the other extremity of the park.

I found my patient, a man somewhat advanced in years, but of a robust conformation, in bed; he had been seized with a fit, which was supposed to be apoplectic, a few hours before; but was already sensible and out of immediate danger. After I had prescribed a few simple remedies, I took aside the patient's wife, and went with her to the parlor below stairs, to make some inquiry about her husband's ordinary regimen and habits of life. These seemed sufficiently regular; I could discover no apparent cause for the attack, which presented symptoms not familiar to my experience. "Has your husband ever had such fits before?"

"Never!"

"Had he experienced any sudden emotion? Had he heard any unexpected news? or had anything happened to put him out?"

The woman looked much disturbed at these inquiries. I pressed them more urgently. At last she burst into tears, and clasping my hand, said: "Oh! doctor, I ought to tell you — I sent for you on purpose — yet I fear you will not believe me: my good man has seen a ghost!"

"A ghost!" said I, repressing a smile. "Well, tell me all, that I may prevent the ghost coming again."

The woman's story was prolix. Its substance was this: Her husband, habitually an early riser, had left his bed that morning still earlier than usual, to give directions about some cattle that were to be sent for sale to a neighboring fair. An hour afterwards he had been found by a shepherd near the mausoleum, apparently lifeless. On being removed to his own house, he had recovered speech, and bidding all except his wife leave the room, he then told her that on walking across the park towards the cattle-sheds, he had seen, what appeared to him at first, a pale light by the iron door of the mausoleum. On approaching nearer, this light changed into the distinct and visible form of his master, Sir Philip Derval, who was then abroad — supposed to be in the East, where he had resided for many years. The impression on the steward's mind was so strong, that he called out, "Oh! Sir Philip!" when, looking still more intently, he perceived that the face was that of a corpse. As he continued to gaze, the apparition seemed gradually to recede, as if vanishing into the sepulchre itself. He knew no more; he became unconscious. It was the excess of the poor woman's alarm, on hearing this strange tale, that made her resolve to send for me instead of the parish apothecary. She fancied so astounding a cause for her husband's seizure could only be properly dealt with by some medical man reputed to have more than ordinary learning. And the steward himself objected to the apothecary in the immediate neighborhood, as more likely to annoy him by gossip than a physician from a comparative distance.

I took care not to lose the confidence of the good wife by parading too quickly my disbelief in the phantom her husband declared that he had seen; but as the story itself seemed at once to decide the nature of the fit to be epileptic, I began to tell her of similar delusions which, in my experience, had occurred to those subjected to epilepsy, and finally soothed her into the conviction that the apparition was clearly reducible to natural causes. Afterwards, I led her on to talk about Sir Philip Derval, less from any curiosity I felt about the absent proprietor than from a desire to re-familiarize her own mind to his image as a living man. The steward had been in the service of Sir Philip's father, and had known Sir Philip himself from a child. He was warmly attached to his master, whom the old woman described as a man of rare benevolence and great eccentricity, which last she imputed to his studious habits. He had succeeded to the title and estates as a minor. For the first few years after attaining his majority, he had mixed much in the world. When at Derval Court his house had been filled with gay companions, and was the scene of lavish hospitality. But the estate was not in proportion to the grandeur of the mansion, still less to the expenditure of the owner. He had become greatly embarrassed; and some love disappointment (so it was rumored) occurring simultaneously with his pecuniary difficulties, he had suddenly changed his way of life, shut himself up from his old friends, lived in seclusion, taking to books and scientific pursuits, and as the old woman said, vaguely and expressively, "to old ways." He had gradually by an economy that, towards himself, was penurious, but which did not preclude much judicious generosity to others, cleared off his debts, and once more rich, he had suddenly quitted the country, and taken to a life of travel. He was now about forty-eight years old, and had been eighteen years abroad. He wrote frequently to his steward, giving him minute and thoughtful instructions in regard to the employment, comforts, and homes of the peasantry, but peremptorily ordering him to spend no money on the grounds and mansion, stating as a reason why the latter might be allowed to fall into decay, his intention to pull it down whenever he returned to England.

I stayed sometime longer than my engagements well warranted at my patient's house, not leaving till the sufferer, after a quiet sleep, had removed from his bed to his arm-chair, taken food, and seemed perfectly recovered from his attack.

Riding homeward, I mused on the difference that education makes, even pathologically, between man and man. Here was a brawny inhabitant of rural fields, leading the healthiest of lives, not conscious of the faculty we call imagination, stricken down almost to Death's door by his fright at an optical illusion, explicable, if examined, by the same simple causes which had impressed me the night before with a moment's belief in a sound and a spectre — me who, thanks to sublime education, went so quietly to sleep a few minutes after, convinced that no phantom, the ghostliest that ear ever heard or eye ever saw, can be anything else but a nervous phenomenon.

CHAPTER XXII.

THAT evening I went to Mrs. Poyntz's; it was one of her ordinary "reception nights," and I felt that she would naturally expect my attendance as "a proper attention."

I joined a group engaged in general conversation, of which Mrs. Poyntz herself made the centre, knitting as usual, rapidly while she talked, slowly when she listened.

Without mentioning the visit I had paid that morning, I turned the conversation on the different country places in the neighborhood, and then incidentally asked,

"What sort of a man is Sir Philip Derval? Is it not strange that he should suffer so fine a place to fall into decay?" The answers I received added little to the information I had already obtained. Mrs. Poyntz knew nothing of Sir Philip Derval, except as a man of large estates, whose rental had been greatly increased by a rise in the value of property he possessed in the town of L——, and which lay contiguous to that of her husband. Two or three of the older inhabitants of the Hill had remembered Sir Philip in his early days, when he was gay, high-spirited, hospitable, lavish. One observed that the only person in L—— whom he had admitted to his subsequent seclusion was Dr. Lloyd, who was then without practice, and whom he had employed as an assistant in certain chemical experiments.

Here a gentleman struck into the conversation. He was a stranger to me and to L——, a visitor to one of the dwellers on the Hill, who had asked leave to present him to its queen as a great traveller and an accomplished antiquary.

Said this gentleman: "Sir Philip Derval! I know him. I met him in the East. He was then still, I believe, very fond of chemical science; a clever, odd, philanthropical man; had studied medicine, or at least practised it; was said to have made many marvellous cures. I became acquainted with him in Aleppo. He had come to that town, not much frequented by English travellers, in order to inquire into the murder of two men, of whom one was his friend and the other his countryman."

"This is interesting," said Miss Poyntz, dryly. "We who live on this innocent Hill all love stories of crime; murder is the pleasantest subject you could have hit on. Pray give us the details."

"So encouraged," said the traveller, good-humoredly, "I will not hesitate to communicate the little I know. In Aleppo, there had lived for some years a man who was held by the natives in great reverence. He had the reputation of extraordinary wisdom, but was difficult of access; the lively imagination of the Orientals invested his character with the fascinations of fable; in short, Haroun of Aleppo was popularly considered a magician. Wild stories were told of his powers, of his preternatural age, of his hoarded treasures. Apart from such disputable titles to homage, there seemed no question, from all I heard, that his learning was considerable, his charities extensive, his manner of life irreproachably ascetic. He appears to have resembled those Arabian sages of the Gothic age to whom modern science is largely indebted—a mystic enthusiast, but an earnest scholar. A wealthy and singular Englishman, long resident in another part of the East, afflicted by some languishing disease, took a journey to Alleppo to cousult this sage, who, among his other acquirements, was held to have discovered rare secrets in medicine—his countrymen said in 'charms.' One morning, not long after the Englishman's arrival, Haroun was found dead in his bed, apparently strangled, and the Englishman, who lodged in another part of the town, had disappeared; but some of his clothes, and a crutch on which he habitually supported himself, were found a few miles distant from Aleppo, near the roadside. There appeared no doubt that he, too, had been murdered, but his corpse could not be discovered. Sir Philip Derval had been a loving disciple of this Sage of Aleppo, to whom he assured me he owed not only that knowledge of medicine which, by report, Sir Philip possessed, but the insight into various truths of nature, on the promulgation of which, it was evident, Sir Philip cherished the ambition to found a philosophical celebrity for himself."

"Of what description were those truths of nature?" I asked, somewhat sarcastically.

"Sir, I am unable to tell you, for Sir Philip did not inform me, nor did I much care to ask; for what may be revered as truths in Asia are usually despised as dreams in Europe. To return to my story. Sir Philip had been in Aleppo a little time before the murder; had left the Englishman under the care of Haroun; he returned to Aleppo on hearing the tragic events I have related, and was busied in collecting such evidence as could be gleaned, and instituting inquiries after our missing countryman, at the time I myself chanced to arrive in the city. I assisted in his researches, but without avail. The assassins remained undiscovered. I do not myself doubt that they were mere vulgar robbers. Sir

Philip had a darker suspicion, of which he made no secret to me; but as I confess that I thought the suspicion groundless, you will pardon me if I do not repeat it. Whether, since I left the East, the Englishman's remains have been discovered, I know not. Very probably; for I understand that his heirs have got hold of what fortune he left—less than was generally supposed. But it was reported that he had buried great treasures, a rumor, however absurd, not altogether inconsistent with his character."

"What was his character?" asked Mrs. Poyntz.

"One of evil and sinister repute. He was regarded with terror by the attendants who had accompanied him to Alleppo. But he had lived in a very remote part of the East, little known to Europeans, and, from all I could learn, had there established an extraordinary power, strengthened by superstitious awe. He was said to have studied deeply that knowledge which the philosophers of old called 'occult,' not, like the Sage of Aleppo, for benevolent, but for malignant ends. He was accused of conferring with evil spirits, and filling his barbaric court (for he lived in a kind of savage royalty) with charmers and sorcerers. I suspect, after all, that he was only, like myself, an ardent antiquary, and cunningly made use of the fear he inspired in order to secure his authority, and prosecute in safety researches into ancient sepulchres or temples. His great passion was, indeed, in excavating such remains, in his neighborhood; with what result I know not, never having penetrated so far into regions infested by robbers and pestiferous with malaria. He wore the Eastern dress, and always carried jewels about him. I came to the conclusion that for the sake of these jewels he was murdered, perhaps by some of his own servants (and, indeed, two at least of his suite were missing), who then at once buried his body, and kept their own secret. He was old, very infirm; could never have got very far from the town without assistance."

"You have not yet told us his name," said Mrs. Poyntz.

"His name was Grayle."

"Grayle!" exclaimed Mrs. Poyntz, dropping her work, "Louis Grayle?"

"Yes; Louis Grayle. You could not have known him?"

"Known him! No. But I have often heard my father speak of him. Such was then the tragic end of that strange dark creature, for whom, as a young girl in the nursery, I used to feel a kind of fearful, admiring interest?"

"It is your turn to narrate now," said the traveller.

And we all drew closer round our hostess, who remained silent some moments, her brow thoughtful, her work suspended.

"Well," said she at last, looking round us with a lofty air, which seemed half-defying, "force and courage are always fascinating, even when they are quite in the wrong. I go with the world, because the world goes with me; if it did not ——." Here she stopped for a moment, clenched the firm, white hand, and then scornfully waved it, left the sentence unfinished, and broke into another:

"Going with the world, of course we must march over those who stand against it. But when one man stands single-handed against our march, we do not despise him; it is enough to crush. I am very glad I did not see Louis Grayle when I was a girl of sixteen." Again she paused a moment—and resumed: "Louis Grayle was the only son of a usurer, infamous for the rapacity with which he had acquired enormous wealth. Old Grayle desired to rear his heir as a gentleman; sent him to Eton; boys are always aristocratic; his birth was soon thrown in his teeth; he was fierce; he struck boys bigger than himself—fought till he was half-killed. My father was at school with him; described him as a tiger-whelp. One day he—still a fag—struck a sixth-form boy. Sixth-form boys do not fight fags; they punish them. Louis Grayle was ordered to hold out his hand to the cane; he received the blow, drew forth his school-boy knife, and stabbed the punisher. After that he left Eton. I don't think he was publicly expelled—too mere a child for that honor—but he was taken or sent away; educated with great care under the first masters at home; when he was of age to enter the University, old Grayle was dead. Louis was sent by his guardians to Cambridge, with acquirements far exceeding the average of young men, and with unlimited command of money. My father was at the same college, and described him again — haughty, quarrelsome, reckless, handsome, aspiring, brave. Does that kind of creature interest you, my dears?" (appealing to the ladies).

"La!" said Miss Brabazon; "a horrid usurer's son!"

"Ay, true; the vulgar proverb says it is good to be born with a silver spoon in one's mouth; so it is when one has one's own family crest on it; but when it is a spoon on which people recognize their family crest, and cry out, 'Stolen from our plate-chest,' it is a heritage that outlaws a babe in his cradle. However, young men at college who want money are less scrupulous about descent than boys at Eton are. Louis Grayle found, while at college, plenty of well-born acquaintances willing to recover from him some of the plunder his father had extorted from theirs. He was too wild to distinguish himself by academical honors, but my father said that the tutors of the college declared there were not six undergraduates in the University who knew as much hard and dry science as wild Louis Grayle. He went into the world, no doubt, hoping to shine; but his father's name was too notorious to admit the son into good society. The Polite World, it is true, does not examine a scutcheon with the nice eye of a herald, nor look upon riches with the stately contempt of a stoic — still the Polite World has its family pride and its moral sentiment. It does not like to be cheated — I mean, in money matters; and when the son of the man who has emptied its purse and foreclosed on its acres, rides by its club-windows, hand on haunch, and head in the air, no lion has a scowl more awful, no hyæna a laugh more dread, than that same easy, good-tempered, tolerant, polite, well-bred World which is so pleasant an acquaintance, so languid a friend, and — so remorseless an enemy. In short, Louis Grayle claimed the right to be courted — he was shunned; to be admired — he was loathed. Even his old college acquaintances were shamed out of knowing him. Perhaps he could have lived through all this had he sought to glide quietly into position; but he wanted the tact of the well-bred, and strove to storm his way, not to steal it. Reduced for companions to needy parasites, he braved and he shocked all decorous opinion by that ostentation of excess, which made Richelieus and Lauzuns the rage. But then Richelieus and Lauzuns were dukes! He now very naturally took the Polite World into hate — gave it scorn for scorn. He would ally himself with Democracy; his wealth could not get him into a club, but it would buy him into parliament; he could not be a Lauzun, nor, perhaps, a Mirabeau, but he might be a Danton. He had plenty of knowledge and audacity, and with knowledge and audacity a good hater is sure to be eloquent. Possibly, then, this poor Louis Grayle might have made a great figure, left his mark on his age and his name in history; but in contesting the borough, which he was sure to carry, he had to face an opponent in a real fine gentleman whom his father had ruined, cool and high-bred, with a tongue like a rapier, a sneer like an adder. A quarrel of course; Louis Grayle sent a challenge. The fine gentleman, known to be no coward (fine gentlemen never are), was at first disposed to refuse with contempt. But Grayle had made himself the idol of the mob; and at a word from Grayle, the fine gentleman might have been ducked at a pump, or tossed in a blanket — that would have made him ridiculous; — to be shot at is a trifle, to be laughed at is serious. He therefore condescended to accept the challenge, and my father was his second.

"It was settled, of course, according to English custom, that both combatants should fire at the same time, and by signal. The antagonist fired at the right moment; his ball grazed Louis Grayle's temple. Louis Grayle had not fired. He now seemed to the seconds to take slow and deliberate aim. They called out to him not to fire — they were rushing to prevent him — when the trigger was pulled, and his opponent fell dead on the field. The fight was, therefore, considered unfair; Louis Grayle was tried for his life; he did not stand the trial in person.* He escaped to the Continent; hurried on to some distant, uncivilized lands; could not be traced; reappeared in England no more. The lawyer who conducted his defence pleaded skilfully. He argued that the delay in firing was not

* Mrs. Poyntz here makes a mistake in law, which, though very evident, her listeners do not seem to have noticed. Her mistake will be referred to later.

intentional, therefore not criminal—the effect of the stun which the wound in the temple had occasioned. The judge was a gentleman, and summed up the evidence so as to direct the jury to a verdict against the low wretch who had murdered a gentleman. But the jurors were not gentlemen, and Grayle's advocate had of course excited their sympathy for a son of the people whom a gentleman had wantonly insulted—the verdict was manslaughter. But the sentence emphatically marked the aggravated nature of the homicide—three years' imprisonment. Grayle eluded the prison, but he was a man disgraced and an exile—his ambition blasted, his career an outlaw's, and his age not yet twenty-three. My father said that he was supposed to have changed his name; none knew what had become of him. And so this creature, brilliant and daring, whom if born under better auspices we might now be all fawning on, cringing to—after living to old age, no one knows how—dies murdered at Aleppo, no one, you say, knows by whom."

"I saw some account of his death in the papers about three years ago," said one of the party; "but the name was misspelt, and I had no idea that it was the same man who had fought the duel which Mrs. Colonel Poyntz has so graphically described. I have a very vague recollection of the trial; it took place when I was a boy, more than forty years since. The affair made a stir at the time, but was soon forgotten."

"Soon forgotten," said Mrs. Poyntz; "ay, what is

not? Leave your place in the world for ten minutes, and when you come back somebody else has taken it; but when you leave the world for good, who remembers that you had ever a place even in the parish register?'

"Nevertheless," said I, "a great poet has said, finely and truly,

'The sun of Homer shines upon us still.'"

"But it does not shine upon Homer; and learned folks tell me that we know no more who and what Homer was, if there was ever a single Homer at all, or, rather, a whole herd of Homers, than we know about the man in the moon — if there be one man there, or millions of men. Now, my dear Miss Brabazon, it will be very kind in you to divert our thoughts into channels less gloomy. Some pretty French air —— Dr. Fenwick, I have something to say to you." She drew me towards the window. "So Anne Ashleigh writes me word that I am not to mention your engagement. Do you think it quite prudent to keep it a secret?"

"I do not see how prudence is concerned in keeping it secret one way or the other — it is a mere matter of feeling. Most people wish to abridge, as far as they can, the time in which their private arrangements are the topic of public gossip."

"Public gossip is sometimes the best security for the due completion of private arrangements. As long as a girl is not known to be engaged, her betrothed must be prepared for rivals. Announce the engagement, and rivals are warned off."

"I fear no rivals."

"Do you not?" Bold man! I suppose you will write to Lilian?"

"Certainly."

"Do so, and constantly. By-the-way, Mrs. Ashleigh, before she went, asked me to send her back Lady Haughton's letter of invitation. What for? to show to you?"

"Very likely. Have you the letter still? May I see it?"

"Not just at present. When Lilian or Mrs. Ashleigh writes to you, come and tell me how they like their visit, and what other guests form the party."

Therewith she turned away and conversed apart with the traveller.

Her words disquieted me, and I felt that they were meant to do so—wherefore I could not guess. But there is no language on earth which has more words with a double meaning than that spoken by the Clever Woman, who is never so guarded as when she appears to be frank.

As I walked home thoughtfully, I was accosted by a young man, the son of one of the wealthiest merchants in the town. I had attended him with success, some months before, in a rheumatic fever; he and his family were much attached to me.

"Ah, my dear Fenwick, I am so glad to see you; I

owe you an obligation of which you are not aware — an exceedingly pleasant travelling companion. I came with him to-day from London, where I have been sight-seeing and holiday-making for the last fortnight."

"I suppose you mean that you kindly bring me a patient?"

"No, only an admirer. I was staying at Fenton's Hotel. It so happened one day that I had left in the coffee-room your last work on the Vital Principle, which, by-the-by, the bookseller assures me is selling immensely among readers as non-professional as myself. Coming into the coffee-room again, I found a gentleman reading the book. I claimed it politely; he as politely tendered his excuse for taking it. We made acquaintance on the spot. The next day we were intimate. He expressed great interest and curiosity about your theory and your experiments. I told him I knew you. You may guess if I described you as less clever in your practice than you are in your writings. And, in short, he came with me to L——, partly to see our flourishing town, principally on my promise to introduce him to you. My mother, you know, has what she calls a *dējeuner* to-morrow — *dējeuner* and dance. You will be there?"

"Thank you for reminding me of her invitation. I will avail myself of it if I can. Your new friend will be present? Who and what is he? A medical student?"

"No, a mere gentleman at ease; but seems to have a good deal of general information. Very young;

apparently very rich; wonderfully good looking. I am sure you will like him; everybody must."

"It is quite enough to prepare me to like him that he is a friend of yours." And so we shook hands and parted.

CHAPTER XXIII.

It was late in the afternoon of the following day before I was able to join the party assembled at the merchant's house; it was a villa about two miles out of the town, pleasantly situated, amidst flower-gardens, celebrated in the neighborhood for their beauty. The breakfast had been long over; the company was scattered over the lawn; some formed into a dance on the smooth lawn; some seated under shady awnings; others gliding amidst parterres, in which all the glow of color took a glory yet more vivid under the flush of a brilliant sunshine, and the ripple of a soft, western breeze. Music, loud and lively, mingled with the laughter of happy children, who formed much the larger number of the party.

Standing at the entrance of an arched trellis, that led from the hardier flowers of the lawn to a rare collection of tropical plants under a lofty glass dome (connecting, as it were, the familiar vegetation of the North with that of the remotest East,) was a form that instantaneously caught and fixed my gaze. The entrance of the arcade was filled with parasite creepers, in prodigal luxuriance, of variegated, gorgeous tints — scarlet, golden, purple; and the form, an idealized picture of man's youth fresh from the hand of Nature, stood literally in a frame of blooms.

Never have I seen human face so radiant as that young man's. There was in the aspect an indescribable something that literally dazzled. As one continued to gaze, it was with surprise; one was forced to acknowledge that in the features themselves there was no faultless regularity; nor was the young man's stature imposing — about the middle height. But the effect of the whole was not less transcendent. Large eyes, unspeakably lustrous; a most harmonious coloring; an expression of contagious animation and joyousness; and the form itself so critically fine, that the welded strength of its sinews was best shown in the lightness and grace of its movements.

He was resting one hand carelessly on the golden locks of a child that had nestled itself against his knees, looking up in his face in that silent, loving wonder with which children regard something too strangely beautiful for noisy admiration; he himself was conversing with the host, an old, grey-haired, gouty man, propped on his crutched stick, and listening with a look of mournful envy. To the wealth of the old man all the flowers in that garden owed their renewed delight in the summer air and sun. Oh! that his wealth could renew to himself one hour of the youth whose incarnation stood beside him, Lord, indeed, of Creation; its splendor woven into his crown of beauty, its enjoyments subject to his sceptre of hope and gladness.

I was startled by the hearty voice of the merchant's son: "Ah, my dear Fenwick, I was afraid you would not come—you are late. There is the new friend of whom I spoke to you last night; let me now make you acquainted with him." He drew my arm in his, and led me up to the young man, where he stood under the arching flowers, and whom he then introduced to me by the name of Margrave.

Nothing could be more frankly cordial than Mr. Margrave's manner. In a few minutes I found myself conversing with him familiarly, as if we had been reared in the same home, and sported together in the same playgrounds. His vein of talk was peculiar, offhand, careless, shifting from topic to topic with a bright rapidity.

He said that he liked the place; proposed to stay in it some weeks; asked my address, which I gave to him; promised to call soon at an early hour, while my time was yet free from professional visits. I endeavored, when I went away, to analyze to myself the fascination which this young stranger so notably exercised over all who approached him; and it seemed to me, ever seeking to find material causes for all moral effects, that it rose from the contagious vitality of that rarest of all rare gifts in highly-civilized circles—perfect health; that health which is in itself the most exquisite luxury; which, finding happiness in the mere sense of existence, diffuses round it, like an atmosphere, the harmless hilarity of its bright animal being. Health, to the utmost perfection, is seldom known after childhood; health to the utmost cannot be enjoyed by those who overwork the brain, or admit the sure wear and tear of the passions. The creature I had just seen gave me the notion of youth in the golden age of the poets—the youth of the careless Arcadian, before nymph or shepherdess had vexed his heart with a sigh.

CHAPTER XXIV.

THE house I occupied at L—— was a quaint, old-fashioned building—a corner-house. One side, in which was the front entrance, looked upon a street which, as there were no shops in it, and it was no direct thoroughfare to the busy centres of the town, was always quiet, and at some hours of the day almost deserted. The other side of the house fronted a lane; opposite to it was the long and high wall of the garden to a Young Ladies' Boarding-School. My stables adjoined the house, abutting on a row of smaller buildings, with little gardens before them, chiefly occupied by mercantile clerks and retired tradesmen. By the lane there was a short and ready access both to the high turnpike-road, and to some pleasant walks through green meadows and along the banks of a river.

This house I had inhabited since my arrival at L——, and it had to me so many attractions, in a situation sufficiently central to be convenient for patients, and yet free from noise, and favorable to ready outlet into the country for such foot or horse exercise as my professional avocations would allow me to carve for myself out of what the Latin poet calls the "solid day," that I had refused to change it for one better suited to my increased income; but it was not a house which Mrs. Ashleigh would have liked for Lilian. The main objection to it in the eyes of the "genteel" was, that it had formerly belonged to a member of the healing profession, who united the shop of an apothecary to the diploma of a surgeon; but that shop had given the house a special attraction to me; for it had been built out on the side of the house which fronted the lane, occupying the greater portion of a small gravel court, fenced from the road by a low iron palisade, and separated from the body of the house itself by a short and narrow corridor that communicated with the entrance-hall. This shop I turned into a rude study for scientific experiments, in which I generally spent some early hours of the morning, before my visiting patients began to arrive. I enjoyed the stillness of its separation from the rest of the house; I enjoyed the glimpse of the great chestnut-trees, which overtopped the wall of the school-garden; I enjoyed the ease with which, by opening the glazed sash-door, I could get out, if disposed for a short walk, into the pleasant fields; and so completely had I made this sanctuary my own, that not only my man-servant knew that I was never to be disturbed when in it, except by the summons of a patient, but even the house-maid was forbidden to enter it with broom or duster, except upon special invitation. The last thing at night, before retiring to rest, it was the man-servant's business to see that the sash-window was closed, and the gate to the iron palisade locked; but during the day-time I so often went out of the house by that private way that the gate was then very seldom locked, nor the sash-door bolted from within. In the town of L—— there was little apprehension of house-robberies—especially in the daylight—and certainly in this room, cut off from the main building, there was nothing to attract a vulgar cupidity. A few of the apothecary's shelves and cases still remained on the walls, with, here and there, a bottle of some chemical preparation for experiment. Two or three worm-eaten, wooden chairs; two or three shabby old tables; an old walnut-tree bureau, without a lock, into which odds and ends were confusedly thrust, and sundry ugly-looking inventions of mechanical science, were, assuredly, not the articles which a timid proprietor would guard with jealous care from the chances of robbery. It will be seen later why I have been thus prolix in description. The morning after I had met the young stranger by whom I had been so favorably impressed, I was up as usual, a little before the sun, and long before any of my servants were astir. I went first into the room I have mentioned, and which I shall henceforth designate as my study, opened the window, unlocked the gate, and sauntered for some minutes up and down the silent lane skirting the opposite wall, and overhung by the chestnut-trees rich in the garniture of a glorious summer; then, refreshed for work, I re-entered my study and was soon absorbed in the examination of that now well-known machine, which was then, to me at least, a novelty; invented, if I remember right, by Dubois-Reymond, so distinguished by his researches into the mysteries of organic electricity. It is a wooden cylinder fixed against the edge of a table; on the table two vessels filled with salt and water are so placed that, as you close your hand on the cylinder, the fore-finger of each hand can drop into the water; each of the vessels has a metallic plate, and communicates by wires with a galvanometer with its needle. Now the theory is, that if you clutch the cylinder firmly with the right hand, leaving the left perfectly passive, the needle in the galvanometer will move from west to south; if, in like manner, you exert the left arm, leaving the right arm passive, the needle will deflect from west to north. Hence, it is argued that the electric current is induced through the agency of the nervous system, and that, as human Will produces the muscular contraction requisite, so is it human Will that causes the deflection of the needle. I imagined that if this theory were substantiated by experiment, the discovery might lead to some sublime and unconjectured secret of science. For human Will, thus actively effective on the electric current, and all matter, animate or inanimate, having more or less of electricity, a vast field became opened to conjecture. By what series of patient experimental deduction might not science arrive at the solution of problems which the Newtonian law of gravitation does not suffice to solve; and —— But here I halt. At the date which my story has reached my mind never lost itself long in the Cloud-land of Guess.

I was dissatisfied with my experiment. The needle stirred, indeed, but erratically, and not in directions which, according to the theory, should correspond to my movement. I was about to dismiss the trial with some uncharitable contempt of the foreign philosopher's dogmas, when I heard a loud ring at my street door. While I paused to conjecture whether my servant was yet up to attend to the door, and which of my patients was the most likely to summon me at so unseasonable an hour, a shadow darkened my window. I looked up, and to my astonishment beheld the brilliant face of Mr. Margrave. The sash to the door was already partially opened; he raised it higher, and walked into the room. "Was it you who rang at the street door, and at this hour?" said I.

"Yes; and observing, after I had rung, that all the shutters were still closed, I felt ashamed of my own rash action, and made off rather than brave the reproachful face of some injured housemaid, robbed of her morning dreams. I turned down that pretty lane — lured by the green of the chestnut-trees — caught sight of you through the window, took courage, and here I am! You forgive me?" While thus speaking, he continued to move along the littered floor of the dingy room, with the undulating restlessness of some wild animal in the confines of its den, and he now went on, in short, fragmentary sentences, very slightly linked together, but smoothed, as it were, into harmony by a voice musical and fresh as a sky-lark's warble. "Morning dreams, indeed! dreams that waste the life of such a morning. Rosy magnificence of a summer dawn! Do you not pity the fool who prefers to lie a-bed, and to dream rather than to live? What! and you, strong man, with those noble limbs, in this den! Do you not long for a rush through the green of the fields, a bath in the blue of the river?"

Here he came to a pause, standing, still in the grey light of the growing day, with eyes whose joyous lustre forestalled the sun's, and lips which seemed to laugh even in repose.

But presently those eyes, as quick as they were bright, glanced over the walls, the floor, the shelves, the phials, the mechanical inventions, and then rested full on my cylinder fixed to the table. He approached, examined it curiously, asked what it was? I explained. To gratify him, I sat down and renewed my experiment, with equally ill success. The needle, which should have moved from west to south, describing an angle of from 30 degrees to 40 or even 50 degrees, only made a few troubled, undecided oscillations.

"Tut," cried the young man, "I see what it is; you have a wound in your right hand."

That was true. I had burnt my hand a few days before in a chemical experiment, and the sore had not healed.

"Well," said I, "and what does that matter?"

"Everything; the least scratch in the skin of the hand produces chemical actions on the electric current, independently of your will. Let me try."

He took my place, and in a moment the needle in the galvanometer responded to his grasp on the cylinder, exactly as the inventive philosopher had stated to be the due result of the experiment.

I was startled.

"But how came you, Mr. Margrave, to be so well acquainted with a scientific process little known, and but recently discovered?"

"I well acquainted! not so. But I am fond of all experiments that relate to animal life. Electricity, especially, is full of interest."

On that I drew him out (as I thought), and he talked volubly. I was amazed to find that this young man, in whose brain I had conceived thought kept one careless holiday, was evidently familiar with the physical sciences, and especially with chemistry, which was my own study by predilection. But never had I met with a student in whom a knowledge so extensive was mixed up with notions so obsolete or so crotchety. In one sentence he showed that he had mastered some late discovery by Faraday or Liebig; in the next sentence he was talking the wild fancies of Cardan or Van Helmont. I burst out laughing at some paradox about sympathetic powders, which he enounced as if it were a recognized truth."

"Pray tell me," said I, "who was your master in physics, for a cleverer pupil never had a more crack-brained teacher."

"No," he answered, with his merry laugh, "it is not the teacher's fault. I am a mere parrot; just cry out a few scraps of learning picked up here and there. But, however, I am fond of all researches into Nature; all guesses at her riddles. To tell you the truth, one reason why I have taken to you so heartily is not only that your published work caught my fancy in the dip which I took into its contents (pardon me if I say dip, I never do more than dip into any book), but also because young * * * * tells me that which all whom I have met in this town confirm; viz., that you are one of those few practical chemists who are at once exceedingly cautious and exceedingly bold — willing to try every new experiment, but submitting experiment to rigid tests. Well, I have an experiment running wild in this giddy head of mine, and I want you, some day when at leisure, to catch it, fix it as you have fixed that cylinder; make something of it. I am sure you can."

"What is it?"

"Something akin to the theories in your work. You

would replenish or preserve to each special constitution the special substance that may fail to the equilibrium of its health. But you own that in a large proportion of cases the best cure of disease is less to deal with the disease itself than to support and stimulate the whole system, so as to enable Nature to cure the disease and restore the impaired equilibrium by her own agencies. Thus, if you find that in certain cases of nervous debility a substance like nitric acid is efficacious, it is because the nitric acid has a virtue in locking up, as it were, the nervous energy — that is, preventing all undue waste. Again, in some cases of what is commonly called feverish cold, stimulants like ammonia assist Nature itself to get rid of the disorder that oppresses its normal action; and, on the same principle, I apprehend, it is contended that a large average of human lives is saved in those hospitals which have adopted the supporting system of ample nourishment and alcoholic stimulants."

"Your medical learning surprises me," said I, smiling, "and without pausing to notice where it deals somewhat superficially with disputable points in general, and my own theory in particular, I ask you for the deduction you draw from your premises."

"It is simply this: that to all animate bodies, however various, there must be one principle in common — the vital principle itself. What, if there be one certain means of recruiting that principle? and what if that secret can be discovered?"

"Pshaw! The old illusion of the mediæval empirics."

"Not so. But the mediæval empirics were great discoverers. You sneer at Van Helmont, who sought, in water, the principle of all things; but Van Helmont discovered in his search those invisible bodies called gases. Now the principle of life must be certainly ascribed to a gas.* And whatever is a gas, chemistry

* "According to the views we have mentioned, we must ascribe life to a gas, that is, to an aëriform body."—LIEBIG, *Organic Chemistry, Playfair's translation*, p. 363. It is perhaps not less superfluous to add that Liebig does not support the views "according to which life must be ascribed to a gas," than it would be to state, had Dugald Stewart been quoted as writing, "According to the views we have mentioned the mind is but a bundle of impressions," that Dugald Stewart was not supporting, but opposing, the views of David Hume. The quotation is merely meant to show, in the shortest possible compass, that there are views entertained by speculative reasoners of our day which, according to Liebig, would lead to the inference at which Margrave so boldly arrives. Margrave is, however, no doubt, led to his belief by his reminiscences of Van Helmont, to whose discovery of gas he is referring. Van Helmont plainly affirms "that the arterial spirit of our life is of the nature of a gas;" and in the same chapter (on the fiction of elementary complexions and mixtures) says, "Seeing that the spirit of our life, since it is a gas, is most mightily and swiftly affected by any other gas," &c. He repeats the same dogma in his treatise on Long Life, and indeed very generally throughout his writings, observing, in his Chapter on the "Vital Air," that the spirit of life is a salt, sharp vapor, made of the arterial blood, &c. Liebig, therefore, in confuting some modern notions as to the nature of contagion by miasma, is leading their reasonings back to that assumption in the dawn of physiological science by which the discoverer of gas exalted into the principle of life the substance to which he first gave the name now so familiarly known. It is nevertheless just to Van Helmont to add that his conception of the vital prin-

should not despair of producing! But I can argue no longer now — never can argue long at a stretch — we are wasting the morning; and, joy! the sun is up! See! Out! come out! out! and greet the great Life-giver face to face."

I could not resist the young man's invitation. In a few minutes we were in the quiet lane under the glinting chestnut-trees. Margrave was chanting, low, a wild tune — words in a strange language.

"What words are those? no European language, I think; for I know a little of most of the languages which are spoken in our quarter of the globe, at least by its more civilized races."

"Civilized race! What is civilization? Those words were uttered by men who founded empires when Europe itself was not civilized! Hush, is it not a grand old air?" and lifting his eyes towards the sun, he gave vent to a voice clear and deep as a mighty bell! The

ciple was very far from being as purely materialistic as it would seem to those unacquainted with his writings; for he carefully distinguishes that principle of life which he ascribes to a gas, and by which he means the sensuous animal life, from the intellectual, immortal principle of soul. Van Helmont, indeed, was a sincere believer of Divine Revelation. "The Lord Jesus is the way, the truth, and the life," says with earnest humility this daring genius, in that noble Chapter "on the completing of the mind by the 'prayer of silence,' and the loving offering up of the heart, soul, and strength to the obedience of the Divine will," from which some of the most eloquent of recent philosophers, arguing against materialism, have borrowed largely in support and in ornament of their lofty cause.

air was grand — the words had a sonorous swell that suited it, and they seemed to me jubilant and yet solemn. He stopped abruptly, as a path from the lane had led us into the fields, already half-bathed in sunlight — dews glittering on the hedgerows.

"Your song," said I, "would go well with the clash of cymbals or the peal of the organ. I am no judge of melody, but this strikes me as that of a religious hymn."

"I compliment you on the guess. It is a Persian fire-worshipper's hymn to the sun. The dialect is very different from modern Persian. Cyrus the Great might have chanted it on his march upon Babylon."

"And where did you learn it?"

"In Persia itself."

"You have travelled much — learned much — and are so young and so fresh. Is it an impertinent question if I ask whether your parents are yet living, or are you wholly lord of yourself?"

"Thank you for the question — pray make my answer known in the town. Parents I have not — never had."

"Never had parents!"

"Well, I ought rather to say that no parents ever owned me. I am a natural son — a vagabond — a nobody. When I came of age I received an anonymous letter, informing me that a sum—I need not say what—but more than enough for all I need, was lodged at an English banker's in my name; that my mother had died in my infancy; that my father was also dead —

but recently; that as I was a child of love, and he was unwilling that the secret of my birth should ever be traced, he had provided for me, not by will, but in his life, by a sum consigned to the trust of the friend who now wrote to me; I need give myself no trouble to learn more; faith, I never did. I am young, healthy, rich — yes, rich! Now you know all, and you had better tell it, that I may win no man's courtesy and no maiden's love upon false pretences. I have not even a right, you see, to the name I bear. Hist! let me catch that squirrel."

With what a panther-like bound he sprang! The squirrel eluded his grasp, and was up the oak-tree; in a moment he was up the oak-tree too. In amazement I saw him rising from bough to bough — saw his bright eyes and glittering teeth through the green leaves; presently I heard the sharp piteous cry of the squirrel—echoed by the youth's merry laugh—and down, through that maze of green, Margrave came, dropping on the grass and bounding up, as Mercury might have bounded with his wings at his heels.

"I have caught him — what pretty brown eyes!"

Suddenly the gay expression of his face changed to that of a savage; the squirrel had wrenched itself half-loose, and bitten him. The poor brute! In an instant its neck was wrung — its body dashed on the ground; and that fair young creature, every feature quivering with rage, was stamping his foot on his victim again and again! it was horrible. I caught him by the arm indignantly. He turned round on me like a wild beast disturbed from its prey. His teeth set, his hand lifted, his eyes like balls of fire.

"Shame!" said I, calmly; "shame on you!"

He continued to gaze on me a moment or so; his eye glaring—his breath panting—and then, as if mastering himself with an involuntary effort, his arm dropped to his side, and he said quite humbly, "I beg your pardon; indeed I do. I was beside myself for a moment; I cannot bear pain;" and he looked in deep compassion for himself at his wounded hand. "Venomous brute!" And he stamped again on the body of the squirrel, already crushed out of shape.

I moved away in disgust, and walked on.

But presently I felt my arm softly drawn aside, and a voice, dulcet as the coo of a dove, stole its way into my ears. There was no resisting the charm with which this extraordinary mortal could fascinate even the hard and the cold; nor them, perhaps, the least. For as you see in extreme old age, when the heart seems to have shrunk into itself, and to leave but meagre and nipped affections for the nearest relations if grown up, the indurated egotism softens at once towards a playful child; or as you see in middle life, some misanthrope, whose nature has been soured by wrong and sorrow, shrink from his own species, yet make friends with inferior races and respond to the caress of a dog—so, for the worldling or the cynic, there was an attraction in the freshness of this joyous favorite of Nature — an attraction like that of a beautiful child, spoilt and wayward, or of a graceful animal, half docile, half fierce.

"But'," said I, with a smile, as I felt all displeasure gone, "such indulgence of passion for such a trifle is surely unworthy a student of philosophy!"

"Trifle," he said, dolorously. "But I tell you it is pain; pain is no trifle. I suffer. Look!"

I looked at the hand, which I took in mine. The bite no doubt had been sharp; but the hand that lay in my own was that which the Greek sculptor gives to a gladiator; not large (the extremities are never large in persons whose strength comes from the just proportion of all the members, rather than the factitious and partial force which continued muscular exertion will give to one part of the frame, to the comparative weakening of the rest), but the firm-knit joints, the solid fingers, the finished nails, the massive palm, the supple, polished skin, in which we recognize what Nature designs the human hand to be — the skilled, swift, mighty doer of all those marvels which win Nature herself from the wilderness.

"It is strange," said I, thoughtfully; "but your susceptibility to suffering confirms my opinion, which is different from the popular belief, viz., that pain is most acutely felt by those in whom the animal organization being perfect, and the sense of vitality exquisitely keen, every injury or lesion finds the whole system rise, as it were, to repel the mischief and communicate the consciousness of it to all those nerves which are the sentinels to the garrison of life. Yet my theory is scarcely borne out by general fact. The Indian savages must have a health as perfect as yours; a nervous system as fine. Witness their marvellous accuracy of ear, of eye, of scent, probably also of touch, yet they are indifferent to physical pain; or must I mortify your pride by saying that they have some moral quality defective in you which enables them to rise superior to it?"

"The Indian savages," said Margrave, sullenly, "have not a health as perfect as mine, and in what you call vitality—the blissful consciousness of life—they are as sticks and stones compared to me."

"How do you know?"

"Because I have lived with them. It is a fallacy to suppose that the savage has a health superior to that of the civilized man — if the civilized man be but temperate; and even if not, he has the stamina that can resist for years the effect of excesses which would destroy the savage in a month. As to the savage's fine perceptions of sense, such do not come from exquisite equilibrium of system, but are hereditary attributes transmitted from race to race, and strengthened by training from infancy. But is a pointer stronger and healthier than a mastiff, because the pointer through long descent and early teaching creeps stealthily to his game and stands to it motionless? I will talk of this later; now I suffer! Pain, pain! Has life any ill but pain?"

It so happened that I had about me some roots of the white lily, which I meant, before returning home, to leave with a patient suffering from one of those acute local inflammations, in which that simple remedy often affords great relief. I cut up one of these roots, and bound the cooling leaves to the wounded hand with my handkerchief.

"There," said I. "Fortunately, if you feel pain more sensibly than others, you will recover from it more quickly."

And in a few minutes my companion felt perfectly relieved, and poured out his gratitude with an extravagance of expression and a beaming delight of countenance which positively touched me.

"I almost feel," said I, "as I do when I have stilled an infant's wailing, and restored it smiling to its mother's breast."

"You have done so. I am an infant, and Nature is my mother. Oh, to be restored to the full joy of life, the scent of wild flowers, the song of birds, and this air—summer air—summer air!"

I know not why it was, but at that moment, looking at him and hearing him, I rejoiced that Lilian was not at L——.

"But I came out to bathe. Can we not bathe in that stream?"

"No. You would derange the bandage round your hand; and for all bodily ills, from the least to the gravest, there is nothing like leaving Nature at rest the moment we have hit on the means which assists her own efforts at cure."

"I obey, then; but I so love the water."

"You swim, of course?"

"Ask the fish if it swim. Ask the fish if it can escape me! I delight to dive down—down; to plunge after the startled trout, as an otter does; and then to get amongst those cool, fragrant reeds and bulrushes, or that forest of emerald weed which one sometimes finds waving under clear rivers. Man! man! could you live but an hour of my life you would know how horrible a thing it is to die!"

"Yet the dying do not think so; they pass away calm and smiling, as you will one day."

"I—I! die one day—die!" and he sank on the grass, and buried his face amongst the herbage, sobbing aloud.

Before I could get through half a dozen words, meant to soothe, he had once more bounded up, dashed the tears from his eyes, and was again singing some wild, barbaric chant. Abstracting itself from the appeal to its outward sense by melodies of which the language was unknown, my mind soon grew absorbed in meditative conjectures on the singular nature, so wayward, so impulsive, which had forced intimacy on a man grave and practical as myself.

I was puzzled how to reconcile so passionate a childishness, so undisciplined a want of self-control, with an experience of mankind so extended by travel, with an education, desultory and irregular indeed, but which must, at some time or other, have been familiarized to severe reasonings and laborious studies. In Margrave there seemed to be wanting that mysterious something which is needed to keep our faculties, however severally brilliant, harmoniously locked together—as the string by which a child mechanically binds the wild flowers it gathers; shaping them at choice into the garland or the chain.

CHAPTER XXV.

My intercourse with Margrave grew habitual and familiar. He came to my house every morning before sunrise; in the evenings we were again brought together; sometimes in the houses to which we were both invited, sometimes at his hotel, sometimes in my own home.

Nothing more perplexed me than his aspect of extreme youthfulness, contrasted with the extent of the travels, which, if he were to be believed, had left little of the known world unexplored. One day I asked him, bluntly, how old he was?

"How old do I look? How old should you suppose me to be?"

"I should have guessed you to be about twenty, till you spoke of having come of age some years ago."

"Is it a sign of longevity when a man looks much younger than he is?"

"Conjoined with other signs, certainly."

"Have I the other signs?"

"Yes, a magnificent, perhaps a matchless, constitutional organization. But you have evaded my question as to your age; was it an impertinence to put it?"

"No. I came of age—let me see—three years ago."

"So long since? Is it possible? I wish I had your secret!"

"Secret! What secret?"

"The secret of preserving so much of the boyish freshness in the wear and tear of man-like passions and man-like thoughts."

"You are still young yourself—under forty?"

"Oh, yes! some years under forty."

"And nature gave you a grander frame and a finer symmetry of feature than she bestowed on me."

"Pooh! pooh! You have the beauty that must charm the eyes of women, and that beauty in its sunny forenoon of youth. Happy man! if you love—and wish to be sure that you are loved again."

"What you call love—the unhealthy sentiment, the feverish folly—I left behind me, I think forever, when —"

"Ay, indeed—when?"

"I came of age!"

"Hoary cynic! and you despise love! So did I once. Your time may come."

"I think not. Does any animal, except man, love its fellow she-animal as man loves woman?"

"As man loves woman? No, I suppose not."

"And why should the subject animals be wiser than their king? But, to return — you would like to have my youth and my careless enjoyment of youth?"

"Can you ask—who would not?" Margrave looked at me for a moment with unusual seriousness, and then, in the abrupt changes common to his capricious temperament, began to sing softly one of his barbaric chants — a chant, different from any I had heard him sing before — made, either by the modulation of his voice or the nature of the tune, so sweet that, little as music generally affected me, this thrilled to my very heart's core. I drew closer and closer to him, and murmured when he paused.

"Is not that a love-song?"

"No," said he, "it is the song by which the serpent-charmer charms the serpent."

CHAPTER XXVI.

INCREASED intimacy with my new acquaintance did not diminish the charm of his society, though it brought to light some startling defects, both in his mental and moral organization. I have before said that his knowledge, though it had swept over a wide circuit and dipped into curious unfrequented recesses, was desultory and erratic. It certainly was not that knowledge, sustained and aspiring, which the poet ussures us is "the wing on which we mount to heaven." So, in his faculties themselves there were singular inequalities, or contradictions. His power of memory in some things seemed prodigious, but when examined it was seldom accurate; it could apprehend, but did not hold together with a binding grasp what metaphysicians call "complex ideas." He thus seemed unable to put it to any steadfast purpose in the sciences of which it retained, vaguely and loosely, many recondite principles. For the sublime and beautiful in literature he had no taste whatever. A passionate lover of nature, his imagination had no response to the arts by which nature is expressed or idealized; wholly unaffected by poetry or painting. Of the fine arts, music alone attracted and pleased him. His conversation was often eminently suggestive, touching on much, whether in books or mankind, that set one thinking, but I never remember him to have uttered any of those lofty or tender sentiments which form the connecting links between youth and genius. For if poets sing to the young, and the young hail their own interpreters in poets, it is because the tendency of both is to idealize the realities of life; finding everywhere in the Real a something that is noble or fair, and making the fair yet fairer, and the noble nobler still.

In Margrave's character there seemed no special

vices, no special virtues; but a wonderful vivacity, joyousness, animal good humor. He was singularly temperate, having a dislike to wine, perhaps from that purity of taste which belongs to health absolutely perfect. No healthful child likes alcohols, no animal except man, prefers wine to water.

But his main moral defect seemed to me, in a want of sympathy, even where he professed attachment. He who could feel so acutely for himself, be unmanned by the bite of a squirrel, and sob at the thought that he should one day die, was as callous to the sufferings of another as a deer who deserts and butts from him a wounded comrade.

I give an instance of this hardness of heart where I should have least expected to find it in him:

He had met and joined me as I was walking to visit a patient on the outskirts of the town, when we fell in with a group of children, just let loose for an hour or two from their day-school. Some of these children joyously recognized him as having played with them at their homes; they ran up to him, and he seemed as glad as themselves at the meeting.

He suffered them to drag him along with them, and became as merry and sportive as the youngest of the troop.

"Well, said I, laughing, "if you are going to play at leap-frog, pray don't let it be on the high road, or you will be run over by carts and draymen; see that meadow just in front to the left—off with you there!"

"With all my heart," cried Margrave, "while you pay your visit. Come along, boys."

A little urchin, not above six years old, but who was lame, began to cry, he could not run — he should be left behind.

Margrave stooped: "Climb on my shoulder, little one, and I'll be your horse."

The child dried its tears, and delightedly obeyed.

"Certainly," said I to myself, "Margrave, after all, must have a nature as gentle as it is simple. What other young man, so courted by all the allurements that steal innocence from pleasure, would stop in the thoroughfare to play with children?"

The thought had scarcely passed through my mind when I heard a scream of agony. Margrave had leaped the railing that divided the meadow from the road, and, in so doing, the poor child, perched on his shoulder, had, perhaps from surprise or fright, loosened its hold and fallen heavily — its cries were piteous. Margrave clapped his hands to his ears — uttered an exclamation of anger — and not even stopping to lift up the boy, or examine what the hurt was, called to the other children to come on, and was soon rolling with them on the grass, and pelting them with daisies. When I came up, only one child remained by the sufferer — his little brother, a year older than himself. The child had fallen on his arm, which was not broken, but violently contused. The pain must have been intense. I carried the child to his home, and had to remain there some time. I did not see Margrave till the next morning. When he then called, I felt so indignant that I could scarcely speak to him. When at last I rebuked him for his inhumanity, he seemed surprised; with difficulty remembered the circumstance, and then merely said — as if it were the most natural confession in the world —

"Oh, nothing so discordant as a child's wail. I hate discords. I am pleased with the company of children; but they must be children who laugh and play. Well! why do you look at me so sternly? What have I said to shock you?"

"Shock me — you shock manhood itself! Go; I cannot talk to you now. I am busy."

But he did not go; and his voice was so sweet, and his ways so winning, that disgust insensibly melted into that sort of forgiveness one accords (let me repeat the illustration) to the deer that forsakes its comrade. The poor thing knows no better. And what a graceful, beautiful thing *this* was!

The fascination — I can give it no other name — which Margrave exercised was not confined to me, it was universal — old, young, high, low, man, woman, child, all felt it. Never in Low Town had stranger, even the most distinguished, met with a reception so cordial — so flattering. His frank confession that he was a natural son, far from being to his injury, served to interest people more in him, and to prevent all those inquiries in regard to his connections and antecedents, which would otherwise have been afloat. To be sure, he was evidently rich; at least he had plenty of money. He lived in the best rooms in the principal hotel; was very hospitable; entertained the families with whom he had grown intimate; made them bring their children—music and dancing after dinner. Among the houses in which he had established familiar acquaintance was that of the mayor of the town, who had bought Dr. Lloyd's collection of subjects in natural history. To that collection the mayor had added largely by a very recent purchase. He had arranged these various specimens, which his last acquisitions had enriched by the interesting carcasses of an elephant and a hippopotamus, in a large wooden building contiguous to his dwelling, which had been constructed by a former proprietor (a retired fox-hunter) as a riding-house. And being a man who much affected the diffusion of knowledge, he proposed to open the museum to the admiration of the general public, and at his death, to bequeath it to the Athenæum or Literary Institute of his native town. Margrave, seconded by the influence of the mayor's daughter, had scarcely been three days at L—— before he had persuaded this excellent and public spirited functionary to inaugurate the opening of his museum by the popular ceremony of a ball. A temporary corridor should unite the drawing-rooms, which were on the ground floor, with the building that contained the collection; and thus the fête would be elevated above the frivolous character of a fashionable amusement, and consecrated to the solemnization of an intellectual institute. Dazzled by the brilliancy of this idea, the mayor announced his intention to give a ball that should include the surrounding neighborhood, and be worthy, in all expensive respects, of the dignity of himself and the occasion. A night had been fixed for the ball — a night that became memorable indeed to me! The entertainment was anticipated with a lively interest, in which even the Hill condescended to share. The Hill did not patronize mayors in general; but when a mayor gave a ball for a purpose so patriotic, and on a scale so splendid, the Hill liberally acknowledged that Commerce was, on the whole, a thing which the Eminence might, now and then, condescend to acknowledge without absolutely derogating from the rank which Providence had assigned to it amongst the High Places of earth. Accordingly, the Hill was permitted by its Queen to honor the first magistrate of Low Town by a promise to attend his ball. Now, as this festivity had originated in the suggestion of Margrave, so, by a natural association of ideas, every one, in talking of the ball, talked also of Margrave.

The Hill had at first affected to ignore a stranger whese début had been made in the mercantile circle of Low Town. But the Queen of the Hill now said, sententiously, "This new man in a few days has become a Celebrity. It is the policy of the Hill to adopt Celebrities, if the Celebrities pay respect to the Proprieties. Dr. Fenwick is requested to procure Mr. Margrave the advantage of being known to the Hill."

I found it somewhat difficult to persuade Margrave to accept the Hill's condescending overture. He seemed to have a dislike to all societies pretending to aristocratic distinction — a dislike expressed with a fierceness so unwonted, that it made one suppose he had, at some time or other, been subjected to mortification by the supercilious airs that blow upon heights so elevated. However, he yielded to my instances, and accompanied me one evening to Mrs. Poyntz's house. The Hill was encamped there for the occasion. Mrs. Poyntz was exceedingly civil to him, and after a few commonplace speeches, hearing that he was fond of music, consigned him to the caressing care of Miss Brabazon, who was at the head of the musical department in the Queen of the Hill's administration.

Mrs. Poyntz retired to her favorite seat near the window, inviting me to sit beside her; and while she knitted in silence, in silence my eye glanced toward Margrave in the midst of the group assembled round the piano.

Whether he was in more than usually high spirits, or whether he was actuated by a malign and impish desire to upset the established laws of decorum by which the gaieties of the Hill were habitually subdued into a serene and somewhat pensive pleasantness, I know not; but it was not many minutes before the orderly aspect of the place was grotesquely changed.

Miss Brabazon having come to the close of a complicated and dreary sonata, I heard Margrave abruptly ask her if she could play the Tarantella, that famous Neapolitan air which is founded on the legendary belief that the bite of the tarantula excites an irresistible desire to dance. On that high-bred spinster's confession that she was ignorant of the air, and had not even heard of the legend, Margrave said, "Let me play it to you, with variations of my own." Miss Brabazon graciously yielded her place at the instrument. Margrave seated himself — there was great curiosity to hear his performance. Margrave's fingers rushed over the keys, and there was a general start, the prelude was so unlike any known combination of harmonious sounds. Then he began a chant — song I can scarcely call it — words certainly not in Italian, perhaps in some uncivilized tongue, perhaps in impromptu gibberish. And the torture of the instrument now commenced in good earnest; it shrieked, it groaned, wilder and noisier. Beethoven's Storm, roused by the fell touch of a German pianist, were mild in comparison; and the mighty voice, dominating the anguish of the cracking keys, had the full diapason of a chorus. Certainly I am no judge of music, but to my ear the discord was terrific — to the ears of better informed amateurs it seemed ravishing. All were spellbound; even Mrs. Poyntz paused from her knitting, as the Fates paused from their web at the lyre of Orpheus. To this breathless delight, however, soon succeeded a general desire for movement. To my amazement I beheld these formal matrons and sober fathers of families forming themselves into a dance, turbulent as a children's ball at Christmas. And when, suddenly desisting from his music, Margrave started up, caught the skeleton hand of lean Miss Brabazon, and whirled her into the centre of the dance, I could have fancied myself at a witch's sabbat. My eye turned in scandalous alarm towards Mrs. Poyntz. That great creature seemed as much astounded as myself. Her eyes were fixed on the scene in a stare of positive stupor. For the first time, no doubt, in her life, she was overcome, deposed, dethroned. The awe of her presence was literally whirled away. The dance ceased as suddenly as it had begun. Darting from the galvanized mummy whom he had selected as his partner, Margrave shot to Mrs. Poyntz's side, and said, "Ten thousand pardons for quitting you so soon, but the clock warns me that I have an engagement elsewhere." In another moment he was gone.

The dance halted, people seemed slowly returning to their senses, looking at each other bashfully and ashamed.

"I could not help it, dear," sighed Miss Brabazon at last, sinking into a chair, and casting her deprecating, fainting eyes upon the hostess.

"It is witchcraft," said fat Mrs. Bruce, wiping her forehead.

"Witchcraft!" echoed Mrs. Poyntz; "it does indeed look like it. An amazing and portentous exhibition of animal spirits, and not to be endured by the Proprieties. Where on earth can that young savage have come from?"

"From savage lands," said I. "So he says."

"Do not bring him here again," said Mrs. Poyntz. "He would soon turn the Hill topsy-turvy. But how charming! I should like to see more of him," she added, in an under-voice, "if he would call on me some morning, and not in the presence of those for whose Proprieties I am responsible. Jane must be out in her ride with the Colonel."

Margrave never again attended the patrician festivities of the Hill. Invitations were poured upon him, especially by Miss Brabazon and the other old maids, but in vain.

"Those people," said he, "are too tamed and civilized for me; and so few young persons among them. Even that girl Jane is only young on the surface; inside, as old as the World, or her mother. I like youth, real youth—I am young, I am young!"

And, indeed, I observed he would attach himself to some young person, often to some child, as if with cordial and special favor, yet for not more than an hour or so, never distinguishing them by the same preference when he next met them. I made that remark to him, in rebuke of his fickleness, one evening when he had found me at work on my Ambitious Book, reducing to rule and measure the Laws of Nature.

"It is not fickleness," said he, "it is necessity."

"Necessity! Explain yourself."

"I seek to find what I have not found," said he; "it is my necessity to seek it, and among the young; and disappointed in one, I turn to another. Necessity again. But find it at last I must."

"I suppose you mean what the young usually seek in the young; and if, as you said the other day, you have left love behind you, you now wander back to re-find it."

"Tush! If I may judge by the talk of young fools, love may be found every day by him who looks out for it. What I seek is among the rarest of all discoveries. You might aid me to find it, and in so doing aid yourself to a knowledge far beyond all that your formal experiments can bestow."

"Prove your words, and command my services," said I, smiling somewhat disdainfully.

"You told me that you had examined into the alleged phenomena of animal magnetism, and proved some persons who pretend to the gift which the Scotch call second sight to be bungling impostors. You were right. I have seen the clairvoyants who drive their trade in this town; a common gipsy could beat them in their own calling. But your experience must have shown you that there are certain temperaments in which the gift of the Pythoness is stored, unknown to the possessor, undetected by the common observer; but the signs of which should be as apparent to the modern physiologist as they were to the ancient priest."

"I at least, as a physiologist, am ignorant of the signs — what are they?"

"I should despair of making you comprehend them

by mere verbal description. I could guide your observation to distinguish them unerringly were living subjects before us. But not one in a million has the gift to an extent available for the purposes to which the wise would apply it. Many have imperfect glimpses, few, few indeed, the unveiled, lucent sight. They who have but the imperfect glimpses, mislead and dupe the minds that consult them, because, being sometimes marvellously right, they excite a credulous belief in their general accuracy; and as they are but translators of dreams in their own brain, their assurances are no more to be trusted than are the dreams of commonplace sleepers. But where the gift exists to perfection, he who knows how to direct and to profit by it should be able to discover all that he desires to know for the guidance and preservation of his own life. He will be forewarned of every danger, forearmed in the means by which danger is avoided. For the eye of the true Pythoness matter has no obstruction, space no confines, time no measurement."

"My dear Margrave, you may well say that creatures so gifted are rare; and, for my part, I would as soon search for a unicorn, as, to use your affected expression, for a Pythoness."

"Nevertheless, whenever there comes across the course of your practice some young creature to whom all the evil of the world is as yet unknown, to whom the ordinary cares and duties of the world are strange and unwelcome; who, from the earliest dawn of reason, has loved to sit apart and to muse; before whose eyes visions pass unsolicited; who converses with those who are not dwellers on the earth, and beholds in the space landscapes which the earth does not reflect."

"Margrave, Margrave! of whom do you speak?"

"Whose frame, though exquisitely sensitive, has still a health and a soundness in which you recognize no disease; whose mind has a truthfulness that you know cannot deceive you, and a simple intelligence too clear to deceive itself; who is moved to a mysterious degree by all the varying aspects of external nature — innocently joyous or unaccountably sad — when, I say, such a being comes across your experience, inform me; and the chances are that the true Pythoness is found."

I had listened with vague terror, and with more than one exclamation of amazement, to descriptions which brought Lilian Ashleigh before me; and I now sat mute, bewildered, breathless, gazing upon Margrave, and rejoicing that, at least, Lilian he had never seen.

He returned my own gaze steadily, searchingly, and then, breaking into a slight laugh, resumed:

"You call my word 'Pythoness' affected. I know of no better. My recollections of classic anecdote and history are confused and dim; but somewhere I have read or heard that the priests of Delphi were accustomed to travel chiefly into Thrace or Thessaly in search of the virgins who might fitly administer their oracles, and that the oracles gradually ceased in repute as the priests became unable to discover the organization requisite in the priestesses, and supplied by craft and imposture, or by such imperfect fragmentary developments as belong now to professional clairvoyants, the gifts which Nature failed to afford. Indeed, the demand was one that must have rapidly exhausted so limited a supply. The constant strain upon faculties so wearing to the vital functions in their relentless exercise, under the artful stimulants by which the priests heightened their power, was mortal, and no Pythoness ever retained her life more than three years from the time that her gift was elaborately trained and developed."

"Pooh! I know of no classical authority for the details you so confidently cite. Perhaps some such legends may be found in the Alexandrian Platonists, but those mysteries are no authority on such a subject. After all," I added, recovering from my first surprise, or awe, "the Delphic oracles were proverbially ambiguous, and their responses might be read either way; a proof that the priests dictated the verses, though their arts on the unhappy priestess might throw her into real convulsions, and the real convulsions, not the false gift, might shorten her life. Enough of such idle subjects! Yet no! one question more. If you found your Pythoness, what then?"

"What then? Why, through her aid I might discover the process of an experiment which your practical science would assist me to complete."

"Tell me of what kind is your experiment; and precisely because such little science as I possess is exclusively practical, I may assist you without the help of the Pythoness."

Margrave was silent for some minutes, passing his hand several times across his forehead, which was a frequent gesture of his, and then rising, he answered, in listless accents:

"I cannot say more now, my brain is fatigued; and you are not yet in the right mood to hear me. By the way, how close and reserved you are with me!"

"How so?"

"You never told me that you were engaged to be married. You leave me, who thought to have won your friendship, to hear what concerns you so intimately from a comparative stranger."

"Who told you?"

"That woman with eyes that pry and lips that scheme, to whose house you took me."

"Mrs. Poyntz! is it possible? When?"

"This afternoon. I met her in the street — she stopped me, and, after some unmeaning talk, asked 'if I had seen you lately; if I did not find you very absent and distracted; no wonder — you were in love. The young lady was away on a visit, and wooed by a dangerous rival!'"

"Wooed by a dangerous rival!"

"Very rich, good looking, young. Do you fear him? You turn pale!"

"I do not fear, except so far as he who loves truly, loves humbly, and fears not that another may be preferred, but that another may be worthier of preference than himself. But that Mrs. Poyntz should tell you all this does amaze me. Did she mention the name of the young lady?"

"Yes; Lilian Ashleigh. Henceforth be more frank with me. Who knows? I may help you. Adieu!"

CHAPTER XXVII.

"WHEN Margrave had gone, I glanced at the clock —not yet nine. I resolved to go at once to Mrs. Poyntz. It was not an evening on which she received, but doubtless she would see me. She owed me an explanation. How thus carelessly divulge a secret she had been enjoined to keep? and this rival, of whom I was ignorant? It was no longer a matter of wonder that Margrave should have described Lilian's peculiar idiosyncrasies in his sketch of his fabulous Pythoness. Doubtless, Mrs. Poyntz had, with unpardonable levity of indiscretion, revealed all of which she disapproved in my choice. But for what object? Was this her boasted friendship for me? Was it consistent with the regard she professed for Mrs. Ashleigh and Lilian? Occupied by these perplexed and indignant thoughts, I arrived at Mrs. Poyntz's house, and was admitted to her presence. She was fortunately alone; her daughter and the Colonel had gone to some party on the Hill. I would not take the hand she held out to me on entrance; seated myself in stern displeasure, and proceeded at once to inquire if she had really betrayed to Mr. Margrave the secret of my engagement to Lilian.

"Yes, Allen Fenwick; I have this day told, not only Mr. Margrave, but every person I met who is likely to tell it to some one else, the secret of your engagement to Lilian Ashleigh. I never promised to conceal it; on the contrary, I wrote word to Anne Ashleigh that I would therein act as my own judgment counselled me. I think my words to you were that 'public gossip was sometimes the best security for the completion of private engagements.'"

"Do you mean that Mrs. or Miss Ashleigh recoils from the engagement with me, and that I should meanly compel them both to fulfil it by calling in the public to censure them — if — if —— Oh, madam, this is worldly artifice indeed!"

"Be good enough to listen to me quietly. I have never yet shown you the letter to Mrs. Ashleigh, written by Lady Haughton, and delivered by Mr. Vigors. That letter I will now show to you; but before doing so I must enter into a preliminary explanation. Lady Haughton is one of those women who love power, and cannot obtain it except through wealth and station — by her own intellect she could never obtain it. When her husband died she was reduced from an income of twelve thousand a year to a jointure of twelve hundred, but with the exclusive guardianship of a young son, a minor, and adequate allowances for the charge; she continued, therefore, to preside as mistress over the establishments in town and country; still had the administration of her son's wealth and rank. She stinted his education, in order to maintain her ascendency over him. He became a brainless prodigal — spendthrift alike of health and fortune. Alarmed, she saw that, probably, he would die young and a beggar; his only hope of reform was in marriage. She reluctantly resolved to marry him to a penniless, well-born, soft-minded young lady whom she knew she could control; just before this marriage was to take place he was killed by a fall from his horse. The Haughton estate passed to his cousin, the luckiest young man alive; the same Ashleigh Sumner who had already succeeded, in default of male issue, to poor Gilbert Ashleigh's landed possessions. Over this young man Lady Haughton could expect no influence. She would be a stranger in his house. But she had a niece! Mr. Vigors assured her the niece was beautiful. And if the niece could become Mrs. Ashleigh Sumner, then Lady Haughton would be a less unimportant Nobody in the world, because she would still have her nearest relation in a Somebody at Haughton Park. Mr. Vigors had his own pompous reasons for approving an alliance which he might help to accomplish. The first step towards that alliance was obviously to bring into reciprocal attraction the natural charms of the young lady and the acquired merits of the young gentleman. Mr. Vigors could easily induce his ward to pay a visit to Lady Haughton, and Lady Haughton had only to extend her invitations to her niece; hence the letter to Mrs. Ashleigh, of which Mr. Vigors was the bearer, and hence my advice to you, of which you can now understand the motive. Since you thought Lilian Ashleigh the only woman you could love, and since I thought there were other women in the world who might do as well for Ashleigh Sumner, it seemed to me fair for all parties that Lilian should not go to Lady Haughton's in ignorance of the sentiments with which she had inspired you. A girl can seldom be sure that she loves until she is sure that she is loved. And now," added Mrs. Poyntz, rising and walking across the room to her bureau — "now I will show you Lady Haughton's invitation to Mrs. Ashleigh. Here it is!"

I ran my eye over the letter, which she thrust into my hand, resuming her knitwork while I read.

The letter was short, couched in conventional terms of hollow affection. The writer blamed herself for having so long neglected her brother's widow and child; her heart had been wrapped up too much in the son she had lost; that loss had made her turn to the ties of blood still left to her; she had heard much of Lilian from their common friend, Mr. Vigors; she longed to embrace so charming a niece. Then followed the invitation and the postscript. The postscript ran thus, so far as I can remember: "Whatever my own grief at my irreparable bereavement, I am no egotist, I keep my sorrow to myself. You will find some pleasant guests at my house, among others our joint connection, young Ashleigh Sumner."

"Women's postscripts are proverbial for their significance," said Mrs. Poyntz, when I had concluded the letter and laid it on the table; "and if I did not at once show you this hypocritical effusion, it was simply because at the name Ashleigh Sumner its object became transparent, not perhaps to poor Anne Ashleigh nor to innocent Lilian, but to my knowledge of the parties concerned, as it ought to be to that shrewd intelligence which you derive partly from nature, partly from the insight into life which a true physician cannot fail to acquire. And if I know anything of you, you would have romantically said, had you seen the letter at first, and understood its covert intention, 'Let me not shackle the choice of the woman I love, and to whom an alliance so coveted in the eyes of the world might, if she were left free, be proffered.'"

"I should not have gathered from the postscript all that you see in it, but had its purport been so suggested to me, you are right, I should have so said. Well, and as Mr. Margrave tells me that you informed him that I have a rival, I am now to conclude that the rival is Mr. Ashleigh Sumner?"

"Has not Mrs. Ashleigh or Lilian mentioned him in writing to you?"

"Yes, both; Lilian very slightly; Mrs. Ashleigh with some praise, as a young man of high character and very courteous to her."

"Yet, though I asked you to come and tell me who were the guests at Lady Haughton's, you never did so."

"Pardon me; but of the guests I thought nothing, and letters addressed to my heart seemed to me too sacred to talk about. And Ashleigh Sumner then courts Lilian! How do you know?"

"I know everything that concerns me; and here, the explanation is simple. My aunt, Lady Delafield, is staying with Lady Haughton. Lady Delafield is one of the women of fashion who shine by their own light; Lady Haughton shines by borrowed light, and borrows every ray she can find."

"And Lady Delafield writes you word——"

"That Ashleigh Sumner is caught by Lilian's beauty."

"And Lilian herself——"

"Women like Lady Delafield do not readily believe that any girl could refuse Ashleigh Sumner; considered in himself, he is steady and good-looking; considered as owner of Kirby Hall and Haughton Park, he has, in the eyes of any sensible mother, the virtues of Cato and the beauty of Antinous."

I pressed my hand to my heart—close to my heart lay a letter from Lilian—and there was no word in that letter which showed that *her* heart was gone from mine. I shook my head gently, and smiled in confiding triumph.

Mrs. Poyntz surveyed me with a bent brow and a compressed lip.

"I understand your smile," she said, ironically. "Very likely Lilian may be quite untouched by this young man's admiration, but Anne Ashleigh may be dazzled by so brilliant a prospect for her daughter. And, in short, I thought it desirable to let your engagement be publicly known throughout the town to-day; that information will travel — it will reach Ashleigh Sumner through Mr. Vigors, or others in this neighborhood, with whom I know that he corresponds. It will bring affairs to a crisis, and before it may be too late. I think it well that Ashleigh Sumner should leave that house; if he leave it for good, so much the better. And, perhaps, the sooner Lilian returns to L—— the lighter your own heart will be."

"And for these reasons you have published the secret of——"

"Your engagement? Yes. Prepare to be congratulated wherever you go. And now, if you hear either from mother or daughter, that Ashleigh Sumner has proposed, and been, let us say, refused, I do not doubt that, in the pride of your heart, you will come and tell me."

"Rely upon it, I will; but before I take leave, allow me to ask, why you described to a young man like Mr. Margrave — whose wild and strange humors you have witnessed and not approved — any of those traits of character in Miss Ashleigh which distinguish her from other girls of her age?"

"I? You mistake. I said nothing to him of her character. I mentioned her name, and said she was beautiful — that was all."

"Nay, you said that she was fond of musing, of solitude; that in her fancies she believed in the reality of visions which might flit before her eyes as they flit before the eyes of all imaginative dreamers."

"Not a word did I say to Mr. Margrave of such peculiarities in Lilian; not a word more than what I have told you, on my honor!"

Still incredulous, but disguising my incredulity with that convenient smile by which we accomplish so much of the polite dissimulation indispensable to the decencies of civilized life, I took my departure, returned home, and wrote to Lilian.

CHAPTER XXVIII.

The conversation with Mrs. Poyntz left my mind restless and disquieted. I had no doubt, indeed, of Lilian's truth, but could I be sure that the attentions of a young man, with advantages of fortune so brilliant, would not force on her thoughts the contrast of the humbler lot and the duller walk of life in which she had accepted as companion a man removed from her romantic youth less by disparity of years than by gravity of pursuits? And would my suit now be as welcomed as it had been by a mother even so unworldly as Mrs. Ashleigh? Why, too, should both mother and daughter have left me so unprepared to hear that I had a rival? Why not have implied some consoling assurance that such rivalry need not cause me alarm? Lilian's letters, it is true, touched but little on any of the persons round her — they were filled with the outpourings of an ingenuous heart, colored by the glow of a golden fancy. They were written as if in the wide world we two stood apart alone, consecrated from the crowd by the love that, in linking us together, had hallowed each to the other. Mrs. Ashleigh's letters were more general and diffusive, detailed the habits of the household, sketched the guests, intimated her continued fear of Lady Haughton, but had said nothing more of Mr. Ashleigh Sumner than I had repeated to Mrs. Poyntz. However, in my letter to Lilian I related the intelligence that had reached me, and impatiently I awaited her reply.

Three days after the interview with Mrs. Poyntz, and two days before the long-anticipated event of the mayor's ball, I was summoned to attend a nobleman who had lately been added to my list of patients, and whose residence was about twelve miles from L——. The nearest way was through Sir Philip Derval's park. I went on horseback, and proposed to stop on the way to inquire after the steward, whom I had seen but once since his fit, and that was two days after it, when he called himself at my house to thank me for my attendance, and to declare that he was quite recovered.

As I rode somewhat fast through the park, I came, however, upon the steward, just in front of the house. I reined in my horse and accosted him. He looked very cheerful.

"Sir," said he, in a whisper, "I have heard from Sir Philip; his letter is dated since — since — my good woman told you what I saw — well, since then. So that it must have been all a delusion of mine, as you told her. And yet, well — well — we will not talk of it, doctor. But I hope you have kept the secret. Sir Philip would not like to hear of it if he comes back."

"Your secret is quite safe with me. But is Sir Philip likely to come back?"

"I hope so, doctor. His letter is dated Paris, and that's nearer home than he has been for many years; and — but bless me — some one is coming out of the house? a young gentleman! Who can it be?"

I looked, and to my surprise I saw Margrave descending the stately stairs that led from the front door. The steward turned towards him, and I mechanically followed, for I was curious to know what had brought Margrave to the house of the long-absent traveller.

It was easily explained. Mr. Margrave had heard at L—— much of the pictures and internal decorations of the mansion. He had, by dint of coaxing (he said, with his enchanting laugh), persuaded the old housekeeper to show him the rooms.

"It is against Sir Philip's positive orders to show the house to any stranger, sir; and the housekeeper has done very wrong," said the steward.

"Pray don't scold her. I dare say Sir Philip would not have refused me a permission he might not give to every idle sight-seer. Fellow-travellers have a freemasonry with each other; and I have been much in the same far countries as himself. I heard of him there, and could tell you more about him, I dare say, than you know yourself."

"You, sir! pray do, then."

"The next time I come," said Margrave, gaily; and, with a nod to me, he glided off through the trees of the neighboring grove, along the winding footpath that led to the lodge.

"A very cool gentleman," muttered the steward; "but what pleasant ways he has! You seem to know him, sir. Who is he — may I ask?"

"Mr. Margrave. A visitor at L——, and he has been a great traveller, as he says; perhaps he met Sir Philip abroad."

"I must go and hear what he said to Mrs. Gates; excuse me, sir, but I am so anxious about Sir Philip."

"If it be not too great a favor, may I be allowed the same privilege granted to Mr. Margrave? To judge by the outside of the house, the inside must be worth seeing; still, if it be against Sir Philip's positive orders ——"

"His orders were, not to let the Court become a show-house — to admit none without my consent — but I should be ungrateful indeed, doctor, if I refused that consent to you."

I tied my horse to the rusty gate of the terrace-walk, and followed the steward up the broad stairs of the terrace. The great doors were unlocked. We entered a lofty hall with a domed ceiling; at the back of the hall the grand staircase ascended by a double flight. The design was undoubtedly Vanbrugh's, an architect who, beyond all others, sought the effect of grandeur less in space than in proportion. But Vanbrugh's designs need the relief of costume and movement, and the forms of a more pompous generation, in the bravery of velvets and laces, glancing amid those gilded columns, or descending with stately tread those broad palatial stairs. His halls and chambers are so made for festival and throng, that they become like deserted theatres, inexpressibly desolate, as we miss the glitter of the lamps and the movement of the actors.

The housekeeper had now appeared; a quiet, timid old woman. She excused herself for admitting Margrave — not very intelligibly. It was plain to see that she had, in truth, been unable to resist what the steward termed his "pleasant ways."

As if to escape from a scolding she talked volubly all the time, bustling nervously through the rooms, along which I followed her guidance with a hushed footstep. The principal apartments were on the ground-floor, or rather a floor raised some ten or fifteen feet above the ground; they had not been modernized since the date in which they were built. Hangings of faded silk; tables of rare marble and mouldered gilding; comfortless chairs at drill against the walls; pictures, of which connoisseurs alone could estimate the value, darkened by dust or blistered by sun and damp, made a general character of discomfort. On not one room, on not one nook, still lingered some old smile of home.

Meanwhile I gathered from the housekeeper's rambling answers to questions put to her by the steward, as I moved on, glancing at the pictures, that Margrave's visit that day was not his first. He had been to the house twice before; his ostensible excuse that he was an amateur in pictures (though, as I had before observed, for that department of art he had no taste); but each time he had talked much of Sir Philip. He said, that though not personally known to him, he had resided in the same towns abroad, and had friends equally intimate with Sir Philip; but when the steward inquired if the visitor had given any information as to the absentee, it became very clear that Margrave had been rather asking questions than volunteering intelligence.

We had not come to the end of the state apartments, the last of which was a library. "And," said the old woman, "I don't wonder the gentleman knew Sir Philip, for he seemed a scholar, and looked very hard over the books, especially those old ones by the fireplace, which Sir Philip, Heaven bless him, was always poring into."

Mechanically I turned to the shelves by the fireplace, and examined the volumes ranged in that department. I found they contained the works of those writers whom we may class together under the title of mystics — Iamblichus and Plotinus; Swedenborg and Behmen; Sandivogius, Van Helmont, Paracelsus, Cardan. Works, too, were there, by writers less renowned, on astrology, geomancy, chiromancy, &c. I began to understand among what class of authors Margrave had picked up the strange notions with which he was apt to interpolate the doctrines of practical philosophy.

"I suppose this library was Sir Philip's usual sitting room?" said I.

"No, sir; he seldom sat here. This was his study;" and the old woman opened a small door, masked by false book-backs. I followed her into a room of moderate size, and evidently of much earlier date than the rest of the house. "It is the only room left of an older mansion," said the steward, in answer to my remark. "I have heard it was spared on account of the chimney-piece. But there is a Latin inscription which will tell you all about it. I don't know Latin myself."

The chimney-piece reached to the ceiling. The frieze of the lower part rested on rude stone caryatides; the upper part was formed of oak-panels very curiously carved in the geometrical designs favored by the taste prevalent in the reigns of Elizabeth and James, but different from any I had ever seen in the drawings of old houses. And I was not quite unlearned in such matters, for my poor father was a passionate antiquary in all that relates to mediæval art. The design in the oak panels was composed of triangles interlaced with varied ingenuity, and enclosed in circular bands inscribed with the signs of the Zodiac.

On the stone frieze supported by the caryatides, immediately under the wood-work, was inserted a metal plate, on which was written, in Latin, a few lines to the effect that "in this room, Simon Forman, the seeker of hidden truth, taking refuge from unjust persecution, made those discoveries in nature which he committed, for the benefit of a wiser age, to the charge of his protector and patron, the worshipful Sir Miles Derval, knight."

Forman! The name was not quite unfamiliar to me; but it was not without an effort that my memory enabled me to assign it to one of the most notorious of those astrologers or soothsayers whom the superstition of an earlier age alternately persecuted and honored.

The general character of the room was more cheerful than the statelier chambers I had hitherto passed through, for it had still the look of habitation. The arm-chair by the fire-place; the knee-hole writing-table beside it; the sofa near the recess of a large bay-window, with book-prop and candlestick screwed to its back; maps, coiled in their cylinder, ranged under the cornice; low strong safes, skirting two sides of the room, and apparently intended to hold papers and title-deeds; seals carefully affixed to their jealous locks. Placed on the top of these oldfashioned receptacles were articles familiar to modern use; a fowling-piece here; fishing-rods there; two or three simple flower vases; a pile of music books; a box of crayons. All in this room seemed to speak of residence and ownership—of the idiosyncrasies of a lone single man, it is true, but of a man of one's own time—a country gentleman of plain habits but not uncultivated tastes.

I moved to the window; it opened by a sash upon a large balcony, from which a wooden stair wound to a little garden, not visible in front of the house, surrounded by a thick grove of evergreens, through which one broad vista was cut; and that vista was closed by a view of the mausoleum.

I stepped out into the garden—a patch of sward with a fountain in the centre—and parterres, now more filled with weeds than flowers. At the left corner was a tall wooden summer-house or pavilion—its door wide open. "Oh, that's where Sir Philip used to study many a long summer's night," said the steward.

"What! in that damp pavilion?"

"It was a pretty place enough then, sir; but it is very old. They say as old as the room you have just left."

"Indeed, I must look at it then."

The walls of this summer-house had once been

painted in the arabesques of the Renaissance period; but the figures were now scarcely traceable. The wood-work had started in some places, and the sun-beams stole through the chinks and played on the floor, which was formed from old tiles quaintly tesselated and in triangular patterns, similar to those I had observed in the chimney-piece. The room in the pavilion was large, furnished with old worm-eaten tables and settles.

"It was not only here that Sir Philip studied, but sometimes in the room above," said the steward.

"How do you get to the room above? Oh! I see; a staircase in the angle." I ascended the stairs with some caution, for they were crooked and decayed; and, on entering the room above, comprehended at once why Sir Philip had favored it.

The cornice of the ceiling rested on pilasters, within which the compartments were formed into open un-glazed arches, surrounded by a railed balcony. Through these arches, on three sides of the room, the eye commanded a magnificent extent of prospect. On the fourth side the view was bounded by the mansoleum. In this room was a large telescope, and on stepping into the balcony, I saw that a winding stair mounted thence to a platform on the top of the pavilion — perhaps once used as an observatory by Forman himself.

"The gentleman who was here to-day was very much pleased with this look-out, sir," said the housekeeper.

"Who would not be? I suppose Sir Philip has a taste for astronomy."

"I dare say, sir," said the steward, looking grave; "he likes most out-of-the-way things."

The position of the sun now warned me that my time pressed, and that I should have to ride fast to reach my new patient at the hour appointed. I therefore hastened back to my horse, and spurred on, wondering whether, in the chain of association which so subtly links our pursuits in manhood to our impressions in childhood, it was the Latin inscription on the chimney-piece that had originally biassed Sir Philip Derval's literary taste towards the mystic jargon of the books at which I had contemptuously glanced.

CHAPTER XXIX.

I DID not see Margrave the following day, but the next morning, a little after sunrise, he walked into my study, according to his ordinary habit.

"So you know something about Sir Philip Derval?" said I. "What sort of a man is he?"

"Hateful!" cried Margrave; and then checking himself, burst out into his merry laugh. "Just like my exaggerations! I am not acquainted with anything to his prejudice. I came across his track once or twice in the East. Travellers are always apt to be jealous of each other."

"You are a strange compound of cynicism and credulity. But I should have fancied that you and Sir Philip would have been congenial spirits, when I found, among his favorite books, Van Helmont and Paracelsus. Perhaps you, too, study Swedenborg, or, worse still, Ptolemy and Lilly?"

"Astrologers? No! They deal with the future! I live for the day; only I wish the day never had a morrow!"

"Have you not, then, that vague desire for the *something beyond;* that not unhappy, but grand discontent with the limits of the immediate Present, from which man takes his passion for improvement and progress, and from which some sentimental philosophers have deduced an argument in favor of his destined immortality?"

"Eh!" said Margrave, with as vacant a stare as that of a peasant whom one has addressed in Hebrew. "What farrago of words is this? I do not comprehend you."

"With your natural abilities," I asked with interest "do you never feel a desire for fame?"

"Fame? Certainly not. I cannot even understand it!"

"Well, then, would you have no pleasure in the thought that you had rendered a service to humanity?"

Margrave looked bewildered; after a moment's pause, he took from the table a piece of bread that chanced to be there, opened the window, and threw the crumbs into the lane. The sparrows gathered round the crumbs.

"Now," said Margrave, "the sparrows come to that dull pavement for the bread that recruits their lives in this world; do you believe that one sparrow would be silly enough to fly to a house-top for the sake of some benefit to other sparrows, or to be chirruped about after he was dead? I care for science as the sparrow cares for bread; it may help me to something good for my own life; and as for fame and humanity, I care for them as the sparrow cares for the general interest and posthumous approbation of sparrows!"

"Margrave; there is one thing in you that perplexes me more than all else — human puzzle as you are — in your many eccentricities and self-contradictions."

"What is that one thing in me most perplexing?"

"This; that in your enjoyment of Nature you have all the freshness of a child, but when you speak of Man and his objects in the world, you talk in the vein of some worn-out and hoary cynic. At such times, were I to close my eyes, I should say to myself, 'What weary old man is thus venting his spleen against the ambition which has failed, and the love which has forsaken him?' Outwardly the very personation of youth, and revelling like a butterfly in the warmth of the sun and the tints of the herbage, why have you none of the golden passions of the young? their bright dreams of some impossible love — their sublime enthusiasm for some unattainable glory? The sentiment you have just clothed in the illustration by which you place yourself on a level with the sparrows is too mean and too gloomy to be genuine at your age. Misanthropy is among the dismal fallacies of greybeards. No man, till man's energies leave him, can divorce himself from the bonds of our social kind."

"Our kind — your kind, possibly! But I——." He swept his hand over his brow, and resumed, in strange, absent, and wistful accents: "I wonder what it is that is wanting here, and of which at moments I have a dim reminiscence." Again he paused, and gazing on me, said with more appearance of friendly interest than I had ever before remarked in his countenance, "You are not looking well. Despite your great physical strength, you suffer like your own sickly patients."

"True! I suffer at this moment, but not from bodily pain."

"You have some cause of mental disquietude?"

"Who in this world has not?"

"I never have."

"Because you own you have never loved; certainly, you never seem to care for any one but yourself; and in yourself you find an unbroken sunny holiday — high spirits, youth, health, beauty, wealth. Happy boy!"

At that moment my heart was heavy within me.

Margrave resumed: —

"Among the secrets which your knowledge places at the command of your art, what would you give for one which would enable you to defy and to deride a rival where you place your affections, which could lock to yourself, and imperiously control, the will of the being whom you desire to fascinate, by an influence paramount, transcendent?"

"Love has that secret," said I, "and love alone."

"A power stronger than love can suspend, can change love itself. But if love be the object or dream of your life, love is the rosy associate of youth and beauty. Beauty soon fades, youth soon departs. What if in nature there were means by which beauty and youth can be fixed into blooming duration — means that could arrest the course, nay, repair the effects, of time on the elements that make up the human frame?"

"Silly boy! Have the Rosicrucians bequeathed to you a prescription for the elixir of life?"

"If I had the prescription I should not ask your aid to discover its ingredients."

"And is it in the hope of that notable discovery you have studied chemistry, electricity, and magnetism? Again I say, Silly boy!"

Margrave did not heed my reply. His face was overcast, gloomy, troubled.

"That the vital principle is a gas," said he, abruptly, "I am fully convinced. Can that gas be the one which combines caloric with oxygen?"

"Phosoxygen? Sir Humphry Davy demonstrates that gas not to be, as Lavoisier supposed, caloric, but light, combined with oxygen; and he suggests, not indeed that it is the vital principle itself, but the pabulum of life to organic beings." *

"Does he?" said Margrave, his face clearing up. "Possibly, possibly then, here we approach the great secret of secrets. Look you, Allen Fenwick, I promise to secure to you unfailing security from all the jealous fears that now torture your heart; if you care for that fame which to me is not worth the scent of a flower, the balm of a breeze, I will impart to you a knowledge which, in the hands of ambition, would dwarf into commonplace the boasted wonders of recognized science. I will do all this, if, in return, but for one month you will give yourself up to my guidance in whatever experiments I ask, no matter how wild they may seem to you."

"My dear Margrave, I reject your bribes as I would reject the moon and the stars which a child might offer to me in exchange for a toy. But I may give the child its toy for nothing, and I may test your experiments for nothing some day when I have leisure."

I did not hear Margrave's answer, for at that moment my servant entered with letters. Lilian's hand! Tremblingly, breathlessly, I broke the seal. Such a loving, bright, happy letter; so sweet in its gentle chiding of my wrongful fears. It was implied rather than said that Ashleigh Sumner had proposed and been refused. He had now left the house. Lilian and her mother were coming back; in a few days we should meet. In

* See Sir Humphry Davy on Heat, Light, and the Combinations of Light.

this letter were enclosed a few lines from Mrs. Ashleigh. She was more explicit about my rival than Lilian had been. If no allusion to his attentions had been made to me before, it was from a delicate consideration for myself. Mrs. Ashleigh said that "the young man had heard from L—— of our engagement, and—disbelieved it;" but, as Mrs. Poyntz had so shrewdly predicted, hurried at once to the avowal of his own attachment, and the offer of his own hand. On Lilian's refusal his pride had been deeply mortified. He had gone away manifestly in more anger than sorrow. "Lady Delafield, dear Margaret Poyntz's aunt, had been most kind in trying to soothe Lady Haughton's disappointment, which was rudely expressed—so rudely," added Mrs. Ashleigh, "that it gives us an excuse to leave sooner than had been proposed—which I am very glad of. Lady Delafield feels much for Mr. Sumner; has invited him to visit her at a place she has near Worthing; she leaves to-morrow in order to receive him; promises to reconcile him to our rejection, which, as he was my poor Gilbert's heir, and was very friendly at first, would be a great relief to my mind. Lilian is well, and so happy at the thoughts of coming back."

When I lifted my eyes from these letters I was as a new man, and the earth seemed a new earth. I felt as if I *had* realized Margrave's idle dreams—as if youth could never fade, love could never grow cold.

"You care for no secrets of mine at this moment," said Margrave, abruptly.

"Secrets," I murmured; "none now are worth knowing. I am loved — I am loved!"

"I bide my time," said Margrave; and as my eyes met his, I saw there a look I had never seen in those eyes before — sinister, wrathful, menacing. He turned away, went out through the sash door of the study; and as he passed towards the fields under the luxuriant chestnut-trees, I heard his musical, barbaric chant — the song by which the serpent-charmer charms the serpent — sweet, so sweet — the very birds on the boughs hushed their carol as if to listen.

CHAPTER XXX.

I CALLED that day on Mrs. Poyntz, and communicated to her the purport of the glad news I had received.

She was still at work on the everlasting knitting, her firm fingers linking mesh into mesh as she listened; and when I had done, she laid her skein deliberately down, and said, in her favorite characteristic formula,

"So, at last? — that is settled!"

She rose and paced the room as men are apt to do in reflection — women rarely need such movement to aid their thoughts — her eyes were fixed on the floor, and one hand was lightly pressed on the palm of the other — the gesture of a musing reasoner who is approaching the close of a difficult calculation.

At length she paused, fronting me, and said, dryly,

"Accept of my congratulations — life smiles on you now — guard that smile, and when we meet next, may we be even firmer friends than we are now!"

"When we meet next — that will be to-night — you surely go to the mayor's great ball? All the Hill descends to Low Town to-night."

"No; we are obliged to leave L—— this afternoon — in less than two hours we shall be gone — a family engagement. We may be weeks away; you will excuse me, then, if I take leave of you so unceremoniously. Stay, a motherly word of caution. That friend of yours, Mr. Margrave! Moderate your intimacy with him; and especially after you are married. There is in that stranger, of whom so little is known, a something which I cannot comprehend — a something that captivates, and yet revolts. I find him disturbing my thoughts, perplexing my conjectures, haunting my fancies — I, plain woman of the world! Lilian is imaginative; beware of her imagination, even when sure of her heart. Beware of Margrave. The sooner he quits L——, the better, believe me, for your peace of mind. Adieu! I must prepare for our journey."

"That woman," muttered I, on quitting her house, "seems to have some strange spite against my poor Lilian, ever seeking to rouse my own distrust of that exquisite nature which has just given me such proof of its truth. And yet — and yet — is that woman so wrong here? True! Margrave with his wild notions, his strange beauty! — true — true — he might dangerously encourage that turn for the mystic and visionary which distresses me in Lilian. Lilian should not know him. How induce him to leave L——? Ah — those experiments on which he asks my assistance! I might commence them when he comes again, and then invent some excuse to send him for completer tests to the famous chemists of Paris or Berlin."

CHAPTER XXXI.

It is the night of the mayor's ball! The guests are assembling fast; county families twelve miles round have been invited, as well as the principal families of the town. All, before proceeding to the room set apart for the dance, moved in procession through the museum — homage to science before pleasure!

The building was brilliantly lighted, and the effect was striking, perhaps because singular and grotesque. There, amidst stands of flowers and evergreens, lit up with colored lamps, were grouped the dead representatives of races all inferior — some deadly — to man. The fancy of the ladies had been permitted to decorate and arrange these types of the animal world. The tiger glared with glass eyes from amidst artificial reeds and herbage, as from his native jungle; the grisly white bear peered from a mimic iceberg. There, in front, stood the sage elephant, facing a hideous hippopotamus; whilst an anaconda twined its long spire round the stem of some tropical tree in zinc. In glass cases, brought into full light by festooned lamps, were dread specimens of the reptile race — scorpion and vampire, and cobra capella, with insects of gorgeous hues, not a few of them with venomed stings.

But the chief boast of the collection was in the varieties of the Genus Simia — baboons and apes, chimpanzees, with their human visage, mockeries of man, from the dwarf monkeys perched on boughs lopped from the mayor's shrubberies, to the formidable orang-outang, leaning on his huge club.

Every one expressed to the mayor admiration — to each other antipathy, for this unwonted and somewhat ghastly, though instructive, addition to the revels of a ball-room.

Margrave, of course, was there, and seemingly quite at home, gliding from group to group of gaily-dressed ladies, and brilliant with a childish eagerness to play off the showman. Many of these grim fellow-creatures he declared he had seen, played, or fought with. He had something true or false to say about each. In his high spirits he contrived to make the tiger move, and imitated the hiss of the terrible anaconda. All that he did had its grace, its charm; and the buzz of admiration and the flattering glances of ladies' eyes followed him wherever he moved.

However, there was a general feeling of relief when

the mayor led the way from the museum into the ball-room. In provincial parties guests arrive pretty much within the same hour, and so few who had once paid their respects to the apes and serpents, the hippopotamus and the tiger, were disposed to repeat the visit, that long before eleven o'clock the museum was as free from the intrusion of human life as the wilderness in which its dead occupants had been born.

I had gone my round through the rooms, and, little disposed to be social, had crept into the retreat of a window-niche, pleased to think myself screened by its draperies; not that I was melancholy, far from it — for the letter I had received that morning from Lilian had raised my whole being into a sovereignty of happiness high beyond the reach of the young pleasure-hunters, whose voices and laughter blended with that vulgar music.

To read her letter again I had stolen to my nook — and, now, sure that none saw me kiss it, I replaced it in my bosom. I looked through the parted curtain; the room was comparatively empty; but there, through the open folding-doors, I saw the gay crowd gathered round the dancers, and there again, at right angles, a vista along the corridor afforded a glimpse of the great elephant in the deserted museum.

Presently I heard, close beside me, my host's voice.

"Here's a cool corner, a pleasant sofa, you can have it all to yourself; what an honor to receive you under my roof, and on this interesting occasion! Yes, as you say, there are great changes in L—— since you left us. Society has much improved. I must look about and find some persons to introduce to you. Clever! oh, I know your tastes. We have a wonderful man—a new doctor. Carries all before him—very high character, too—good old family—greatly looked up to, even apart from his profession. Dogmatic a little—a Sir Oracle—'Lets no dog bark;' you remember the quotation—Shakespeare. Where on earth is he? My dear Sir Philip, I am sure you would enjoy his conversation."

Sir Philip! Could it be Sir Philip Derval, to whom the mayor was giving a flattering, yet scarcely propitiatory, description of myself? Curiosity combined with a sense of propriety in not keeping myself an unsuspected listener: I emerged from the curtain, but silently, and reached the centre of the room before the mayor perceived me. He then came up to me eagerly, linked his arm in mine, and leading me to a gentleman seated on a sofa, close by the window I had quitted, said:

"Doctor, I must present you to Sir Philip Derval, just returned to England, and not six hours in L——. If you would like to see the museum again, Sir Philip, the doctor, I am sure, will accompany you."

"No, I thank you; it is painful to me at present, to see, even under your roof, the collection which my poor dear friend, Dr. Lloyd, was so proudly beginning to form when I left these parts."

"Ay, Sir Philip—Dr. Lloyd was a worthy man in his way, but sadly duped in his latter years; he took to mesmerism, only think! But our young doctor here showed him up, I can tell you."

Sir Philip, who had acknowledged my first introduction to his acquaintance by the quiet courtesy with which a well-bred man goes through a ceremony that custom enables him to endure with equal ease and indifference, now evinced by a slight change of manner how little the mayor's reference to my dispute with Dr. Lloyd advanced me in his good opinion. He turned away with a bow more formal than his first one, and said calmly:

"I regret to hear that a man so simple-minded and so sensitive as Dr. Lloyd should have provoked an encounter in which I can well conceive him to have been worsted. With your leave, Mr. Mayor, I will look into your ball-room. I may perhaps find there some old acquaintance."

He walked towards the dancers, and the mayor, linking his arm in mine, followed close behind, saying in his loud, hearty tones:

"Come along, you too, Dr. Fenwick, my girls are there; you have not spoken to them yet."

Sir Philip, who was then half way across the room, turned round abruptly, and, looking me full in the face, said:

"Fenwick, is your name Fenwick?—Allen Fenwick?"

"That is my name, Sir Philip."

"Then permit me to shake you by the hand; you are

no stranger, and no mere acquaintance to me. Mr. Mayor, we will look into your ball-room later; do not let us keep you now from your other guests."

The mayor, not in the least offended by being thus summarily dismissed, smiled, walked on, and was soon lost amongst the crowd.

Sir Philip, still retaining my hand, reseated himself on the sofa, and I took my place by his side. The room was still deserted; now and then a straggler from the ball-room looked in for a moment, and then sauntered back to the central place of attraction.

"I am trying to guess," said I, "how my name should be known to you. Possibly you may, in some visit to the Lakes, have known my father?"

"No; I know none of your name but yourself—if, indeed, as I doubt not, you are the Allen Fenwick to whom I owe no small obligation. You were a medical student at Edinburgh in the year ——?"

"Yes."

"So! At that time there was also at Edinburgh a young man, named Richard Strahan. He lodged in a fourth flat in the Old Town."

"I remember him very well."

"And you remember, also, that a fire broke out at night in the house in which he lodged; that, when it was discovered, there seemed no hope of saving him. The flames wrapt the lower part of the house; the staircase had given way. A boy, scarcely so old as himself, was the only human being in the crowd who dared to scale the ladder, that even then scarcely reached the windows from which the smoke rolled in volumes; that boy penetrated into the room — found the inmate almost insensible — rallied, supported, dragged him to the window — got him on the ladder — saved his life then — and his life later, by nursing with a woman's tenderness, through the fever caused by terror and excitement, the fellow-creature he had rescued by a man's daring. The name of that gallant student was Allen Fenwick, and Richard Strahan is my nearest living relation. Are we friends now?"

I answered confusedly. I had almost forgotten the circumstances referred to. Richard Strahan had not been one of my more intimate companions; and I had never seen nor heard of him since leaving college. I inquired what had become of him.

"He is at the Scotch bar," said Sir Philip, "and of course without practice. I understand that he has fair average abilities, but no application. If I am rightly informed, he is, however, a thoroughly honorable, upright man, and of an affectionate and grateful disposition."

"I can answer for all you have said in his praise. He had the qualities you name too deeply rooted in youth to have lost them now."

Sir Philip remained for some moments in a musing silence. And I took advantage of that silence to examine him with more minute attention than I had done before, much as the first sight of him had struck me.

He was somewhat below the common height. So delicately formed that one might call him rather fragile than slight. But in his carriage and air there was remarkable dignity. His countenance was at direct variance with his figure. For as delicacy was the attribute of the last, so power was unmistakably the characteristic of the first. He looked fully the age his steward had ascribed to him — about forty-eight; at a superficial glance, more; for his hair was prematurely white—not grey, but white as snow. But his eyebrows were still jet black, and his eyes, equally dark, were serenely bright. His forehead was magnificent; lofty, and spacious, and with only one slight wrinkle between the brows. His complexion was sunburnt, showing no sign of weak health. The outline of his lips was that which I have often remarked in men accustomed to great dangers, and contracting in such dangers the habit of self-reliance; firm and quiet, compressed without an effort. And the power of this very noble countenance was not intimidating, not aggressive; it was mild — it was benignant. A man oppressed by some formidable tyranny, and despairing to find a protector, would, on seeing that face, have said, "Here is one who can protect me, and who will!"

Sir Philip was the first to break the silence.

"I have so many relations scattered over England, that fortunately not one of them can venture to calculate on my property if I die childless, and therefore not one of them can feel himself injured when, a few weeks hence, he shall read in the newspapers, that Philip

Derval is married. But for Richard Strahan, at least, though I never saw him, I must do something before the newspapers make that announcement. His sister was very dear to me."

"Your neighbors, Sir Philip, will rejoice at your marriage, since, I presume, it may induce you to settle amongst them at Derval Court."

"At Derval Court! No! I shall not settle there." Again he paused a moment or so, and then went on: "I have long lived a wandering life, and in it learned much that the wisdom of cities cannot teach. I return to my native land with a profound conviction that the happiest life is the life most in common with all. I have gone out of my way to do what I deemed good, and to avert or mitigate what appeared to me evil. I pause now and ask myself, whether the most virtuous existence be not that in which virtue flows spontaneously from the springs of quiet everyday action — when a man does good without restlessly seeking it, does good unconsciously, simply because he is good and he lives? Better, perhaps, for me, if I had thought so long ago! And now I come back to England with the intention of marrying, late in life though it be, and with such hopes of happiness as any matter-of-fact man may form. But my hope will not be at Derval Court. I shall reside either in London or its immediate neighborhood, and seek to gather round me minds by which I can correct, if I cannot confide to them, the knowledge I myself have acquired."

"Nay, if, as I have accidentally heard, you are fond of scientific pursuits, I cannot wonder that, after so long an absence from England, you should feel interest in learning what new discoveries have been made, what new ideas are unfolding the germs of discoveries yet to be. But, pardon me, if in answer to your concluding remark, I venture to say that no man can hope to correct any error in his own knowledge, unless he has the courage to confide the error to those who can correct. La Place has said, '*Tout se tient dans te chaîne immense des vérités;*' and the mistake we make in some science we have specially cultivated is often only to be seen by the light of a separate science as specially cultivated by another. Thus, in the investigation of truth, frank exposition to congenial minds is essential to the earnest seeker."

"I am pleased with what you say," said Sir Philip, "and I shall be still more pleased to find in you the very confidant I require. But what was your controversy with my old friend, Dr. Lloyd? Do I understand our host rightly, that it related to what in Europe has of late days obtained the name of mesmerism?"

I had conceived a strong desire to conciliate the good opinion of a man who had treated me with so singular and so familiar a kindness, and it was sincerely that I expressed my regret at the acerbity with which I had assailed Dr. Lloyd; but of his theories and pretensions I could not disguise my contempt. I enlarged on the extravagant fallacies involved in a fabulous "clairvoyance," which always failed when put to plain test by sober-minded examiners. I did not deny the effects of imagination on certain nervous constitutions. "Mesmerism could cure nobody; credulity could cure many. There was the well-known story of the old woman tried as a witch; she cured agues by a charm; she owned the impeachment, and was ready to endure gibbet or stake for the truth of her talisman; more than a mesmerist would for the truth of his passes! And the charm was a scroll of gibberish sown in an old bag and given to the woman in a freak by the judge himself when a young scamp on the circuit. But the charm cured? Certainly; just as mesmerism cures. Fools believed in it. Faith, that moves mountains, may well cure agues."

Thus I ran on, supporting my views with anecdote and facts, to which Sir Philip listened with placid gravity.

When I had come to an end, he said, "Of mesmerism, as practised in Europe, I know nothing, except by report. I can well understand that medical men may hesitate to admit it amongst the legitimate resources of orthodox pathology; because, as I gather from what you and others say of its practice, it must, at the best, be far too uncertain in its application to satisfy the requirements of science. Yet an examination of its pretensions may enable you to perceive the truth that lies hid in the powers ascribed to witchcraft; benevolence is but a weak agency compared to malignity;

magnetism perverted to evil may solve half the riddles of sorcery. On this, however, I say no more at present. But as to that which you appear to reject as the most preposterous and incredible pretension of the mesmerists, and which you designate by the word 'clairvoyance,' it is clear to me that you have never yourself witnessed even those very imperfect exhibitions which you decide at once to be imposture. I say imperfect, because it is only a limited number of persons whom the eye or the passes of the mesmerist can affect, and by such means, unaided by other means, it is rarely indeed that the magnetic sleep advances beyond the first vague shadowy twilight dawn of that condition to which only in its fuller developments I would apply the name of 'trance.' But still trance is as essential a condition of being as sleep or as waking, having privileges peculiar to itself. By means within the range of the science that explores its nature and its laws, trance, unlike the clairvoyance you describe, is producible in every human being, however unimpressible to mere mesmerism."

"Producible in every human being! Pardon me if I say that I will give any enchanter his own terms who will produce that effect upon me."

"Will you? You consent to have the experiment tried on yourself?"

"Consent most readily."

"I will remember that promise. But to return to the subject. By the word trance I do not mean exclusively the spiritual trance of the Alexandrian Platonists. There is one kind of trance — that to which all human beings are susceptible — in which the soul has no share; for of this kind of trance, and it was of this I spoke, some of the inferior animals are susceptible; and, therefore, trance is no more a proof of soul than is the clairvoyance of the mesmerists, or the dream of our ordinary sleep, which last has been called a proof of soul, though any man who has kept a dog must have observed that dogs dream as vividly as we do. But in this trance there is an extraordinary cerebral activity — a projectile force given to the mind, distinct from the soul—by which it sends forth its own emanations to a distance in spite of material obstacles, just as a flower, in an altered condition of atmosphere, sends forth the particles of its aroma. This should not surprise you. Your thought travels over land and sea in your waking state; thought, too, can travel in trance, and in trance may acquire an intensified force. There is, however, another kind of trance which is truly called spiritual, a trance much more rare, and in which the soul entirely supersedes the mere action of the mind."

"Stay," said I; "you speak of the soul as something distinct from the mind. What the soul may be, I cannot pretend to conjecture. But I cannot separate it from the intelligence!"

"Can you not? A blow on the brain can destroy the intelligence! Do you think it can destroy the soul?

'From Marlbro's eyes the tears of dotage flow
And Swift expires, a driveller and a show.'

Towards the close of his life even Kant's giant intellect left him. Do you suppose that in these various archetypes of intellectual man the soul was worn out by the years that loosened the strings, or made tuneless the keys, of the perishing instrument on which the mind must rely for all notes of its music? If you cannot distinguish the operations of the mind from the essence of the soul, I know not by what rational inductions you arrive at the conclusion that the soul is imperishable."

I remained silent. Sir Philip fixed on me his dark eyes quietly and searchingly, and, after a short pause, said:

"Almost every known body in nature is susceptible of three several states of existence — the solid, the liquid, the aëriform. These conditions depend on the quantity of heat they contain. The same object at one moment may be liquid; at the next moment solid; at the next, aëriform. The water that flows before your gaze may stop consolidated into ice, or ascend into air as a vapor. Thus is man susceptible of three states of existence — the animal, the mental, the spiritual — and according as he is brought into relation or affinity with that occult agency of the whole natural world, which we familiarly call HEAT, and which no science has yet explained; which no scale can weigh, and no eye discern; one or the other of these three states of being prevails, or is subjected."

I still continued silent, for I was unwilling discourteously to say to a stranger, so much older than myself, that he seemed to me to reverse all the maxims of the philosophy to which he made pretence, in founding speculations audacious and abstruse upon unanalogous comparisons that would have been fantastic even in a poet. And Sir Philip, after another pause, resumed with a half smile:

"After what I have said, it will perhaps not very much surprise you when I add that but for my belief in the powers I ascribe to trance, we should not be known to each other at this moment."

"How—pray explain!"

"Certain circumstances which I trust to relate to you in detail hereafter, have imposed on me the duty to discover and to bring human laws to bear upon a creature armed with terrible powers of evil. This monster, for, without metaphor, monster it is, not man like ourselves, has, by arts superior to those of ordinary fugitives, however dexterous in concealment, hitherto for years eluded my research. Through the trance of an Arab child, who, in her waking state, never heard of his existence, I have learned that this being is in England—is in L——. I am here to encounter him. I expect to do so this very night, and under this very roof."

"Sir Philip!"

"And if you wonder, as you well may, why I have been talking to you with this startling unreserve, know that the same Arab child, on whom I thus implicitly rely, informs me that your life is mixed up with that of the being I seek to unmask and disarm — to be destroyed by his arts or his agents — or to combine in the causes by which the destroyer himself shall be brought to destruction."

"My life! — your Arab child named me, Allen Fenwick?"

"My Arab child told me that the person in whom I should thus naturally seek an ally was he who had saved the life of the man whom I then meant for my heir, if I died unmarried and childless. She told me that I should not be many hours in this town, which she described minutely, before you would be made known to me. She described this house, with yonder lights, and yon dancers. In her trance she saw us sitting together, as we now sit. I accepted the invitation of our host, when he suddenly accosted me on entering the town, confident that I should meet you here, without even asking whether a person of your name were a resident in the place; and now you know why I have so freely unbosomed myself of much that might well make you, a physician, doubt the soundness of my understanding. The same infant, whose vision has been realized up to this moment, has warned me also that I am here at great peril. What that peril may be I have declined to learn, as I have ever declined to ask from the future, what affects only my own life on this earth. That life I regard with supreme indifference, conscious that I have only to discharge, while it lasts, the duties for which it is bestowed on me, to the best of my imperfect power; and aware that minds the strongest and souls the purest may fall into the sloth habitual to predestinarians, if they suffer the action due to the present hour to be awed and paralyzed by some grim shadow on the future! It is only where, irrespectively of aught that can menace myself, a light not struck out of my own reason can guide me to disarm evil or minister to good, that I feel privileged to avail myself of those mirrors on which things, near and far, reflect themselves calm and distinct as the banks and the mountain peak are reflected in the glass of a lake. Here, then, under this roof, and by your side, I shall behold him who — Lo! the moment has come — I behold him now!"

As he spoke these last words, Sir Philip had risen, and, startled by his action and voice, I involuntarily rose too.

Resting one hand on my shoulder, he pointed with the other towards the threshold of the ball-room. There, the prominent figure of a gay group — the sole male amidst a fluttering circle of silks and lawn, of flowery wreaths, of female loveliness, and female frippery — stood the radiant image of Margrave. His eyes were not turned towards us. He was looking down, and his light laugh came soft, yet ringing, through the general murmur.

I turned my astonished gaze back to Sir Philip — yes, unmistakably it was on Margrave that his look was fixed.

Impossible to associate crime with the image of that fair youth! Eccentric notions — fantastic speculations — vivacious egotism—defective benevolence—yes. But crime! — No — impossible.

"Impossible," I said, aloud. As I spoke the group had moved on. Margrave was no longer in sight. At the same moment some other guests came from the ball-room, and seated themselves near us.

Sir Philip looked round, and, observing the deserted museum at the end of the corrider, drew me into it.

When we were alone, he said in a voice quick and low, but decided:

"It is of importance that I should convince you at once of the nature of that prodigy which is more hostile to mankind than the wolf is to the sheepfold. No words of mine could at present suffice to clear your sight from the deception which cheats it. I must enable you to judge for yourself. It must be now and here. He will learn this night, if he has not learned already, that I am in the town. Dim and confused though his memories of myself may be, they are memories still; and he well knows what cause he has to dread me. I must put another in possession of his secret. Another, and at once! For all his arts will be brought to bear against me, and I cannot foretell their issue. Go, then; enter that giddy crowd — select that seeming young man — bring him hither. Take care only not to mention my name; and when here, turn the key in the door, so as to prevent interruption — five minutes will suffice."

"Am I sure that I guess whom you mean? The young, light-hearted man, known in this place, under the name of Margrave? — the young man with the radiant eyes, and the curls of a Grecian statue?"

"The same; him whom I pointed out; quick, bring him hither."

My curiosity was too much roused to disobey. Had I conceived that Margrave, in the heat of youth, had committed some offence which placed him in danger of the law and in the power of Sir Philip Derval, I possessed enough of the old borderers' black-mail loyalty to have given the man whose hand I had familiarly clasped a hint and a help to escape. But all Sir Philip's talk had been so out of the reach of common sense, that I rather expected to see him confounded by some egregious illusion than Margrave exposed to any well-grounded accusation. All, then, that I felt as I walked into the ball-room and approached Margrave, was that curiosity which, I think, any one of my readers will acknowledge that, in my position, he himself would have felt.

Margrave was standing near the dancers, not joining them, but talking with a young couple in the ring. I drew him aside.

"Come with me for a few minutes into the museum; I wish to talk to you."

"What about? — an experiment?"

"Yes, an experiment."

"Then I am at your service."

In a minute more he had followed me into the desolate dead museum. I looked round, but did not see Sir Philip.

CHAPTER XXXII.

MARGRAVE threw himself on a seat just under the great anaconda; I closed and locked the door. When I had done so, my eye fell on the young man's face, and I was surprised to see that it had lost its color; that it showed great anxiety, great distress; that his hands were visibly trembling.

"What is this?" he said, in feeble tones, and raising himself half from his seat as if with great effort. "Help me up — come away! Something in this room is hostile to me — hostile, overpowering! What can it be?"

"Truth and my presence," answered a stern, low voice; and Sir Philip Derval, whose slight form the huge bulk of the dead elephant had before obscured from my view, came suddenly out from the shadow into the full rays of the lamps which lit up, as if for Man's revel, that mocking catacomb for the playmates of Nature which he enslaves for his service or slays for his sport. As Sir Philip spoke and advanced, Margrave sank back into his seat, shrinking, collapsing, nerveless; terror the most abject expressed in his staring eyes and parted lips. On the other hand, the simple dignity of Sir Philip Derval's bearing, and the mild power of his countenance, were alike inconceivably heightened. A change had come over the whole man, the more impressive because wholly undefinable.

Halting opposite Margrave, he uttered some words in a language unknown to me, and stretched one hand over the young man's head. Margrave at once became stiff and rigid as if turned to stone. Sir Philip said to me:

"Place one of those lamps on the floor — there, by his feet."

I took down one of the colored lamps from the mimic tree round which the huge anaconda coiled its spires, and placed it as I was told.

"Take the seat opposite to him and watch."

I obeyed.

Meanwhile Sir Philip had drawn from his breast-pocket a small steel casket, and I observed, as he opened it, that the interior was subdivided into several compartments, each with its separate lid; from one of these he took and sprinkled over the flame of the lamp a few grains of a powder, colorless and sparkling as diamond dust; in a second or so a delicate perfume, wholly unfamiliar to my sense, rose from the lamp.

"You would test the condition of trance; test it, and in the spirit."

And, as he spoke, his hand rested lightly on my

head. Hitherto, amidst a surprise not unmixed with awe, I had preserved a certain defiance, a certain distrust. I had been, as it were, on my guard.

But as those words were spoken, as that hand rested on my head, as that perfume arose from the lamp, all power of will deserted me. My first sensation was that of passive subjugation; but soon I was aware of a strange intoxicating effect from the odor of the lamp, round which there now played a dazzling vapor. The room swam before me. Like a man oppressed by a nightmare, I tried to move, to cry out — feeling that to do so would suffice to burst the thrall that bound me — in vain.

A time that seemed to me inexorably long, but which, as I found afterwards, could only have occupied a few seconds, elapsed in this preliminary state, which, however powerless, was not without a vague luxurious sense of delight. And then suddenly came pain — pain, that in rapid gradations passed into a rending agony. Every bone, sinew, nerve, fibre of the body, seemed as if wrenched open, and as if some hitherto unconjectured Presence in the vital organization were forcing itself to light with all the pangs of travail. The veins seemed swollen to bursting, the heart laboring to maintain its action by fierce spasms. I feel in this description how language fails me. Enough, that the anguish I then endured surpassed all that I have ever experienced of physical pain. This dreadful interval subsided as suddenly as it had commenced. I felt as if a something undefinable by any name had rushed from me, and in that rush that a struggle was over. I was sensible of the passive bliss which attends the release from torture, and then there grew on me a wonderful calm, and, in that calm, a consciousness of some lofty intelligence immeasurably beyond that which human memory gathers from earthly knowledge. I saw before me the still rigid form of Margrave, and my sight seemed with ease to penetrate through its covering of flesh, and to survey the mechanism of the whole interior being.

"View that tenement of clay which now seems so fair, as it was when I last beheld it, three years ago, in the house of Haroun of Aleppo!"

I looked, and gradually, and as shade after shade falls on the mountain side while the clouds gather and the sun vanishes at last, so the form and face on which I looked changed from exuberant youth into infirm old age. The discolored, wrinkled skin, the bleared, dim eye, the flaccid muscles, the brittle, sapless bones. Nor was the change that of age alone; the expression of the countenance had passed into gloomy discontent, and in every furrow a passion or a vice had sown the seeds of grief.

And the brain now opened on my sight, with all its labyrinth of cells. I seemed to have the clue to every winding in the maze.

I saw therein a moral world, charred and ruined, as, in some fable I have read, the world of the moon is described to be; yet withal it was a brain of magnificent formation. The powers abused to evil had been originally of rare order—imagination and scope; the energies that dare; the faculties that discover. But the moral part of the brain had failed to dominate the mental. Defective veneration of what is good or great; cynical disdain of what is right and just; in fine, a great intellect, first misguided, then perverted, and now falling with the decay of the body into ghastly but imposing ruins. Such was the world of that brain as it had been three years ago. And still continuing to gaze thereon, I observed three separate emanations of light; the one of a pale red hue, the second of a pale azure, the third a silvery spark.

The red light, which grew paler and paler as I looked, undulated from the brain along the arteries, the veins, the nerves. And I murmur to myself, "Is this the principle of animal life?"

The azure light equally permeated the frame, crossing and uniting with the red, but in a separate and distinct ray, exactly as, in the outer world, a ray of light crosses or unites with a ray of heat, though in itself a separate individual agency. And again I murmured to myself, "Is this the principle of intellectual being, directing or influencing that of animal life; with it, yet not of it?"

But the silvery spark! What was that? Its centre seemed the brain. But I could fix it to no single organ. Nay, wherever I looked through the system, it reflected itself as a star reflects itself upon water. And I observed that while the red light was growing feebler and feebler, and the azure light was confused, irregular — now obstructed, now hurrying, now almost lost — the silvery spark was unaltered, undisturbed. So independent of all which agitated and vexed the frame, that I became strangely aware that if the heart stopped in its action, and the red light died out, if the brain were paralyzed, that energetic mind smitten into idiocy, and the azure light wandering objectless as a meteor wanders over the morass—still that silver spark would shine the same, indestructible by aught that shattered its tabernacle. And I murmured to myself, "Can that starry spark speak the presence of the soul? Does the silver light shine within creatures to which no life immortal has been promised by Divine Revelation?"

Involuntarily I turned my sight towards the dead forms in the motley collection, and lo, in my trance or my vision, life returned to them all! To the elephant and the serpent; to the tiger, the vulture, the beetle, the moth; to the fish and the polypus, and to yon mockery of man in the giant ape.

I seemed to see each as it lived in its native realm of earth, or of air, or of water; and the red light played more or less warm, through the structure of each, and the azure light, though duller of hue, seemed to shoot through the red, and communicate to the creatures an intelligence far inferior indeed to that of man, but sufficing to conduct the current of their will, and influence the cunning of their instincts. But in none, from the elephant to the moth, from the bird in which brain was the largest, to the hybrid in which life seemed to live as in plants — in none was visible the starry silver spark. I turned my eyes from the creatures around, back again to the form cowering under the huge anaconda, and in terror at the animation which the carcasses took in the awful illusions of that marvellous trance. For the tiger moved as if scenting blood, and to the eyes of the serpent the dread fascination seemed slowly returning.

Again I gazed on the starry spark in the form of the man. And I murmured to myself, "But if this be the soul, why is it so undisturbed and undarkened by the sins which have left such trace and such ravage in the world of the brain?" And gazing yet more intently on the spark, I became vaguely aware that it was not the soul, but the halo around the soul, as the star we see in heaven is not the star itself, but its circle of rays. And if the light itself was undisturbed and undarkened, it was because no sins done in the body could annihilate its essence, nor affect the eternity of its duration. The light was clear within the ruins of its lodgment, because it might pass away, but could not be extinguished.

But the soul itself in the heart of the light reflected back on my own soul within me its ineffable trouble, humiliation, and sorrow; for those ghastly wrecks of power placed at its sovereign command it was responsible; and, appalled by its own sublime fate of duration, was about to carry into eternity the account of its mission in time. Yet it seemed that while the soul was still there, though so forlorn and so guilty, even the wrecks around it were majestic. And the soul, whatever sentence it might merit, was not among the hopelessly lost. For in its remorse and its shame, it might still have retained what could serve for redemption. And I saw that the mind was storming the soul in some terrible rebellious war — all of thought, of passion, of desire, through which the azure light poured its restless flow, were surging up around the starry spark, as in siege. And I could not comprehend the war, nor guess what it was that the mind demanded the soul to yield. Only the distinction between the two was made intelligible by their antagonism. And I saw that the soul, sorely tempted, looked afar for escape from the subjects it had ever so ill controlled, and who sought to reduce to their vassal the power which had lost authority as their king. I could feel its terror in the sympathy of my own terror, the keenness of my own supplicating pity. I knew that it was imploring release from the perils it confessed its want of strength to encounter. And suddenly the starry spark rose from the ruins and the tumult around it—rose into space and vanished. And where my soul had recognized the presence of soul, there was a void. But the red light burned still, becoming more and more vivid; and, as it thus repaired and recruited its lustre, the whole animal form which had been so decrepit, grew restored from decay, grew into vigor and youth: and I saw Margrave as I had seen him in the waking world, the radiant image of animal life in the beauty of its fairest bloom.

And over this rich vitality and this symmetric mechanism now reigned only, with the animal life, the mind. The starry light fled and the soul vanished, still was left visible the mind: mind, by which sensations convey and cumulate ideas, and muscles obey volition: mind, as in those animals that have more than the elementary instincts: mind, as it might be in men, were men not immortal. As my eyes, in the Vision, followed the azure light, undulating, as before, through the cells of the brain, and crossing the red amidst the labyrinth of the nerves, I perceived that the essence of that azure light had undergone a change: it had lost that faculty of continuous and concentred power by which man improves on the works of the past, and weaves schemes to be developed in the future of remote generations; it had lost all sympathy in the past, because it had lost all conception of a future beyond the grave; it had lost conscience; it had lost remorse; the being it informed was no longer accountable through eternity for the employment of time. The azure light was even more vivid in certain organs useful to the conservation of existence, as in those organs I had observed it more vivid among some of the inferior animals than it is in man — secretiveness, destructiveness, and the ready perception of things immediate to the wants of the day. And the azure light was brilliant in cerebral cells, where before it had been dark, such as those which harbor mirthfulness and hope, for there the light was recruited by the exuberant health of the joyous animal being. But it was lead-like, or dim, in the great social organs through which man subordinates his own interest to that of his species, and utterly lost in those through which man is reminded of his duties to the throne of his Maker.

In that marvellous penetration with which the Vision endowed me, I perceived that this mind — though in energy far superior to many; though retaining, from memories of the former existence, the relics of a culture wide and in some things profound; though sharpened into formidable, if desultory, force whenever it schemed or aimed at the animal self-conservation which now made its master impulse or instinct; and though among the reminiscences of its state before its change were arts which I could not comprehend, but which I felt were dark and terrible, lending to a will never checked by remorse, arms that no healthfnl philosophy has placed in the arsenal of disciplined genius; though the mind in itself had an ally in a body as perfect in strength and elasticity as man can take from the favor of nature — still, I say, I felt that that mind wanted *the something,* without which men never could found cities, frame laws, bind together, beautify, exalt the elements of this world, by creeds that habitually subject them to a reference to another. The ant, and the bee, and the beaver congregate and construct; but they do not improve. Man improves because the future impels onward that which is not found in the ant, the bee and the beaver — that which was gone from the being before me.

I shrank appalled into myself, covered my face with my hands, and groaned aloud: "Have I ever then doubted that soul is distinct from mind?"

A hand here again touched my forehead, the light in the lamp was extinguished, I became insensible, and when I recovered I found myself back in the room in which I had first conversed with Sir Philip Derval, and seated, as before, on the sofa, by his side.

CHAPTER XXXIII.

My recollections of all that I have just attempted to describe were distinct and vivid, except with respect to time; it seemed to me as if many hours must have elapsed since I had entered the museum with Margrave; but the clock on the mantelpiece met my eyes as I turned them wistfully round the room; and I was indeed amazed to perceive that five minutes had sufficed for all which it has taken me so long to narrate, and which in their transit had hurried me through ideas and emotions so remote from my anterior experience.

To my astonishment now succeeded shame and indignation — shame that I, who had scoffed at the possibility of the comparatively credible influences of mesmeric action, should have been so helpless a puppet under the hand of the slight fellow-man beside me, and so morbidly impressed by phantasmagorical illusions; indignation that, by some fumes which had special potency over the brain, I had thus been, as it were, conjured out of my senses; and, looking full into the calm face at my side, I said, with a smile to which I sought to convey disdain:

"I congratulate you, Sir Philip Derval, on having learned in your travels in the East so expert a familiarity with the tricks of the jugglers."

"The East has a proverb," answered Sir Philip, quietly, "that the juggler may learn much from the dervish, but the dervish can learn nothing from the juggler. You will pardon me, however, for the effect produced on you for a few minutes, whatever the cause of it may be, since it may serve to guard your whole life from calamities to which it might otherwise have been exposed. And however you may consider that which you have just experienced to be a mere optical illusion, or the figment of a brain super-excited by the fumes of a vapor, look within yourself and tell me if you do not feel an inward and unanswerable conviction that there is more reason to shun and to fear the creature you left asleep under the dead jaws of the giant serpent, than there would be in the serpent itself, could hunger again move its coils, and venom again arm its fangs."

I was silent, for I could not deny that that conviction had come to me.

"Henceforth, when you recover from the confusion or anger which now disturbs your impressions, you will be prepared to listen to my explanations and my recital, in a spirit far different from that with which you would have received them before you were subjected to the experiment, which, allow me to remind you, you invited and defied. You will now, I trust, be fitted to become my confidant and my assistant — you will advise with me how, for the sake of humanity, we should act together against the incarnate lie, the anomalous prodigy which glides through the crowd in the image of joyous beauty. For the present I quit you. I have an engagement, on worldly affairs, in the town this night. I am staying at L——, which I shall leave for Derval Court to-morrow evening. Come to me there the day after to-morrow, at any hour that may suit you the best. Adieu!"

Here, Sir Philip Derval rose and left the room. I made no effort to detain him. My mind was too occupied in striving to recompose itself, and account for the phenomena that had scared it, and for the strength of the impressions it still retained.

I sought to find natural and accountable causes for effects so abnormal.

Lord Bacon suggests that the ointments with which witches anointed themselves might have had the effect of stopping the pores and congesting the brain, and thus impressing the sleep of the unhappy dupes of their own imagination with dreams so vivid that, on waking, they were firmly convinced that they had been borne through the air to the *Sabbat.*

I remember also having heard a distinguished French traveller — whose veracity was unquestionable — say, that he had witnessed extraordinary effects produced on the sensorium by certain fumigations used by an African pretender to magic. A person, of however healthy a brain, subjected to the influence of these fumigations, was induced to believe that he saw the most frightful apparitions.

However extraordinary such effects, they were not incredible — not at variance with our notions of the known laws of nature. And to the vapor or the odors which a powder applied to a lamp had called forth, I was, therefore, prepared to ascribe properties similar to those which Bacon's conjecture ascribed to the witches' ointment, and the French traveller to the fumigations of the African conjuror.

But, as I came to that conclusion, I was seized with an intense curiosity to examine for myself those agencies with which Sir Philip Derval appeared so familiar; —to test the contents in that mysterious casket of steel. I also felt a curiosity no less eager, but more, in spite of myself, intermingled with fear, to learn all that Sir

Philip had to communicate of the past history of Margrave. I could but suppose that the young man must indeed be a terrible criminal, for a person of years so grave, and station so high, to intimate accusations so vaguely dark, and to use means so extraordinary, in order to enlist my imagination rather than my reason against a youth in whom there appeared none of the signs which suspicion interprets into guilt.

While thus musing, I lifted my eyes and saw Margrave himself there, at the threshold of the ball-room — there, where Sir Philip had first pointed him out as the criminal he had come to L—— to seek and disarm; and now, as then, Margrave was the radiant centre of a joyous group: not the young boy-god Iacchus, amidst his nymphs, could, in Grecian frieze or picture, have seemed more the type of the sportive, hilarious vitality of sensuous nature. He must have passed, unobserved by me in my preoccupation of thought, from the museum and across the room in which I sat; and now there was as little trace in that animated countenance of the terror it had exhibited at Sir Philip's approach, as of the change it had undergone in my trance or my phantasy.

But he caught sight of me — left his young companions — came gaily to my side.

"Did you not ask me to go with you into that museum about half an hour ago, or did I dream that I went with you?"

"Yes; you went with me into that museum."

"Then pray what dull theme did you select to set me asleep there?"

I looked hard at him, and made no reply. Somewhat to my relief, I now heard my host's voice:

"Why, Fenwick, what has become of Sir Philip Derval?"

"He has left; he had business." And, as I spoke, again I looked hard on Margrave.

His countenance now showed a change; not surprise, not dismay, but rather a play of the lip, a flash of the eye, that indicated complacency — even triumph.

"So! Sir Philip Derval! He is in L——; he has been here to-night? So! as I expected."

"Did you expect it?" said our host. "No one else did. Who could have told you?"

"The movements of men so distinguished need never take us by surprise. I knew he was in Paris the other day. It is natural enough that he should come here. I was prepared for his coming."

Margrave here turned away towards the window, which he threw open and looked out.

"There is a storm in the air," said he, as he continued to gaze into the night.

Was it possible that Margrave was so wholly unconscious of what had passed in the museum, as to include in oblivion even the remembrance of Sir Philip Derval's presence before he had been rendered insensible, or laid asleep? Was it now only for the first time that he learned of Sir Philip's arrival in L——, and visit to that house? Was there any intimation of menace in his words and his aspect?

I felt that the trouble of my thoughts communicated itself to my countenance and manner; and, longing for solitude and fresh air, I quitted the house. When I found myself in the street, I turned round and saw Margrave still standing at the open window, but he did not appear to notice me; his eyes seemed fixed abstractedly on space.

CHAPTER XXXIV.

I WALKED on slowly and with the downcast brow of a man absorbed in meditation. I had gained the broad place in which the main streets of the town converged, when I was overtaken by a violent storm of rain. I sought shelter under the dark archway of that entrance to the district of Abbey Hill, which was still called Monk's Gate. The shadow within the arch was so deep that I was not aware that I had a companion till I heard my own name, close at my side. I recognized the voice, before I could distinguish the form, of Sir Philip Derval.

"The storm will soon be over," said he, quietly. "I saw it coming on in time. I fear you neglected the first warning of those sable clouds, and must be already drenched."

I made no reply, but moved involuntarily away towards the mouth of the arch.

"I see that you cherish a grudge against me!" resumed Sir Philip. "Are you, then, by nature vindictive?"

Somewhat softened by the friendly tone of this reproach, I answered, half in jest, half in earnest:

"You must own, Sir Philip, that I have some little reason for the uncharitable anger your question imputes to me. But I can forgive you on one condition."

"What is that?"

"The possession, for half an hour, of that mysterious steel casket which you carry about with you, and full permission to analyze and test its contents."

"Your analysis of the contents," returned Sir Philip, dryly, "would leave you as ignorant as before of the uses to which they can be applied. But I will own to you frankly, that it is my intention to select some confidant among men of science, to whom I may safely communicate the wonderful properties which certain essences in that casket possess. I invite your acquaintance, nay, your friendship, in the hope that I may find such a confidant in you. But the casket contains other combinations, which, if wasted, could not be re-supplied; at least by any process which the great Master from whom I received them placed within reach of my knowledge. In this they resemble the diamond; when the chemist has found that the diamond affords no other substance by its combustion than pure carbonic acid gas, and that the only chemical difference between the costliest diamond and a lump of pure charcoal is a proportion of hydrogen less than $\frac{1}{50000}$ part of the weight of the substance — can the chemist make you a diamond?

"These, then, the more potent, but also the more perilous of the casket's contents, shall be explored by no science, submitted to no test. They are the keys to masked doors in the ramparts of Nature, which no mortal can pass through without rousing dread sentries never seen upon this side her wall. The powers they confer are secrets locked in my breast, to be lost in my grave; as the casket which lies on my breast shall not be transferred to the hands of another, till all the rest of my earthly possessions pass away with my last breath in life, and my first in eternity."

"Sir Philip Derval," said I, struggling against the appeals to fancy or to awe, made in words so strange, uttered in a tone of earnest conviction, and heard amidst the glare of the lightning, the howl of the winds, and the roll of the thunder — "Sir Philip Derval, you accost me in language which, but for my experience of the powers at your command, I should hear with the contempt that is due to the vaunts of a mountebank, or the pity we give to the morbid beliefs of his dupe. As it is, I decline the confidence with which you would favor me, subject to the conditions which it seems you would impose. My profession abandons to quacks all drugs which may not be analyzed — all secrets which may not be fearlessly told. I cannot visit you at Derval Court. I cannot trust myself, voluntarily, again in the power of a man, who has arts of which I may not examine the nature, by which he can impose on my imagination and steal away my reason."

"Reflect well before you decide," said Sir Philip with a solemnity that was stern. "If you refuse to be warned and to be armed by me, your reason and your imagination will alike be subjected to influences which I can only explain by telling you that there is truth in those immemorial legends which depose to the existence of magic."

"Magic!"

"There is magic of two kinds — the dark and evil, appertaining to witchcraft or necromancy; the pure and beneficent, which is but philosophy applied to certain mysteries in Nature remote from the beaten tracks of science, but which deepened the wisdom of ancient sages, and can yet unriddle the myths of departed races."

"Sir Philip," I said, with impatient and angry interruption, "if you think that a jargon of this kind be worthy a man of your acquirements and station, it is at least a waste of time to address it to me. I am led to conclude that you desire to make use of me for some purpose which I have a right to suppose honest and blameless, because all you know of me is, that I rendered to your relation services which cannot lower my character in your eyes. If your object be, as you have intimated, to aid you in exposing and disabling a man whose antecedents have been those of guilt, and who threatens with danger the society which receives him, you must give me proofs that are not reducible to magic; and you must prepossess me against the person you accuse, not by powders and fumes that disorder the brain, but by substantial statements, such as justify one man in condemning another. And, since you have thought fit to convince me that there are chemical means at your disposal, by which the imagination can be so affected as to accept, temporarily, illusions for realities, so I again demand, and now still more decidedly than before, that while you address yourself to my reason, whether to explain your object or to vindicate your charges against a man whom I have admitted to my acquaintance, you will divest yourself of all means and agencies to warp my judgment, so illicit and fraudulent as those which you own yourself to possess. Let the casket, with all its contents, be transferred to my hands, and pledge me your word that, in giving that casket, you reserve to yourself no other means by which chemistry can be abused to those influences over physical organization, which ignorance or imposture may ascribe to — magic."

"I accept no conditions for my confidence, though I think the better of you for attempting to make them. If I live, you will seek me yourself, and implore my aid. Meanwhile, listen to me, and ——"

"No; I prefer the rain and the thunder to the whispers that steal to my ear in the dark from one of whom I have reason to beware."

So saying, I stepped forth, and at that moment the lightning flashed through the arch, and brought into full view the face of the man beside me. Seen by that glare, it was pale as the face of a corpse, but its expression was compassionate and serene.

I hesitated, for the expression of that hueless countenance touched me; it was not the face which inspires distrust or fear.

"Come," said I, gently; "grant my demand. The casket—"

"It is no scruple of distrust that now makes that demand; it is a curiosity which in itself is a fearful tempter. Did you now possess what at this moment you desire, how bitterly you would repent!"

"Do you still refuse my demand?"

"I refuse."

"If then you really need me, it is you who will repent."

I passed from the arch into the open space. The rain had passed, the thunder was more distant. I looked back when I had gained the opposite side of the way, at the angle of a street which led to my own house. As I did so, again the skies lightened, but the flash was comparatively slight and evanescent; it did not penetrate the gloom of the arch; it did not bring the form of Sir Philip into view; but, just under the base of the outer buttress to the gateway, I descried the outline of a dark figure, cowering down, huddled up for shelter, the outline so indistinct, and so soon lost to sight as the flash faded, that I could not distinguish if it were man or brute. If it were some chance passer-by, who had sought refuge from the rain, and overheard any part of our strange talk, "the listener," thought I, with a half-smile, "must have been mightily perplexed."

CHAPTER XXXV.

On reaching my own home, I found my servant sitting up for me with the information that my attendance was immediately required. The little boy whom Margrave's carelessness had so injured, and for whose injuries he had shown so little feeling, had been weakened by the confinement which the nature of the injury required, and for the last few days had been generally ailing. The father had come to my house a few minutes before I reached it, in great distress of mind, saying that his child had been seized with fever, and had become delirious. Hearing that I was at the mayor's house, he had hurried thither in search of me.

I felt as if it were almost a relief to the troubled and haunting thoughts which tormented me, to be summoned to the exercise of a familiar knowledge. I hastened to the bedside of the little sufferer, and soon forgot all else in the anxious struggle for a human life. The struggle promised to be successful; the worst symptoms began to yield to remedies prompt and energetic, if simple. I remained at the house, rather to comfort and support the parents than because my continued attendance was absolutely needed, till the night was well-nigh gone; and all cause of immediate danger having subsided, I then found myself once more in the streets. An atmosphere palely clear in the grey of dawn had succeeded to the thunder-clouds of the stormy night; the street lamps, here and there, burned wan and still. I was walking slowly and wearily, so tired out that I was scarcely conscious of my own thoughts, when, in a narrow lane, my feet stopped almost mechanically before a human form stretched at full length in the centre of the road, right in my path. The form was dark in the shadow thrown from the neighboring houses. "Some poor drunkard," thought I, and the humanity, inseparable from my calling, not allowing me to leave a fellow-creature thus exposed to the risk of being run over by the first drowsy wagoner who might pass along the thoroughfare, I stooped to rouse and to lift the form. What was my horror when my eyes met the rigid stare of a dead man's. I started, looked again; it was the face of Sir Philip Derval! He was lying on his back, the countenance upturned, a dark stream oozing from the breast — murdered by two ghastly wounds — murdered not long since; the blood was still warm. Stunned and terror-stricken, I stood bending over the body. Suddenly I was touched on the shoulder.

"Hollo! what is this?" said a gruff voice.

"Murder!" I answered, in hollow accents, which sounded strangely to my own ear.

"Murder! so it seems." And the policeman who had thus accosted me lifted the body.

"A gentleman by his dress. How did this happen? How did you come here?" and the policeman glanced suspiciously at me.

At this moment, however, there came up another policeman, in whom I recognized the young man whose sister I had attended and cured.

"Dr. Fenwick," said the last, lifting his hat respectfully, and at the sound of my name his fellow-policeman changed his manner, and muttered an apology.

I now collected myself sufficiently to state the name and rank of the murdered man. The policemen bore the body to their station, to which I accompanied them. I then returned to my own house, and had scarcely sunk on my bed when sleep came over me. But what a sleep! Never till then had I known how awfully distinct dreams can be. The phantasmagoria of the naturalist's collection revived. Life again awoke in the serpent and the tiger, the scorpion moved, and the vulture flapped its wings. And there was Margrave, and there Sir Philip; but their position of power was reversed. And Margrave's foot was on the breast of the dead man. Still I slept on, till I was roused by the summons to attend on Mr. Vigors, the magistrate to whom the police had reported the murder.

I dressed hastily and went forth. As I passed through the street, I found that the dismal news had already spread. I was accosted on my way to the magistrate by a hundred eager, tremulous, inquiring tongues.

The scanty evidence I could impart was soon given.

My introduction to Sir Philip at the mayor's house, our accidental meeting under the arch, my discovery of the corpse some hours afterwards on my return from my patient, my professional belief that the deed must have been done a very short time, perhaps but a few minutes, before I chanced upon its victim. But, in that case, how account for the long interval that had elapsed between the time in which I had left Sir Philip under the arch, and the time in which the murder must have been committed? Sir Philip could not have been wandering through the streets all those hours. This doubt, however, was easily and speedily cleared up. A Mr. Jeeves, who was one of the principal solicitors in the town, stated that he had acted as Sir Philip's legal agent and adviser ever since Sir Philip came of age, and was charged with the exclusive management of some valuable house property which the deceased had possessed in L——; that when Sir Philip had arrived in the town late in the afternoon of the previous day, he had sent for Mr. Jeeves; informed him that he, Sir Philip, was engaged to be married; that he wished to have full and minute information as to the details of his house property (which had greatly increased in value since his absence from England), in connection with the settlements his marriage would render necessary; and that this information was also required by him in respect to a codicil he desired to add to his will.

He had accordingly requested Mr. Jeeves to have all the books and statements concerning the property ready for his inspection that night, when he would call, after leaving the ball which he had promised the mayor, whom he had accidentally met on entering the town, to attend. Sir Philip had also asked Mr. Jeeves to detain one of his clerks in his office, in order to serve, conjointly with Mr. Jeeves, as a witness to the codicil he desired to add to his will. Sir Philip had accordingly come to Mr. Jeeves's house a little before midnight; had gone carefully through all the statements prepared for him, and had executed the fresh codicil to his testament, which testament he had in their previous interview given to Mr. Jeeves's care sealed up. Mr. Jeeves stated that Sir Philip, though a man of remarkable talents and great acquirements, was extremely eccentric, and of a very peremptory temper, and that the importance attached to a promptitude for which there seemed no pressing occasion, did not surprise him in Sir Philip as it might have done in an ordinary client. Sir Philip said, indeed, that he should devote the next morning to the draft for his wedding settlements, according to the information of his property which he had acquired; and after a visit of very brief duration to Derval Court, should quit the neighborhood and return to Paris, where his intended bride then was, and in which city it had been settled that the marriage ceremony should take place.

Mr. Jeeves had, however, observed to him, that if he were so soon to be married, it was better to postpone any revision of testamentary bequests, since after marriage he would have to make a new will altogether.

And Sir Philip had simply answered:

"Life is uncertain; who can be sure of the morrow?"

Sir Philip's visit to Mr. Jeeves's house had lasted some hours, for the conversation between them had branched off from actual business to various topics. Mr. Jeeves had not noticed the hour when Sir Philip went; he could only say that as he attended him to the street-door, he observed, rather to his own surprise, that it was close upon daybreak.

Sir Philip's body had been found not many yards distant from the hotel at which he had put up, and to which, therefore, he was evidently returning when he left Mr. Jeeves: an old-fashioned hotel, which had been the principal one at L—— when Sir Philip left England, though now outrivalled by the new and more central establishment in which Margrave was domiciled.

The primary and natural supposition was that Sir Philip had been murdered for the sake of plunder; and this supposition was borne out by the fact to which his valet deposed, viz:

That Sir Philip had about his person, on going to the

mayor's house, a purse containing notes and sovereigns; and this purse was now missing.

The valet, who, though an Albanian, spoke English fluently, said that the purse had a gold clasp, on which Sir Philip's crest and initials were engraved. Sir Philip's watch was, however, not taken.

And now, it was not without a quick beat of the heart that I heard the valet declare that a steel casket, to which Sir Philip attached extraordinary value, and always carried about him, was also missing.

The Albanian described this casket as of ancient Byzantine workmanship, opening with a peculiar spring, only known to Sir Philip, in whose possession it had been, so far as the servant knew, about three years; when, after a visit to Aleppo, in which the servant had not accompanied him, he had first observed it in his master's hands. He was asked if this casket contained articles to account for the value Sir Philip set on it — such as jewels, bank-notes, letters of credit, &c. The man replied that it might possibly do so; he had never been allowed the opportunity of examining its contents; but that he was certain the casket held medicines, for he had seen Sir Philip take from it some small phials, by which he had performed great cures in the East, and especially during a pestilence which had visited Damascus, just after Sir Philip had arrived at that city on quitting Aleppo. Almost every European traveller is supposed to be a physician; and Sir Philip was a man of great benevolence, and the servant firmly believed him also to be of great medical skill. After this statement, it was very naturally and generally conjectured that Sir Philip was an amateur disciple of homœopathy, and that the casket contained the phials or globules in use among homœopathists.

Whether or not Mr. Vigors enjoyed a vindictive triumph in making me feel the weight of his authority, or whether his temper was ruffled in the excitement of so grave a case, I cannot say, but his manner was stern and his tone discourteous in the questions which he addressed to me. Nor did the questions themselves seem very pertinent to the object of investigation.

"Pray, Dr. Fenwick," said he, knitting his brows, and fixing his eyes on me rudely, "did Sir Philip Derval, in his conversation with you, mention the steel casket which it seems he carried about with him?"

I felt my countenance change slightly as I answered, "Yes."

"Did he tell you what it contained?"

"He said it contained secrets."

"Secrets of what nature? medicinal or chemical? Secrets which a physician might be curious to learn and covetous to possess?"

This question seemed to me so offensively significant that it roused my indignation, and I answered haughtily, that "a physician of any degree of merited reputation did not much believe in, and still less covet, those secrets in his art which were the boast of quacks and pretenders."

"My question need not offend you, Dr. Fenwick. I put it in another shape: Did Sir Philip Derval so boast of the secrets contained in his casket, that a quack or pretender might deem such secrets of use to him?"

"Possibly he might, if he believed in such a boast."

"Humph!—he might, if he so believed. I have no more questions to put to you, at present, Dr. Fenwick."

Little of any importance in connection with the deceased, or his murder, transpired in the course of that day's examination and inquiries.

The next day, a gentleman distantly related to the young lady to whom Sir Philip was engaged, and who had been for some time in correspondence with the deceased, arrived at L——. He had been sent for at the suggestion of the Albanian servant, who said that Sir Philip had stayed a day at this gentleman's house in London, on his way to L——, from Dover.

The new comer, whose name was Danvers, gave a more touching pathos to the horror which the murder had excited. It seemed that the motives which had swayed Sir Philip in the choice of his betrothed, were singularly pure and noble. The young lady's father—an intimate college friend—had been visited by a sudden reverse of fortune, which had brought on a fever that proved mortal. He had died some years ago, leaving his only child penniless, and had bequeathed her to the care and guardianship of Sir Philip.

The orphan received her education at a convent near Paris; and when Sir Philip, a few weeks since, arrived in that city from the East, he offered her his hand and fortune.

"I know," said Mr. Danvers, "from the conversation I held with him when he came to me in London, that he was induced to this offer by the conscientious desire to discharge the trust consigned to him by his old friend. Sir Philip was still of an age that could not permit him to take under his own roof a female ward of eighteen, without injury to her good name. He could only get over that difficulty by making the ward his wife. 'She will be safer and happier with the man she will love and honor for her father's sake,' said the chivalrous gentleman, 'than she will be under any other roof I could find for her.'"

And now there arrived another stranger to L——, sent for by Mr. Jeeves, the lawyer — a stranger to L——, but not to me; my old Edinburgh acquaintance, Richard Strahan.

The will in Mr. Jeeves's keeping, with its recent codicil, was opened and read. The will itself bore date about six years anterior to the testator's tragic death; it was very short, and, with the exception of a few legacies, of which the most important was ten thousand pounds to his ward, the whole of his property was left to Richard Strahan, on the condition that he took the name and arms of Derval within a year from the date of Sir Philip's decease. The codicil, added to the will the night before his death, increased the legacy to the young lady from ten to thirty thousand pounds, and bequeathed an annuity of one hundred pounds a year to his Albanian servant. Accompanying the will, and within the same envelope, was a sealed letter, addressed to Richard Strahan, and dated at Paris two weeks before Sir Philip's decease. Strahan brought that letter to me. It ran thus: "Richard Strahan, I advise you to pull down the house called Derval Court, and to build another on a better site, the plans of which, to be modified according to your own taste and requirements, will be found among my papers. This is a recommendation, not a command. But I strictly enjoin you entirely to demolish the more ancient part, which was chiefly occupied by myself, and to destroy by fire, without perusal, all the books and manuscripts found in the safes in my study. I have appointed you my sole executor, as well as my heir, because I have no personal friends in whom I can confide as I trust I may do in the man I have never seen, simply because he will bear my name and represent my lineage. There will be found in my writing-desk, which always accompanies me in my travels, an autobiographical work, a record of my own life, comprising discoveries, or hints at discovery, in science, through means little cultivated in our age. You will not be surprised that before selecting you as my heir and executor, from a crowd of relations not more distant, I should have made inquiries in order to justify my selection. The result of those inquiries informs me that you have not yourself the peculiar knowledge nor the habits of mind that could enable you to judge of matters which demand the attainments and the practice of science; but that you are of an honest, affectionate nature, and will regard as sacred the last injunctions of a benefactor. I enjoin you, then, to submit the aforesaid manuscript memoir to some man on whose character for humanity and honor you can place confidential reliance, and who is accustomed to the study of the positive sciences, more especially chemistry, in connection with electricity and magnetism. My desire is that he shall edit and arrange this memoir for publication; and that, wherever he feels a conscientious doubt whether any discovery, or hint of discovery, therein contained, would not prove more dangerous than useful to mankind, he shall consult with any other three men of science whose names are a guarantee for probity and knowledge, and according to the best of his judgment, after such consultation, suppress or publish the passage of which he has so doubted. I own the ambition which first directed me towards studies of a very unusual character, and which has encouraged me in their pursuit through many years of voluntary exile in lands where they could be best facilitated or aided — the ambition of leaving behind me the renown of a bold discoverer in those recesses of nature which philosophy has hitherto abandoned to superstition. But I feel, at the moment in which I trace these lines, a fear lest, in the absorbing interest of researches which tend to increase to a marvellous degree the power of man over all matter, animate or inanimate, I may have blunted my own moral perceptions; and that there may be much in the knowledge I sought and acquired from the pure desire of investigating hidden truths, that could be more abused to purposes of tremendous evil than be likely to conduce to benignant good. And of this a mind disciplined to severe reasoning, and uninfluenced by the enthusiasm which has probably obscured my own judgment, should be the unprejudiced arbiter. Much as I have coveted and still do covet that fame which makes the memory of one man the common inheritance of all, I would infinitely rather that my name should pass away with my breath, than that I should transmit to my fellow-men any portion of a knowledge which the good might forbear to exercise and the bad might unscrupulously pervert. I bear about me, wherever I wander, a certain steel casket. I received this casket, with its contents, from a man whose memory I hold in profound veneration. Should I live to find a person whom, after minute and intimate trial of his character, I should deem worthy of such confidence, it is my intention to communicate to him the secret how to prepare and how to use such of the powders and essences stored within that casket as I myself have ventured to employ. Others I have never tested, nor do I know how they could be re-supplied if lost or wasted. But as the contents of this casket, in the hands of any one not duly instructed as to the mode of applying them, would either be useless, or conduce, through inadvertent and ignorant misapplication, to the most dangerous consequences; so, if I die without having found, and in writing named, such a confidant as I have described above, I command you immediately to empty all the powders and essences found therein into any running stream of water, which will at once harmlessly dissolve them. On no account must they be cast into fire!

"This letter, Richard Strahan, will only come under your eyes in case the plans and the hopes which I have formed for my earthly future should be frustrated by the death on which I do not calculate, but against the chances of which this will and this letter provide. I am about to revisit England, in defiance of a warning that I shall be there subjected to some peril which I refuse to have defined, because I am unwilling that any mean apprehension of personal danger should enfeeble my nerves in the discharge of a stern and solemn duty. If I overcome that peril, you will not be my heir; my testament will be remodelled; this letter will be recalled and destroyed. I shall form ties which promise me the happiness I have never hitherto found, though it is common to all men — the affections of home, the caresses of children, among whom I may find one to whom hereafter I may bequeath, in my knowledge, a far nobler heritage than my lands. In that case, however, my first care would be to assure your own fortunes. And the sum which this codicil assures to my betrothed would be transferred to yourself on my wedding-day. Do you know why, never having seen you, I thus select you for preference to all my other kindred? — why my heart, in writing thus, warms to your image? Richard Strahan, your only sister, many years older than yourself — you were then a child — was the object of my first love. We were to have been wedded, for her parents deceived me into the belief that she returned my affection. With a rare and noble candor she herself informed me that her heart was given to another, who possessed not my worldly gifts of wealth and station. In resigning my claims to her hand, I succeeded in propitiating her parents to her own choice. I obtained for her husband the living which he held, and I settled on your sister the dower which, at her death, passed to you as the brother to whom she had shown a mother's love, and the interest of which has secured you a modest independence.

"If these lines ever reach you, recognize my title to reverential obedience to commands which may seem to you wild, perhaps irrational; and repay, as if a debt due from your own lost sister, the affection I have borne to you for her sake."

While I read this long and strange letter, Strahan sat by my side, covering his face with his hands, and weeping with honest tears for the man whose death had made him powerful and rich.

"You will undertake the trust ordained to me in this letter," said he, struggling to compose himself. "You will read and edit this memoir; you are the very man he himself would have selected. Of your honor and humanity there can be no doubt, and you have studied with success the sciences which he specifies as requisite for the discharge of the task he commands."

At this request, though I could not be wholly unprepared for it, my first impulse was that of a vague terror. It seemed to me as if I were becoming more and more entangled in a mysterious and fatal web. But this impulse soon faded in the eager yearnings of an ardent and irresistible curiosity.

I promised to read the manuscript, and in order that I might fully imbue my mind with the object and wish of the deceased, I asked leave to make a copy of the letter I had just read. To this Strahan readily assented, and that copy I have transcribed in the preceding pages.

I asked Strahan if he had yet found the manuscript; he said, "No, he had not yet had the heart to inspect the papers left by the deceased. He would now do so. He should go in a day or two to Derval Court, and reside there till the murderer was discovered, as doubtless he soon must be through the vigilance of the police. Not till that discovery was made should Sir Philip's remains, though already placed in their coffin, be consigned to the family vault."

Strahan seemed to have some superstitious notion that the murderer might be more secure from justice if his victim were thrust, unavenged, into the tomb.

CHAPTER XXXVI.

The belief prevalent in the town ascribed the murder of Sir Philip to the violence of some vulgar robber, probably not an inhabitant of L——. Mr. Vigors did not favor that belief. He intimated an opinion, which seemed extravagant and groundless, that Sir Philip had been murdered, for the sake not of the missing purse, but of the missing casket. It was currently believed that the solemn magistrate had consulted one of his pretended *clairvoyants*, and that this impostor had gulled him with assurances, to which he attached a credit that perverted into egregiously absurd directions his characteristic activity and zeal.

Be that as it may, the coroner's inquest closed without casting any light on so mysterious a tragedy.

What were my own conjectures I scarcely dared to admit — I certainly could not venture to utter them. But my suspicions centred upon Margrave. That for some reason or other he had cause to dread Sir Philip's presence in L—— was clear, even to my reason. And how could my reason reject all the influences which had been brought to bear on my imagination, whether by the scene in the museum or my conversation with the deceased? But it was impossible to act on such suspicions — impossible even to confide them. Could I have told to any man the effect produced on me in the museum, he would have considered me a liar or a madman. And in Sir Philip's accusations against Margrave there was nothing tangible — nothing that could bear repetition. Those accusations, if analyzed, vanished into air. What did they imply? — that Margrave was a magician, a monstrous prodigy, a creature exceptional to the ordinary conditions of humanity. Would the most reckless of mortals have ventured to bring against the worst of characters such a charge, on the authority of a deceased witness, and to found on evidence so fantastic the awful accusation of murder? But of all men, certainly I — a sober, practical physician — was the last whom the public could excuse for such incredible implications — and certainly, of all men, the last against whom any suspicion of heinous crime would be readily entertained was that joyous youth in whose sunny aspect life and conscience alike seemed to keep careless holiday. But I could not overcome, nor did I attempt to reason against, the horror akin to detestation that had succeeded to the fascinating attraction by which Margrave had before conciliated a liking, founded rather on admiration than esteem.

In order to avoid his visits I kept away from the study in which I had habitually spent my mornings, and to which he had been accustomed to so ready an access. And if he called at the front door, I directed my servant to tell him that I was either from home or engaged. He did attempt for the first few days to visit me as before, but when my intention to shun him became thus manifest, desisted, naturally enough, as any other man so pointedly repelled would have done.

I abstained from all those houses in which I was likely to meet him; and went my professional round of visits in a close carriage, so that I might not be accosted by him in his walks.

One morning, a very few days after Strahan had shown me Sir Philip Derval's letter, I received a note from my old college acquaintance, stating that he was going to Derval Court that afternoon; that he should take with him the memoir which he had found, and begging me to visit him at his new home the next day, and commence my inspection of the manuscript. I consented eagerly.

That morning, on going my round, my carriage passed by another drawn up to the pavement, and I recognized the figure of Margrave standing beside the vehicle, and talking to some one seated within it. I looked back, as my own carriage whirled rapidly by, and saw with uneasiness and alarm that it was Richard Strahan to whom Margrave was thus familiarly addressing himself. How had the two made acquaintance? Was it not an outrage on Sir Philip Derval's memory, that the heir he had selected should be thus apparently intimate with the man whom he had so sternly denounced? I became still more impatient to read the memoir — in all probability it would give such explanations with respect to Margrave's antecedents, as, if not sufficing to criminate him of legal offences, would at least effectually terminate any acquaintance between Sir Philip's successor and himself.

All my thoughts were, however, diverted to channels of far deeper interest even than those in which my mind had of late been so tumultuously whirled along, when, on returning home, I found a note from Mrs. Ashleigh. She and Lilian had just come back to L——, sooner than she had led me to anticipate. Lilian had not seemed quite well the last day or two, and had been anxious to return.

CHAPTER XXXVII.

LET me recall it — softly — softly! Let me recall that evening spent with her! — that evening, the last before darkness rose between us like a solid wall.

It was evening, at the close of summer. The sun had set, the twilight was lingering still. We were in the old monastic garden — garden so quiet, so cool, so fragrant. She was seated on a bench under the one great cedar-tree that rose sombre in the midst of the grassy lawn with its little paradise of flowers. I had thrown myself on the sward at her feet; her hand so confidingly lay in the clasp of mine. I see her still — how young, how fair, how innocent!

Strange, strange! So inexpressibly English; so thoroughly the creature of our sober, homely life! The pretty, delicate white robe that I touch so timorously, and the ribbon-knots of blue that so well become the soft color of the fair cheek, the wavy silk of the brown hair! She is murmuring low her answer to my trembling question.

"As well as when last we parted? Do you love me as well still?"

"There is no 'still' written here," said she, softly pressing her hand to her heart. "Yesterday is as tomorrow in the Forever."

"Ah, Lilian! if I could reply to you in words as akin to poetry as your own."

"Fie! you who affect not to care for poetry!"

"That was before you went away — before I missed you from my eyes, from my life — before I was quite conscious how precious you were to me, more precious than common words can tell! Yes, there is one period in love when all men are poets, however the penury of their language may belie the luxuriance of their fancies. What would become of me if you ceased to love me?"

"Or of me, if you could cease to love?"

"And somehow it seems to me this evening as if my heart drew nearer to you — nearer, as if for shelter."

"It is sympathy," said she, with tremulous eagerness; "that sort of mysterious sympathy which I have often heard you deny or deride; for I, too, feel drawn nearer to you, as if there were a storm at hand. I was oppressed by an indescribable terror in returning home, and the moment I saw you there came a sense of protection."

Her head sank on my shoulder; we were silent some moments; then we both rose by the same involuntary impulse, and round her slight form I twined my strong arm of man. And now we are winding slow under the lilacs and acacias that belt the lawn. Lilian has not yet heard of the murder, which forms the one topic of the town, for all tales of violence and blood affected her as they affect a fearful child. Mrs. Ashleigh, therefore, had judiciously concealed from her the letters and the journals by which the dismal news had been carried to herself. I need scarcely say that the grim subject was not broached by me. In fact, my own mind escaped from the events which had of late so perplexed and tormented it; the tranquillity of the scene, the bliss of Lilian's presence, had begun to chase away even that melancholy foreboding which had overshadowed me in the first moments of our reunion. So we came gradually to converse of the future — of the day, not far distant, when we two should be as one. We planned our bridal excursion. We would visit the scenes endeared to her by song, to me by childhood — the bank and waves of my native Windermere—our one brief holiday before life returned to labor, and hearts now so disquieted by hope and joy settled down to the calm serenity of home.

As we thus talked, the moon, hourly rounded to her full, rose amidst skies without a cloud. We paused to gaze on her solemn, haunting beauty, as where are the lovers who have not paused to gaze? We were then on the terrace-walk, which commanded a view of the town below. Before us was a parapet wall, low on the garden side, but inaccessible on the outer side, forming part of a straggling, irregular street that made one of the boundaries dividing Abbey Hill from Low Town. The lamps of the thoroughfares, in many a line and row beneath us, stretched far away, obscured here and there by intervening roofs and tall church-towers. The hum of the city came to our ears, low and mellowed into a lulling sound. It was not displeasing to be reminded that there was a world without, as close and closer we drew each to each — worlds to one another! Suddenly there carolled forth the song of a human voice — a wild, irregular, half-savage melody — foreign, uncomprehended words — air and words not new to me. I recognized the voice and chant of Margrave. I started, and uttered an angry exclamation.

"Hush!" whispered Lilian, and I felt her frame shiver within my encircling arm. "Hush! listen! Yes; I have heard that voice before — last night."

"Last night! you were not here; you were more than a hundred miles away."

"I heard it in a dream! Hush, hush!"

The song rose louder; impossible to describe its effect, in the midst of the tranquil night, chiming over the serried roof-tops, and under the solitary moon. It was not like the artful song of man, for it was defective in the methodical harmony of tune; it was not like the song of the wild bird, for it had no monotony in its sweetness; it was wandering and various as the sounds from an Æolian harp. But it affected the senses to a powerful degree, as in remote lands and in vast solitudes I have since found the note of the mocking-bird, suddenly heard, affect the listener half with delight, half with awe, as if some demon-creature of the desert were mimicking man for its own merriment. The chant now had changed into an air of defying glee, of menacing exultation; it might have been the triumphant war-song of some antique barbarian race. The note was sinister; a shadow passed through me, and Lilian had closed her eyes, and was sighing heavily; then with a rapid change, sweet as the coo with which an Arab mother lulls her babe to sleep, the melody died away. "There, there, look," murmured Lilian, moving from me, "the same I saw last night in sleep; the same I saw in the space above, on the evening I first knew you!"

Her eyes were fixed — her hand raised; my look followed hers, and rested on the face and form of Margrave. The moon shone full upon him, so full as if concentrating all its light upon his image. The place on which he stood (a balcony to the upper story of a house about fifty yards distant) was considerably above the level of the terrace from which we gazed on him. His arms were folded on his breast, and he appeared to be looking straight towards us. Even at that distance the lustrous youth of his countenance appeared to me terribly distinct, and the light of his wondrous eye seemed to rest upon us in one lengthened, steady ray through the limpid moonshine. Involuntarily I seized Lilian's hand, and drew her away almost by force, for she was unwilling to move, and as I led her back, she turned her head to look round; I too turned in jealous rage! I breathed more freely. Margrave had disappeared!

"How came he there? It is not his hotel. Whose house is it?" I said, aloud, though speaking to myself.

Lilian remained silent; her eyes fixed upon the ground as if in deep reverie. I took her hand; it did not return my pressure. I felt cut to the heart when she drew coldly from me that hand, till then so frankly cordial. I stopped short: "Lilian, what is this? you are chilled towards me. Can the mere sound of that man's voice, the mere glimpse of that man's face, have ——" I paused; I did not dare to complete my question.

Lilian lifted her eyes to mine, and I saw at once in those eyes a change. Their look was cold; not haughty, but abstracted. "I do not understand you," she said, in a weary, listless accent. "It is growing late; I must go in."

So we walked on moodily, no longer arm in arm, nor hand in hand. Then it occurred to me that, the next day Lilian would be in that narrow world of society; that there she could scarcely fail to hear of Margrave, to meet, to know him. Jealousy seized me with all its imaginary terrors, and amidst that jealousy, a nobler, purer apprehension for herself. Had I been Lilian's brother instead of her betrothed, I should not have trembled less to foresee the shadow of Margrave's mysterious influence passing over a mind so predisposed to the charm which Mystery itself has for those whose thoughts fuse their outlines in fancies; whose world melts away into Dreamland. Therefore I spoke.

"Lilian, at the risk of offending you — alas! I have never done so before this night — I must address to you a prayer, which I implore you not to regard as the dictate of a suspicion unworthy you and myself. The person whom you have just heard and seen is, at present, much courted in the circles of this town. I entreat you not to permit any one to introduce him to you. I entreat you not to know him. I cannot tell you all my reasons for this petition; enough that I pledge you my honor that those reasons are grave. Trust then in my truth, as I trust in yours. Be assured that I stretch not the rights which your heart has bestowed upon mine in the promise I ask, as I shall be freed from all fear by a promise which I know will be sacred when once it is given."

"What promise?" asked Lilian, absently, as if she had not heard my words.

"What promise? Why, to refuse all acquaintance with that man; his name is Margrave. Promise me, dearest, promise me."

"Why is your voice so changed?" said Lilian. "Its

tone jars on my ear," she added, with a peevishness so unlike her, that it startled me more than it offended; and, without a word further, she quickened her pace, and entered the house.

For the rest of the evening we were both taciturn and distant towards each other. In vain Mrs. Ashleigh kindly sought to break down our mutual reserve. I felt that I had the right to be resentful, and I clung to that right the more because Lilian made no attempt at reconciliation. This, too, was wholly unlike herself, for her temper was ordinarily sweet — sweet to the extreme of meekness; saddened if the slightest misunderstanding between us had ever vexed me, and yearning to ask forgiveness if a look or a word had pained me. I was in hopes that, before I went away, peace between us would be restored. But long ere her usual hour for retiring to rest, she rose abruptly, and, complaining of fatigue and headache, wished me good-night, and avoided the hand I sorrowfully held out to her as I opened the door.

"You must have been very unkind to poor Lilian," said Mrs. Ashleigh, between jest and earnest, "for I never saw her so cross to you before. And the first day of her return, too!"

"The fault is not mine," said I, somewhat sullenly; "I did but ask Lilian, and that as a humble prayer, not to make the acquaintance of a stranger in this town against whom I have reasons for distrust and aversion. I know not why that prayer should displease her."

"Nor I. Who is the stranger?"

"A person who calls himself Margrave. Let me at least entreat you to avoid him!"

"Oh, I have no desire to make acquaintance with strangers. But, now Lilian is gone, do tell me all about this dreadful murder? The servants are full of it, and I cannot keep it long concealed from Lilian. I was in hopes that you would have broken it to her."

I rose impatiently; I could not bear to talk thus of an event the tragedy of which was associated in my mind with circumstances so mysterious. I became agitated and even angry when Mrs. Ashleigh persisted in rambling woman-like inquiries — "Who was suspected of the deed? Who did I think had committed it? What sort of a man was Sir Philip? What was that strange story about a casket?" Breaking from such interrogations, to which I could give but abrupt and evasive answers, I seized my hat, and took my departure.

CHAPTER XXXVIII.

LETTER FROM ALLEN FENWICK TO LILIAN ASHLEIGH.

"I HAVE promised to go to Derval Court to-day, and shall not return till to-morrow. I cannot bear the thought that so many hours should pass away with one feeling less kind than usual resting like a cloud upon you and me. Lilian, if I offended you, forgive me! Send me one line to say so! — one line which I can place next to my heart and cover with grateful kisses till we meet again!"

REPLY.

"I scarcely know what you mean, nor do I quite understand my own state of mind at this moment. It cannot be that I love you less—and yet—but I will not write more now. I feel glad that we shall not meet for the next day or so, and then I hope to be quite recovered. I am not well at this moment. Do not ask me to forgive you — but, if it is I who am in fault, forgive me, oh forgive me, Allen."

And with this unsatisfactory note—not worn next to my heart, not covered with kisses, but thrust crumpled into my desk like a creditor's unwelcome bill, I flung myself on my horse and rode to Derval Court. I am naturally proud; my pride came now to my aid. I felt bitterly indignant against Lilian, so indignant that I resolved on my return to say to her, "If in those words, 'And yet,' you implied a doubt whether you loved me less, I cancel your vows, I give you back your freedom." And I could have passed from her threshold with a firm foot, though with the certainty that I should never smile again.

Does her note seem to you who may read these pages to justify such resentment? Perhaps not. But there is an atmosphere in the letters of the one we love, which we alone — we who love — can feel, and in the atmosphere of that letter I felt the chill of the coming winter.

I reached the park lodge of Derval Court late in the day. I had occasion to visit some patients whose houses lay scattered many miles apart, and for that reason, as well as from the desire for some quick bodily exercise which is so natural an effect of irritable perturbation of mind, I had made the journey on horseback instead of using a carriage, that I could not have got through the lanes and field-paths by which alone the work set to myself could be accomplished in time.

Just as I entered the park, an uneasy thought seized hold of me with the strength which is ascribed to presentiments. I had passed through my study (which has been so elaborately described) to my stables, as I generally did when I wanted my saddle-horse, and, in so doing, had, doubtless, left open the gate to the iron palisade, and probably the window of the study itself. I had been in this careless habit for several years, without ever once having cause for self-reproach. As I before said, there was nothing in my study to tempt a thief; the study shut out from the body of the house, and the servant sure at nightfall both to close the window and lock the gate; yet now, for the first time, I felt an impulse, urgent, keen, and disquieting, to ride back to the town and see those precautions taken. I could not guess why, but something whispered to me that my neglect had exposed me to some great danger. I even checked my horse and looked at my watch; too late! — already just on the stroke of Strahan's dinner-hour as fixed in his note; my horse, too, was fatigued and spent; besides, what folly! what bearded man can believe in the warnings of a "presentiment?" I pushed on, and soon halted before the old-fashioned flight of stairs that led up to the hall. Here I was accosted by the old steward; he had just descended the stairs, and, as I dismounted, he thrust his arm into mine unceremoniously, and drew me a little aside.

"Doctor, I was right; it *was* his ghost that I saw by the iron door of the mausoleum. I saw it again at the same place last night, but I had no fit then. Justice on his murderer! Blood for blood!"

"Ay!" said I sternly; for if I suspected Margrave before, I felt convinced now that the inexpiable deed was his. Wherefore convinced? Simply because I now hated him more, and hate is so easily convinced! "Lilian! Lilian!" I murmured to myself that name: the flame of my hate was fed by my jealousy. "Ay!" said I, sternly, "murder will out."

"What are the police about?" said the old man, querulously; "days pass on days, and no nearer the truth. But what does the new owner care? He has the rents and acres; what does he care for the dead? I will never serve another master. I have just told Mr. Strahan so. How do I know whether he did not do the deed? Who else had an interest in it?"

"Hush, hush!" I cried; "you do not know how wildly you are talking."

The old man stared at me, shook his head, released my arm, and strode away.

A laboring man came out of the garden, and having unbuckled the saddle-bags, which contained the few things required for so short a visit, I consigned my horse to his care, and ascended the perron. The old housekeeper met me in the hall, conducted me up the great staircase, showed me into a bedroom prepared for me, and told me that Mr. Strahan was already waiting dinner for me. I should find him in the study. I hastened to join him. He began apologizing, very unnecessarily, for the state of his establishment. He had, as yet, engaged no new servants. The housekeeper, with the help of a housemaid, did all the work.

Richard Strahan at college had been as little distinguishable from other young men as a youth neither rich nor poor, neither clever nor stupid, neither handsome nor ugly, neither audacious sinner nor formal saint, possibly could be.

Yet, to those who understood him well, he was not without some of those moral qualities by which a youth of mediocre intellect often matures into a superior man.

He was, as Sir Philip had been rightly informed, thoroughly honest and upright. But with a strong sense of duty, there was also a certain latent hardness. He was not indulgent. He had outward frankness with acquaintances, but was easily roused to suspicion.

He had much of the thriftiness and self-denial of the North countryman, and I have no doubt that he had lived with calm content and systematic economy on an income which made him, as a bachelor, independent of his nominal profession, but would not have sufficed, in itself, for the fitting maintenance of a wife and family. He was, therefore, still single.

It seemed to me, even during the few minutes in which we conversed before dinner was announced, that his character showed a new phase with his new fortunes. He talked in a grandiose style of the duties of station and the woes of wealth. He seemed to be very much afraid of spending, and still more appalled at the idea of being cheated. His temper, too, was ruffled; the steward had given him notice to quit. Mr. Jeeves, who had spent the morning with him, had said the steward would be a great loss, and a steward, at once sharp and honest, was not to be easily found.

What trifles can embitter the possession of great goods! Strahan had taken a fancy to the old house; it was conformable to his notions, both of comfort and pomp, and Sir Philip had expressed a desire that the old house should be pulled down. Strahan had inspected the plans for the new mansion to which Sir Philip had referred, and the plans did not please him; on the contrary, they terrified.

"Jeeves says that I could not build such a house under seventy or eighty thousand pounds, and then it will require twice the establishment which will suffice for this. I shall be ruined," cried the man who had just come into possession of at least ten thousand a year.

"Sir Philip did not enjoin you to pull down the old house; he only advised you to do so. Perhaps he thought the site less healthy than that which he proposes for a new building, or was aware of some other drawback to the house, which you may discover later. Wait a little, and see before deciding."

"But, at all events, I suppose I must pull down this curious old room—the nicest part of the whole house!"

Strahan, as he spoke, looked wistfully round at the quaint oak chimney-piece; the carved ceiling; the well-built, solid walls, with the large mullion casement, opening so pleasantly on the sequestered gardens. He had ensconced himself in Sir Philip's study, the chamber in which the once famous mystic, Forman, had found a refuge.

"So cozy a room for a single man!" sighed Strahan. "Near the stables and dog-kennels, too! But I suppose I must pull it down. I am not bound to do so legally; it is no condition of the will. But in honor and gratitude I ought not to disobey poor Sir Philip's positive injunction."

"Of that," said I, gravely, "there cannot be a doubt."

Here our conversation was interrupted by Mrs. Gates, who informed us that dinner was served in the library. Wine of great age was brought from the long-neglected cellars; Strahan filled and refilled his glass, and, warmed into hilarity, began to talk of bringing old college friends around him in the winter season, and making the roof-tree ring with laughter and song once more.

Time wore away, and night had long set in, when Strahan at last rose from the table, his speech thick and his tongue unsteady. We returned to the study, and I reminded my host of the special object of my visit to him, viz., the inspection of Sir Philip's manuscript.

"It is tough reading," said Strahan; "better put it off till to-morrow. You will stay here two or three days."

"No; I must return to L—— to-morrow. I cannot absent myself from my patients. And it is the more desirable that no time should be lost before examining the contents of the manuscript, because probably they may give some clue to the detection of the murderer."

"Why do you think that?" cried Strahan, startled from the drowsiness that was creeping over him.

"Because the manuscript may show that Sir Philip had some enemy — and who but an enemy could have had a motive for such a crime? Come, bring forth the book. You of all men are bound to be alert in every research that may guide the retribution of justice to the assassin of your benefactor."

"Yes, yes. I will offer a reward of five thousand pounds for the discovery. Allen, that wretched old steward had the insolence to tell me that I was the only man in the world who could have an interest in the death of his master; and he looked at me as if he thought that I had committed the crime. You are right; it becomes me, of all men, to be alert. The assassin must be found. He must hang."

While thus speaking, Strahan had risen, unlocked a desk which stood on one of the safes, and drawn forth a thick volume, the contents of which were protected by a clasp and lock. Strahan proceeded to open this lock by one of a bunch of keys, which he said had been found on Sir Philip's person.

"There, Allen, this is the memoir. I need not tell you what store I place on it; not, between you and me, that I expect it will warrant poor Sir Philip's high opinion of his own scientific discoveries. That part of his letter seems to me very queer, and very flighty. But he evidently set his heart on the publication of his work, in part, if not in whole. And, naturally, I must desire to comply with a wish so distinctly intimated by one to whom I owe so much. I beg you, therefore, not to be too fastidious. Some valuable hints in medicine, I have reason to believe, the manuscript will contain, and those may help you in your profession, Allen."

"You have reason to believe! Why?"

"Oh, a charming young fellow, who, with most of the other gentry resident at L——, called on me at my hotel, told me that he had travelled in the East, and had there heard much of Sir Philip's knowledge of chemistry, and the cures it had enabled him to perform."

"You speak of Mr. Margrave. He called on you?"

"Yes."

"You did not, I trust, mention to him the existence of Sir Philip's manuscript."

"Indeed I did; and I said you had promised to examine it. He seemed delighted at that, and spoke most highly of your peculiar fitness for the task."

"Give me the manuscript," said I, abruptly, "and, after I have looked at it to-night, I may have something to say to you to-morrow in reference to Mr. Margrave."

"There is the book," said Strahan; "I have just glanced at it, and find much of it written in Latin; and I am ashamed to say that I have so neglected the little Latin I learned in our college days, that I could not construe what I looked at."

I sat down and placed the book before me; Strahan fell into a doze, from which he was wakened by the housekeeper, who brought in the tea-things.

"Well," said Strahan, languidly, "Do you find much in the book that explains the many puzzling riddles in poor Sir Philip's eccentric life and pursuits?"

"Yes," said I. "Do not interrupt me."

Strahan again began to doze, and the housekeeper asked if we should want anything more that night, and if I thought I could find my way to my bedroom.

I dismissed her impatiently, and continued to read.

Strahan woke up again as the clock struck eleven,

and finding me still absorbed in the manuscript, and disinclined to converse, lighted his candle, and telling me to replace the manuscript in the desk when I had done with it, and be sure to lock the desk and take charge of the key, which he took off the bunch and gave me, went upstairs, yawning.

I was alone in the wizard Forman's chamber, and bending over a stranger record than had ever excited my infant wonder, or, in later years, provoked my sceptic smile.

CHAPTER XXXIX.

The Manuscript was written in a small and peculiar hand-writing, which, though evidently by the same person whose letter to Strahan I had read, was, whether from haste or some imperfection in the ink, much more hard to decipher. Those parts of the Memoir which related to experiments, or alleged secrets in Nature, that the writer intimated a desire to submit exclusively to scholars or men of science, were in Latin — and Latin which, though grammatically correct, was frequently obscure. But all that detained the eye and attention on the page necessarily served to impress the contents more deeply on remembrance.

The narrative commenced with the writer's sketch of his childhood. Both his parents had died before he attained his seventh year. The orphan had been sent by his guardians to a private school, and his holidays had been passed at Derval Court. Here his earliest reminiscences were those of the quaint old room, in which I now sat, and of his childish wonder at the inscription on the chimney-piece — who and what was the Simon Forman who had there found a refuge from persecution? Of what nature were the studies he had cultivated, and the discoveries he boasted to have made?

When he was about sixteen, Philip Derval had begun to read the many mystic books which the library contained; but without other result on his mind than the sentiment of disappointment and disgust. The impressions produced on the credulous imagination of childhood vanished. He went to the university; was sent abroad to travel; and on his return took that place in the circles of London which is so readily conceded to a young idler of birth and fortune. He passed quickly over that period of his life, as one of extravagance and dissipation, from which he was first drawn by the attachment for his cousin to which his letter to Strahan referred. Disappointed in the hopes which that affection had conceived, and his fortune impaired, partly by some years of reckless profusion, and partly by the pecuniary sacrifices at which he had effected his cousin's marriage with another, he retired to Derval Court, to live there in solitude and seclusion. On searching for some old title-deeds required for a mortgage, he chanced upon a collection of manuscripts, much discolored, and in part eaten away by moth or damp. These, on examination, proved to be the writings of Forman. Some of them were astrological observations and predictions; some were upon the nature of the Cabbala; some upon the invocation of spirits and the magic of the dark ages. All had a certain interest, for they were interspersed with personal remarks, anecdotes of eminent actors in a very stirring time, and were composed as Colloquies, in imitation of Erasmus; the second person in the dialogue being Sir Miles Derval, the patron and pupil; the first person being Forman, the philosopher and expounder.

But along with these shadowy lucubrations were treatises of a more uncommon and a more startling character; discussions on various occult laws of nature, and detailed accounts of analytical experiments. These opened a new, and what seemed to Sir Philip a practical, field of inquiry — a true border-land between natural science and imaginative speculation. Sir Philip had cultivated philosophical science at the university; he resumed the study, and tested himself the truth of various experiments suggested by Forman. Some, to his surprise, proved successful — some wholly failed. These lucubrations first tempted the writer of the memoir towards the studies in which the remainder of his life had been consumed. But he spoke of the lucubrations themselves as valuable only where suggestive of some truths which Forman had accidentally approached, without being aware of their true nature and importance. They were debased by absurd puerilities, and vitiated by the vain and presumptuous ignorance which characterized the astrology of the middle ages. For these reasons the writer intimated his intention (if he lived to return to England) to destroy Forman's manuscripts, together with sundry other books, and a few commentaries of his own upon studies which had for a while misled him — all now deposited in the safes of the room in which I sat.

After some years passed in the retirement of Derval Court, Sir Philip was seized with the desire to travel, and the taste he had imbibed for occult studies led him towards those Eastern lands in which they took their origin, and still retain their professors.

Several pages of the manuscript were now occupied with minute statements of the writer's earlier disappointment in the objects of his singular research. The so-called magicians, accessible to the curiosity of European travellers, were either but ingenious jugglers, or produced effects that perplexed him by practices they had mechanically learned, but of the rationale of which they were as ignorant as himself. It was not till he had resided some considerable time in the East, and acquired a familiar knowledge of its current languages and the social habits of its various populations, that he became acquainted with men in whom he recognized earnest cultivators of the lore which tradition ascribes to the colleges and priesthoods of the ancient world; men generally living remote from others, and seldom to be bribed by money to exhibit their marvels or divulge their secrets. In his intercourse with these sages, Sir Philip arrived at the conviction that there does exist an art of magic, distinct from the guile of the conjuror, and applying to certain latent powers and affinities in nature a philosophy akin to that which we receive in our acknowledged schools, inasmuch as it is equally based upon experiment, and produces from definite causes definite results. In support of this startling proposition, Sir Philip now devoted more than half his volume to the detail of various experiments, to the process and result of which he pledged his guarantee as the actual operator. As most of these alleged experiments appeared to me wholly incredible, and as all of them were unfamiliar to my practical experience, and could only be verified or falsified by tests that would require no inconsiderable amount of time and care, I passed with little heed over the pages in which they were set forth. I was impatient to arrive at that part of the manuscript which might throw light on the mystery in which my interest was the keenest. What were the links which connected the existence of Margrave with the history of Sir Philip Derval? Thus hurrying on, page after page, I suddenly, towards the end of the volume, came upon a name that arrested all my intention — Haroun of Aleppo. He who has read the words addressed to me in my trance may well conceive the thrill that shot through my heart when I came upon that name, and will readily understand how much more vividly my memory retains that part of the manuscript to which I now proceed, than all which had gone before.

"It was," wrote Sir Philip, "in an obscure suburb of Aleppo that I at length met with the wonderful man from whom I have acquired a knowledge immeasurably more profound and occult than that which may be tested in the experiments to which I have devoted so large a share of this memoir. Haroun of Aleppo had, indeed, mastered every secret in nature which the nobler or theurgic magic seeks to fathom.

"He had discovered the great Principle of Animal Life, which had hitherto baffled the subtlest anatomist; provided only that the great organs were not irreparably destroyed, there was no disease that he could not cure; no decrepitude to which he could not restore vigor; yet his science was based on the same theory as that espoused by the best professional practitioners of medicine — viz., that the true art of healing is to assist nature to throw off the disease — to summon, as it were, the whole system to eject the enemy that has fastened on a part. And thus his processes, though occasionally varying in the means employed, all combined in this — viz., the reinvigorating and recruiting of the principle of life."

No one knew the birth or origin of Haroun; no one knew his age. In outward appearance he was in the strength and prime of mature manhood. But, according to testimonies in which the writer of the memoir expressed a belief that, I need scarcely say, appeared to me egregiously credulous, Haroun's existence under the same name, and known by the same repute, could be traced back to more than a hundred years. He told Sir Philip that he had thrice renewed his own life, and had resolved to do so no more — he had grown weary of living on. With all his gifts, Haroun owned himself to be consumed by a profound melancholy. He complained that there was nothing new to him under the sun; he said that, while he had at his command unlimited wealth, wealth had ceased to bestow enjoyment; and he preferred living as simply as a peasant; he had tired out all the affections and all the passions of the human heart; he was in the universe as in a solitude. In a word, Haroun would often repeat with mournful solemnity: "The soul is not meant to inhabit this earth, and in fleshy tabernacle, for more than the period usually assigned to mortals; and when by art in repairing the walls of the body, we so retain it, the soul repines, becomes inert or dejected." "He only," said Haroun, "would feel continued joy in continued existence who could preserve in perfection the sensual part of man, with such mind or reason as may be independent of the spiritual essence; but whom soul itself has quitted! Man, in short, as the grandest of the animals, but without the sublime discontent of earth, which is the peculiar attribute of soul."

One evening Sir Philip was surprised to find at Haroun's house another European. He paused in his narrative to describe this man. He said that for three or four years previously he had heard frequent mention, amongst the cultivators of magic, of an orientalized Englishman engaged in researches similar to his own, and to whom was ascribed a terrible knowledge in those branches of the art which, even in the East, are condemned as instrumental to evil. Sir Philip here distinguished at length, as he had so briefly distinguished in his conversation with me, between the two kinds of magic — that which he alleged to be as pure from sin as any other species of experimental knowledge, and that by which the agencies of witchcraft are invoked for the purposes of guilt.

The Englishman, to whom the culture of this latter and darker kind of magic was ascribed, Sir Philip Derval had never hitherto come across. He now met him at the house of Haroun; decrepit, emaciated, bowed down with infirmities, and racked with pain. Though little more than sixty, his aspect was that of extreme old age, but still on his face there were seen the ruins of a once singular beauty; and still in his mind there was a force that contrasted the decay of the body. Sir Philip had never met with an intellect more powerful and more corrupt. The son of a notorious usurer, heir to immense wealth, and endowed with the talents which justify ambition, he had entered upon life burdened with the odium of his father's name. A duel, to which he had been provoked by an ungenerous taunt on his origin, but in which a temperament fiercely vindictive had led him to violate the usages prescribed by the social laws that regulate such encounters, had subjected him to a trial in which he escaped conviction, either by a flaw in the technicalities of legal procedure, or by the compassion of the jury; * but the moral pre-

* The reader will here observe a discrepancy between Mrs. Poyntz's account and Sir Philip Derval's narrative. According to the former, Louis Grayle was tried in his absence from England, and sentenced to three years' imprisonment, which his flight enabled him to evade. According to the latter, Louis Grayle stood his trial, and obtained an acquittal. Sir Philip's account must, at least, be nearer the truth than the lady's, because Louis Grayle could not, according to English law, have been tried on a capital charge without being present in court. Mrs. Poyntz tells her story as a woman generally does tell a story — sure to make a mistake where she touches on a question of law; and — unconsciously perhaps to herself — the Woman of the World warps the facts in her narrative so as to save the personal dignity of the hero, who has captivated her interest, not from the moral odium of a great crime, but the debasing position of a prisoner at the bar. Allen Fenwick, no doubt, purposely omits to notice the discrepancy between these two statements, or to animadvert on the mistake which, in the eyes of a lawyer, would discredit Mrs. Poyntz's. It is consistent with some of the objects for which Allen Fenwick makes public his Strange Story, to invite the reader to draw his own inferences from the contradictions by which, even in the most commonplace matters (and how much more in any tale of wonder!), a fact stated by one person is made to differ from the same fact stated by another. The rapidity with which a truth becomes transformed into fable, when it is once sent on its travels from lip to lip, is illustrated by an amusement at this moment in fashion. The amusement is this: In a party of eight or ten persons, let one whisper to another an account of some supposed transaction, or a piece of invented gossip relating to absent persons, dead or alive; let the person, who thus first hears the story, proceed to whisper it, as exactly as he can remember what he has just

sumptions against him were sufficiently strong to set an indelible brand on his honor, and an insurmountable barrier to the hopes which his early ambition had conceived. After this trial he had quitted his country to return to it no more. Thenceforth much of his life had been passed out of sight or conjecture of civilized men in remote regions and amongst barbarous tribes. At intervals, however, he had reappeared in European capitals; shunned by and shunning his equals, surrounded by parasites, amongst whom were always to be found men of considerable learning, whom avarice or poverty subjected to the influences of his wealth. For the last nine or ten years he had settled in Persia, purchased extensive lands, maintained the retinue, and

heard, to the next; the next does the same to his neighbor, and so on, till the tale has run the round of the party. Each narrator, as soon as he has whispered his version of the tale, writes down what he has whispered. And though, in this game, no one has had any interest to misrepresent, but, on the contrary, each for his own credit's sake strives to repeat what he has heard as faithfully as he can, it will be almost invariably found that the story told by the first person has received the most material alterations before it has reached the eighth or the tenth. Sometimes, the most important feature of the whole narrative is altogether omitted; sometimes, a feature altogether new and preposterously absurd has been added. At the close of the experiment one is tempted to exclaim: "How, after this, can any of those portions of history, which the chronicler took from hearsay, be believed?" But, above all, does not every anecdote of scandal which has passed, not through ten lips, but perhaps through ten thousand, before it has reached us, become quite as perplexing to him who would get at the truth, as the marvels he recounts are to the bewildered reason of Fenwick the Sceptic?

exercised more than the power, of an Oriental prince. Such was the man who, prematurely worn out, and assured by physicians that he had not six weeks of life, had come to Aleppo with the gaudy escort of an Eastern satrap, had caused himself to be borne in his litter to the mud hut of Haroun the Sage, and now called on the magician, in whose art was his last hope, to reprieve him from the — grave.

He turned round to Sir Philip, when the latter entered the room, and exclaimed in English, "I am here because you are. Your intimacy with this man was known to me. I took your character as the guarantee of his own. Tell me that I am no credulous dupe. Tell him that I, Louis Grayle, am no needy petitioner. Tell me of his wisdom; assure him of my wealth."

Sir Philip looked inquiringly at Haroun, who remained seated on his carpet in profound silence.

"What is it you ask of Haroun?"

"To live on — to live on. For every year of life he can give me, I will load these floors with gold."

"Gold will not tempt Haroun."

"What will?"

"Ask him yourself; you speak his language."

"I have asked him; he vouchsafes me no answer."

Haroun here suddenly roused himself as from a reverie. He drew from under his robe a small phial, from which he let fall a single drop into a cup of water, and said, "Drink this. Send to me to-morrow for such medicaments as I may prescribe. Return hither yourself in three days; not before!"

When Grayle was gone, Sir Philip, moved to pity, asked Haroun if, indeed, it were within the compass of his art to preserve life in a frame that appeared so thoroughly exhausted. Haroun answered, "A fever may so waste the lamp of life that one ruder gust of air could extinguish the flame, yet the sick man recovers. This sick man's existence has been one long fever; this sick man can recover."

"You will aid him to do so?"

"Three days hence I will tell you."

On the third day Grayle revisited Haroun, and, at Haroun's request, Sir Philip came also. Grayle declared that he had already derived unspeakable relief from the remedies administered; he was lavish in expressions of gratitude; pressed large gifts on Haroun, and seemed pained when they were refused. This time Haroun conversed freely, drawing forth Grayle's own irregular, perverted, stormy, but powerful intellect.

I can best convey the general nature of Grayle's share in the dialogue between himself, Haroun, and Derval — recorded in the narrative in words which I cannot trust my memory to repeat in detail — by stating the effect it produced on my own mind. It seemed, while I read, as if there passed before me some convulsion of Nature — a storm, an earthquake. Outcries of rage, of scorn, of despair; a despot's vehemence of will; a rebel's scoff at authority. Yet, ever and anon, some swell of lofty thought, some burst of passionate genius, abrupt variations from the vaunt of superb defiance to the wail of intense remorse.

The whole had in it, I know not what, of uncouth but colossal — like the chant, in the old lyrical tragedy of one of those mythical giants, who, proud of descent from Night and Chaos, had held sway over the elements, while still crude and conflicting, to be crushed under the rocks, upheaved in their struggle, as Order and Harmony subjected a brightening Creation to the milder influences throned in Olympus. But it was not till the later passages of the dialogue in which my interest was now absorbed, that the language ascribed to this sinister personage lost a gloomy pathos not the less impressive for the awe with which it was mingled. For, till then, it seemed to me as if in that tempestuous nature there were still broken glimpses of starry light; that a character originally lofty, if irregular and fierce, had been embittered by early and continuous war with the social world, and had, in that war, become maimed and distorted; that, under happier circumstances, its fiery strength might have been disciplined to good; that even now, where remorse was so evidently poignant, evil could not be irredeemably confirmed.

At length all the dreary compassion previously inspired vanished in one unqualified abhorrence.

The subjects discussed changed from those which, relating to the common world of men, were within the scope of my reason. Haroun led his wild guest to boast of his own proficiency in magic, and, despite my incredulity, I could not overcome the shudder with which fictions, however extravagant, that deal with that dark Unknown abandoned to the chimeras of poets, will, at night and in solitude, send through the veins of men the least accessible to imaginary terrors.

Grayle spoke of the power he had exercised through the agency of evil spirits — a power to fascinate and to destroy. He spoke of the aid revealed to him, now too late, which such direful allies could afford, not only to a private revenge, but to a kingly ambition. Had he acquired the knowledge he declared himself to possess, before the feebleness of the decaying body made it valueless, how he could have triumphed over that world, which had expelled his youth from its pale! He spoke of means by which his influence could work undetected on the minds of others, control agencies that could never betray, and baffle the justice that could never discover. He spoke vaguely of a power by which a spectral reflection of the material body could be cast, like a shadow, to a distance; glide through the walls of a prison, elude the sentinels of a camp — a power that he asserted to be — when enforced by concentred will, and acting on the mind, where, in each individual temptation found mind the weakest — almost infallible in its effect to seduce or to appal. And he closed these and similar boasts of demoniacal arts, which I remember too obscurely to repeat, with a tumultuous imprecation on their nothingness to avail against the gripe of death. All this lore he would communicate to Haroun, in return for what? A boon shared by the meanest peasant — life, common life; to breathe yet a while the air, feel yet a while the sun.

Then Haroun replied. He said, with a quiet disdain, that the dark art to which Grayle made such boastful pretence, was the meanest of all abuses of knowledge, rightly abandoned, in all ages, to the vilest natures. And then, suddenly changing his tone, he spoke, so far as I can remember the words assigned to him in the manuscript, to this effect:

"Fallen and unhappy wretch, and you ask me for prolonged life! — a prolonged curse to the world and to yourself. Shall I employ spells to lengthen the term of the Pestilence, or profane the secrets of Nature to restore vigor and youth to the failing energies of Crime?"

Grayle, as if stunned by the rebuke, fell on his knees with despairing entreaties that strangely contrasted his previous arrogance. "And it was," he said, "because his life had been evil that he dreaded death. If life could be renewed he would repent, he would change; he retracted his vaunts, he would forsake the arts he had boasted, he would re-enter the world as its benefactor."

"So ever the wicked man lies to himself when appalled by the shadow of death," answered Haroun. "But know, by the remorse which preys on thy soul, that it is not thy soul that addresses this prayer to me.

Couldst thou hear, through the storms of the Mind, the Soul's melancholy whisper, it would dissuade thee from a wish to live on. While I speak, I behold it, that SOUL! Sad for the stains on its essence, awed by the account it must render, but dreading, as the direst calamity, a renewal of years below — darker stains and yet heavier accounts? Whatever the sentence it may now undergo, it has a hope for mercy in the remorse which the mind vainly struggles to quell. But darker its doom if longer retained to earth, yoked to the mind that corrupts it, and enslaved to the senses which thou bidst me restore to their tyrannous forces."

And Grayle bowed his head and covered his face with his hands in silence and in trembling.

Then Sir Philip, seized with compassion, pleaded for him. "At least, could not the soul have longer time on earth for repentance?" And while Sir Philip was so pleading, Grayle fell prostrate in a swoon like that of death. When he recovered, his head was leaning on Haroun's knee, and his opening eyes fixed on the glittering phial which Haroun held, and from which his lips had been moistened.

"Wondrous!" he murmured; "how I feel life flowing back to me. And that, then, is the elixir! it is no fable!"

His hands stretched greedily, as to seize the phial, and he cried imploringly, "More, more!" Haroun replaced the vessel in the folds of his robe, and answered:

"I will not renew thy youth, but I will release thee from bodily suffering: I will leave the mind and the soul free from the pangs of the flesh, to reconcile, if yet possible, their long war. My skill may afford thee months yet for repentance; seek, in that interval, to atone for the evil of sixty years; apply thy wealth where it may most compensate for injury done, most relieve the indigent, and most aid the virtuous. Listen to thy remorse. Humble thyself in prayer."

Grayle departed, sighing heavily and muttering to himself.

The next day Haroun summoned Sir Philip Derval, and said to him:

"Depart to Damascus. In that city the Pestilence has appeared. Go thither thou, to heal and to save. In this casket are stored the surest antidotes to the poison of the plague. Of that essence, undiluted and pure, which tempts to the undue prolongation of soul in the prison of flesh, this casket contains not a drop. I curse not my friend with so mournful a boon. Thou hast learned enough of my art to know by what simples the health of the temperate is easily restored to its balance, and their path to the grave smoothed from pain. Not more should Man covet from Nature for the solace and weal of the body. Nobler gifts far than aught for the body this casket contains. Herein are the essences which quicken the life of those duplicate senses that lie dormant and coiled in their chrysalis web, awaiting the wings of a future development—the senses by which we can see, though not with the eye, and hear, but not by the ear. Herein are the links between Man's mind and Nature's; herein are secrets more precious even than these—those extracts of light which enable the Soul to distinguish itself from the Mind, and discriminate the spiritual life, not more from life carnal than life intellectual. Where thou seest some noble intellect, studious of Nature, intent upon Truth, yet ignoring the fact that all animal life has a mind, and Man alone on the earth ever asked, and has asked, from the hour his step trod the Earth and his eye sought the Heaven, 'Have I not a soul—can it perish!'—there, such aids to the soul, in the innermost vision vouchsafed to the mind, thou mayest lawfully use. But the treasures contained in this casket are like all which a mortal can win from the mines he explores;—good or ill in their uses as they pass to the hands of the good or the evil. Thou wilt never confide them but to those who will not abuse; and even then, thou art an adept too versed in the mysteries of Nature not to discriminate between the powers that may serve the good to good ends, and the powers that may tempt the good—where less wise than experience has made thee and me—to the ends that are evil; and not even to thy friend, the most virtuous—if less proof against passion, than thou and I have become—wilt thou confide such contents of the casket as may work on the fancy, to deafen the conscience, and imperil the soul."

Sir Philip took the casket, and with it directions for

use, which he did not detail. He then spoke to Haroun about Louis Grayle, who had inspired him with a mingled sentiment of admiration and abhorrence; of pity and terror. And Haroun answered thus, repeating the words ascribed to him, so far as I can trust, in regard to them — as to all else in this marvellous narrative — to a memory habitually tenacious even in ordinary matters, and strained to the utmost extent of its power, by the strangeness of the ideas presented to it, and the intensity of my personal interest in whatever admitted a ray into that cloud which, gathering fast over my reason, now threatened storm to my affections:

"When the mortal deliberately allies himself to the spirits of evil, he surrenders the citadel of his being to the guard of its enemies; and those who look from without can only dimly guess what passes within the precincts abandoned to Powers whose very nature we shrink to contemplate, lest our mere gaze should invite them. This man, whom thou pitiest, is not yet everlastingly consigned to the fiends, because his soul still struggles against them. His life has been one long war between his intellect which is mighty and his spirit which is feeble. The intellect, armed and winged by the passions, has besieged and oppressed the soul; but the soul has never ceased to repine and to repent. And at moments it has gained its inherent ascendency, persuaded revenge to drop the prey it had seized, turned the mind astray from hatred and wrath into unwonted paths of charity and love. In the long desert of guilt there have been green spots and fountains of good. The fiends have occupied the intellect which invoked them, but they have never yet thoroughly mastered the soul which their presence appals. In the struggle that now passes within that breast, amidst the flickers of waning mortality, only Allah, whose eye never slumbers, can aid."

Haroun then continued, in words yet more strange and yet more deeply graved in my memory:

"There have been men (thou mayst have known such) who, after an illness in which life itself seemed suspended, have arisen, as out of a sleep, with characters wholly changed. Before, perhaps gentle and good and truthful, they now become bitter, malignant and false. To the persons and the things they had before loved, they evince repugnance and loathing. Sometimes this change is so marked and irrational, that their kindred ascribe it to madness. Not the madness which affects them in the ordinary business of life, but that which turns into harshness and discord the moral harmony that results from natures whole and complete. But there are dervishes who hold that in that illness, which had for its time the likeness of death, the soul itself has passed away, and an evil genius has fixed itself into the body and the brain, thus left void of their former tenant, and animates them in the unaccountable change from the past to the present existence. Such mysteries have formed no part of my study, and I tell you the conjecture received in the East without hazarding a comment whether of incredulity or belief. But if, in this war between the mind which the fiends have seized, and the soul which implores refuge of Allah; if, while the mind of yon traveller now covets life lengthened on earth for the enjoyments it had perverted its faculties to seek and to find in sin, and covets so eagerly that it would shrink from no crime, and revolt from no fiend, that could promise the gift — the soul shudderingly implores to be saved from new guilt, and would rather abide by the judgment of Allah on the sins that have darkened it, than pass forever irredeemably away to the demons: if this be so, what if the soul's petition be heard — what if it rise from the ruins around it — what if the ruins be left to the witchcraft that seeks to rebuild them? There, if demons might enter, that which they sought as their prize has escaped them; that which they find would mock them by its own incompleteness even in evil. In vain might animal life the most perfect be given to the machine of the flesh; in vain might the mind, freed from the check of the soul, be left to roam at will through a brain stored with memories of knowledge and skilled in the command of its faculties; in vain, in addition to all that body and brain bestow on the normal condition of man, might unhallowed reminiscences gather all the arts and the charms of the sorcery by which the fiends tempted the soul, before it fled, through the passions of flesh and the cravings of mind; the Thing, thus devoid of a soul, would be an instrument of evil, doubtless, but an instrument that of itself could not design, invent, and complete. The demons themselves could have no permanent hold on the perishable materials. They might enter it for some gloomy end which Allah permits in his inscrutable wisdom; but they could leave it no trace when they pass from it, because there is no conscience where soul is wanting. The human animal without soul, but otherwise made felicitously perfect in its mere vital organization, might ravage and destroy, as the tiger and the serpent may destroy and ravage, and, the moment after, would sport in the sunlight harmless and rejoicing, because, like the serpent and the tiger, it is incapable of remorse."

"Why startle my wonder," said Derval, "with so fantastic an image?"

"Because, possibly the image may come into palpable form! I know, while I speak to thee, that this miserable man is calling to his aid the evil sorcery over which he boasts his control. To gain the end he desires, he must pass through a crime. Sorcery whispers to him how to pass through it, secure from the detection of man. The soul resists, but in resisting, is weak against the tyranny of the mind to which it has submitted so long. Question me no more. But if I vanish from thine eyes, if thou hear that the death which, to my sorrow and in my foolishness I have failed to recognize as the merciful minister of Heaven, has removed me at last from the earth, believe that the Pale Visitant was welcome, and that I humbly accept as blessed release the lot of our common humanity."

Sir Philip went to Damascus. There he found the pestilence raging — there he devoted himself to the cure of the afflicted; in no single instance, so at least he declared, did the antidotes stored in the casket fail in their effect. The pestilence had passed, his medicaments were exhausted, when the news reached him that Haroun was no more. The Sage had been found, one morning, lifeless in his solitary home, and, according to popular rumor, marks on his throat betrayed the murderous hand of the strangler. Simultaneously, Louis Grayle had disappeared from the city, and was supposed to have shared the fate of Haroun, and been secretly buried by the assassins who had deprived him of life. Sir Philip hastened to Aleppo. There, he ascertained that on the night in which Haroun died, Grayle did not disappear alone; with him were also missing two of his numerous suite; the one, an Arab woman, named Ayesha, who had for some years been his constant companion, his pupil and associate in the mystic practices to which his intellect had been debased, and who was said to have acquired a singular influence over him, partly by her beauty, and partly by the tenderness with which she had nursed him through his long decline; the other, an Indian, specially assigned to her service, of whom all the wild retainers of Grayle spoke with detestation and terror. He was believed by them to belong to that murderous sect of fanatics whose existence as a community has only recently been made known to Europe, and who strangle their unsuspecting victim in the firm belief that they thereby propitiate the favor of the goddess they serve. The current opinion at Aleppo was, that if those two persons had conspired to murder Haroun, perhaps for the sake of the treasures he was said to possess, it was still more certain that they had made away with their own English lord, whether for the sake of the jewels he wore about him, or for the sake of treasures less doubtful than those imputed to Haroun — and of which the hiding-place would to them be much better known. "I did not share that opinion," wrote the narrator; "for I assured myself that Ayesha sincerely loved her awful master; and that love need excite no wonder, for Louis Grayle was one whom, if a woman, and especially a woman of the East, had once loved, before old age and infirmity fell on him, she would love and cherish still more devotedly when it became her task to protect the being who, in his day of power and command, had exalted his slave into the rank of his pupil and companion. And the Indian whom Grayle had assigned to her service, was allowed to have that brute kind of fidelity which, though it recoils from no crime for a master, refuses all crime against him.

"I came to the conclusion that Haroun had been murdered by order of Louis Grayle — for the sake of the elixir of life — murdered by Juma the Strangler; and that Grayle himself had been aided in his flight from Aleppo, and tended, through the effects of the life-giving drug thus murderously obtained, by the womanly love of the Arab woman, Ayesha. These convictions (since I could not — without being ridiculed as the wildest of dupes — even hint at the vital elixir) I failed to impress on the Eastern officials, or even on a countryman of my own whom I chanced to find at Aleppo. They only arrived at what seemed the common-sense verdict—viz.: that Haroun might have been strangled, or might have died in a fit (the body, little examined, was buried long before I came to Aleppo); and that Louis Grayle was murdered by his own treacherous dependents. But all trace of the fugitives was lost.

"And now," wrote Sir Philip, "I will state by what means I discovered that Louis Grayle still lived — changed from age into youth; a new form, a new being; realizing, I verily believe, the image which Haroun's words had raised up, in what then seemed to me the metaphysics of phantasy; criminal, without consciousness of crime; the dreadest of the mere animal race; an incarnation of the blind powers of Nature — beautiful and joyous, wanton, and terrible, and destroying! Such as ancient myths have personified in the idols of Oriental creeds; such as Nature, of herself, might form man in her moments of favor, if man were wholly the animal, and spirit were no longer the essential distinction between himself and the races to which by superior formation and subtler perceptions he would still be the king.

"But *this* being is yet more dire and portentous than the mere animal man, for in him are not only the fragmentary memories of a pristine intelligence which no mind, unaided by the presence of soul, could have originally compassed, but amidst that intelligence are the secrets of the magic which is learned through the agencies of spirits the most hostile to our race. And who shall say whether the fiends do not enter at their will this void and deserted temple whence the soul has departed, and use as their tools, passive and unconscious, all the faculties which, skilful in sorcery, still place a mind at the control of their malice?

"It was in the interest excited in me by the strange and terrible fate that befell an Armenian family with which I was slightly acquainted, that I first traced, in the creature I am now about to describe, and whose course I devote myself to watch, and trust to bring to a close—the murderer of Haroun for the sake of the elixir of youth.

"In this Armenian family there were three daughters; one of them ——"

I had just read thus far when a dim shadow fell over the page, and a cold air seemed to breathe on me. Cold—so cold, that my blood halted in my veins as if suddenly frozen! Involuntarily I started, and looked up, sure that some ghastly presence was in the room. And then, on the opposite side of the wall, I beheld an unsubstantial likeness of a human form. Shadow I call it, but the word is not strictly correct, for it was luminous, though with a pale shine. In some exhibition in London there is shown a curious instance of optical illusion; at the end of a corridor you see, apparently in strong light, a human skull. You are convinced it is there as you approach; it is, however, only a reflection from a skull at a distance. The image before me was less vivid, less seemingly prominent than is the illusion I speak of. I was not deceived. I felt it was a spectrum, a phantasm, but I felt no less surely that it was a reflection from an animate form — the form and the face of Margrave; it was there, distinct, unmistakable. Conceiving that he himself must be behind me, I sought to rise, to turn round, to examine. I could not move: limb and muscle were over-mastered by some incomprehensible spell. Gradually my senses forsook me, I became unconscious as well as motionless. When I recovered, I heard the clock strike three. I must have been nearly two hours insensible; the candles before me were burning low; my eyes rested on the table; the dead man's manuscript was gone!

CHAPTER XL.

THE dead man's manuscript was gone. But how? A phantom might delude my eye, a human will, though exerted at a distance, might, if the tales of mesmerism be true, deprive me of movement and of consciousness; but neither phantom nor mesmeric will could surely remove from the table before me the material substance of the book that had vanished! Was I to seek explanation in the arts of sorcery ascribed to Louis Grayle in the narrative? — I would not pursue that conjecture. Against it my reason rose up half alarmed, half disdainful. Some one must have entered the room — some one have removed the manuscript. I looked round. The windows were closed, the curtains partly drawn over the shutters, as they were before my consciousness had left me — all seemed undisturbed. Snatching up one of the candles, fast dying out, I went into the adjoining library, the desolate state-rooms, into the entrance-hall, and examined the outer door. Barred and locked! The robber had left no vestige of his stealthy presence.

I resolved to go at once to Strahan's room and tell him of the loss sustained. A deposit had been confided to me, and I felt as if there were a slur on my honor every moment in which I kept its abstraction concealed from him to whom I was responsible for the trust. I hastily ascended the great staircase, grim with faded portraits, and found myself in a long corridor opening on my own bed-room; no doubt also on Strahan's. Which was his? I knew not. I opened rapidly door after door, peered into empty chambers, went blundering on, when, to the right, down a narrow passage, I recognized the signs of my host's whereabouts — signs familiarly commonplace and vulgar, signs by which the inmate of any chamber in lodging-house or inn makes himself known — a chair before a doorway, clothes negligently thrown on it, beside it a pair of shoes. And so ludicrous did such testimony of common every-day life, of the habits which Strahan would necessarily have contracted in his desultory, unluxurious bachelor's existence — so ludicrous, I say, did these homely details seem to me, so grotesquely at variance with the wonders of which I had been reading, with the wonders yet more incredible of which I myself had been witness and victim, that, as I turned down the passage, I heard my own unconscious, half-hysterical laugh; and, startled by the sound of that laugh as if it came from some one else, I paused, my hand on the door, and asked myself: "Do I dream? Am I awake? And if awake, what am I to say to the commonplace mortal I am about to rouse? Speak to him of a phantom! Speak to him of some weird spell over this strong frame! Speak to him of a mystic trance in which has been stolen what he confided to me, without my knowledge! What will he say? What should I have said a few days ago to any man who told such a tale to me?" I did not wait to resolve these questions. I entered the room. There was Strahan sound asleep on his bed. I shook him roughly. He started up, rubbed his eyes — "You, Allen — you? What the deuce? — what's the matter?"

"Strahan, I have been robbed! — robbed of the manuscript you lent me. I could not rest till I had told you."

"Robbed, robbed! Are you serious?"

By this time Strahan had thrown off the bed-clothes, and sat upright, staring at me.

And then those questions which my mind had suggested while I was standing at his door repeated themselves with double force. Tell this man, this unimaginative, hard-headed, raw-boned, sandy-haired North-countryman — tell this man a story which the most credulous school-girl would have rejected as a fable! Impossible.

"I fell asleep," said I, coloring and stammering, for the slightest deviation from truth was painful to me, "and — and — when I woke — the manuscript was gone. Some one must have entered, and committed the theft ——"

"Some one entered the house at this hour of the night, and then only stolen a manuscript which could be of no value to him? Absurd! If thieves have come in, it must be for other objects — for plate, for money. I will dress; we will see!"

Strahan hurried on his clothes, muttering to himself, and avoiding my eye. He was embarrassed. He did not like to say to an old friend what was on his mind, but I saw at once that he suspected I had resolved to deprive him of the manuscript, and had invented a wild tale in order to conceal my own dishonesty.

Nevertheless he proceeded to search the house. I followed him in silence, oppressed with my own thoughts, and longing for solitude in my own chamber. We found no one, no trace of any one, nothing to excite suspicion. There were but two female servants sleeping in the house — the old housekeeper, and a country girl who assisted her. It was not possible to suspect either of these persons, but in the course of our search we opened the door of their rooms. We saw that they were both in bed, both seemingly asleep; it seemed idle to wake and question them. When the formality of our futile investigation was concluded, Strahan stopped at the door of my bedroom, and for the first time fixing his eyes on me steadily, said:

"Allen Fenwick, I would have given half the fortune I have come into rather than this had happened. The manuscript, as you know, was bequeathed to me as a sacred trust by a benefactor whose slightest wish it is my duty to observe religiously. If it contained aught valuable to a man of your knowledge and profession — why, you were free to use its contents. Let me hope, Allen, that the book will reappear to-morrow."

He said no more, drew himself away from the hand I involuntarily extended, and walked quickly back towards his own room.

Alone once more, I sank on a seat, buried my face in my hands, and strove in vain to collect into some definite shape my own tumultuous and disordered thoughts. Could I attach serious credit to the marvellous narrative I had read? Were there, indeed, such powers given to man? such influences latent in the calm routine of Nature? I could not believe it; I must have some morbid affection of the brain; I must be under an hallucination. Hallucination? The phantom, yes — the trance, yes. But still, how came the book gone? That, at least, was not hallucination.

I left my room the next morning with a vague hope that I should find the manuscript somewhere in the study; that, in my own trance, I might have secreted it, as sleep-walkers are said to secrete things, without remembrance of their acts in their waking state.

I searched minutely in every conceivable place. Strahan found me still employed in that hopeless task. He had breakfasted in his own room, and it was past eleven o'clock when he joined me. His manner was now hard, cold, and distant, and his suspicion so bluntly shown, that my distress gave way to resentment.

"Is it possible," I cried indignantly, "that you who have known me so well can suspect me of an act so base, and so gratuitously base? Purloin, conceal a book confided to me, with full power to copy from it whatever I might desire, use its contents in any way that might seem to me serviceable to science, or useful to me in my own calling!"

"I have not accused you," answered Strahan, sullenly. "But what are we to say to Mr. Jeeves, to all others who know that this manuscript existed? Will they believe what you tell me?"

"Mr. Jeeves," I said, "cannot suspect a fellow townsman, whose character is as high as mine, of untruth and theft. And to whom else have you communicated the facts connected with a memoir and a request of so extraordinary a nature?"

"To young Margrave; I told you so!"

"True, true. We need go no further to find the thief.

Margrave has been in the house more than once. He knows the position of the rooms. You have named the robber!"

"Tut! what on earth could a gay young fellow like Margrave want with a work of such dry and recondite nature as I presume my poor kinsman's memoir must be?"

I was about to answer, when the door was abruptly opened, and the servant girl entered, followed by two men, in whom I recognized the superintendent of the L—— police and the same subordinate who had found me by Sir Philip's corpse.

The superintendent came up to me with a grave face, and whispered in my ear. I did not at first comprehend him. "Come with you," I said, "and to Mr. Vigors, the magistrate? I thought my deposition was closed."

The superintendent shook his head. "I have the authority here, Dr. Fenwick."

"Well, I will come of course. Has anything new transpired?"

The superintendent turned to the servant girl, who was standing with gaping mouth and staring eyes. "Show us Dr. Fenwick's room. You had better put up, sir, whatever things you have brought here. I will go upstairs with you," he whispered again. "Come, Dr. Fenwick, I am in the discharge of my duty."

Something in the man's manner was so sinister and menacing that I felt at once, that some new and strange calamity had befallen me. I turned towards Strahan.

He was at the threshold, speaking in a low voice to the subordinate policeman, and there was an expression of amazement and horror in his countenance. As I came towards him he darted away without a word.

I went up the stairs, entered my bedroom, the superintendent close behind me. As I took up mechanically the few things I had brought with me, the police-officer drew them from me with an abruptness that appeared insolent, and deliberately searched the pockets of the coat which I had worn the evening before, then opened the drawers of the room, and even pried into the bed.

"What do you mean?" I asked, haughtily.

"Excuse me, sir. Duty. You are ——"

"Well, I am what?"

"My prisoner; here is the warrant."

"Warrant! on what charge?"

"The murder of Sir Philip Derval."

"I — I! Murder!" I could say no more.

I must hurry over this awful passage in my marvellous record. It is torture to dwell on the details, and indeed I have so sought to chase them from my recollection, that they only come back to me in hideous fragments, like the incoherent remains of a horrible dream.

All that I need state is as follows: Early on the very morning on which I had been arrested, a man, a stranger in the town, had privately sought Mr. Vigors, and deposed that on the night of the murder, he had been taking refuge from a sudden storm under shelter of the eaves and buttresses of a wall adjoining an old archway; that he had heard men talking within the archway; had heard one say to the other, "You still bear me a grudge." The other had replied, "I can forgive you on one condition." That he then lost much of the conversation that ensued, which was in a lower voice; but he gathered enough to know that the condition demanded by the one was the possession of a casket which the other carried about with him. That there seemed an altercation on this matter between the two men, which, to judge by the tones of voice, was angry on the part of the man demanding the casket; that, finally, this man said in a loud key, "Do you still refuse?" and on receiving the answer which the witness did not overhear, exclaimed threateningly, "It is you who will repent;" and then stepped forth from the arch into the street. The rain had then ceased, but by a broad flash of lightning the witness saw distinctly the figure of the person thus quitting the shelter of the arch; a man of tall stature, powerful frame, erect carriage. A little time afterwards, witness saw a slighter and older man come forth from the arch, whom he could only examine by the flickering ray of the gas-lamp near the wall, the lightning having ceased, but whom he fully believed to be the person he afterwards discovered to be Sir Philip Derval.

He said that he himself had only arrived at the town a few hours before; a stranger to L——, and indeed to England; having come from the United States of

America, where he had passed his life from childhood. He had journeyed on foot to L——, in the hope of finding there some distant relatives. He had put up at a small inn, after which he had strolled through the town, when the storm had driven him to seek shelter. He had then failed to find his way back to the inn, and after wandering about in vain, and seeing no one at that late hour of night of whom he could ask the way, he had crept under a portico and slept for two or three hours. Waking towards the dawn, he had then got up and again sought to find his way to the inn, when he saw, in a narrow street before him, two men, one of whom he recognized as the taller of the two, to whose conversation he had listened under the arch, the other he did not recognize at the moment. The taller man seemed angry and agitated, and he heard him say, "The casket; I will have it." There then seemed to be a struggle between these two persons, when the taller one struck down the shorter, knelt on his breast, and he caught distinctly the gleam of some steel instrument. That he was so frightened that he could not stir from the place, and that though he cried out, he believed his voice was not heard. He then saw the taller man rise, the other resting on the pavement motionless; and a minute or so afterwards beheld policemen coming to the place, on which he, the witness, walked away. He did not know that a murder had been committed; it might be only an assault; it was no business of his, he was a stranger. He thought it best not to interfere, the police having cognizance of the affair. He found out his inn; for the next few days he was absent from L——, in search of his relations, who had left the town, many years ago, to fix their residence in one of the neighboring villages.

He was, however, disappointed, none of these relations now survived. He had now returned to L——, heard of the murder, was in doubt what to do, might get himself into trouble if, a mere stranger, he gave an unsupported testimony. But, on the day before the evidence was volunteered, as he was lounging in the streets, he had seen a gentleman pass by on horseback, in whom he immediately recognized the man who, in his belief, was the murderer of Sir Philip Derval. He inquired of a bystander the name of the gentleman, the answer was "Dr. Fenwick." That, the rest of the day, he felt much disturbed in his mind, not liking to volunteer such a charge against a man of apparent respectability and station. But that his conscience would not let him sleep that night, and he had resolved at morning to go to the magistrate and make a clean breast of it.

The story was in itself so improbable that any other magistrate but Mr. Vigors would perhaps have dismissed it in contempt. But Mr. Vigors, already so bitterly prejudiced against me, and not sorry, perhaps, to subject me to the humiliation of so horrible a charge, immediately issued his warrant to search my house. I was absent at Derval Court; the house was searched

In the bureau in my favorite study, which was left unlocked, the steel casket was discovered, and a large case-knife, on the blade of which the stains of blood were still perceptible. On this discovery I was apprehended, and on these evidences, and on the deposition of this vagrant stranger, I was, not indeed committed to take my trial for murder, but placed in confinement; all bail for my appearance refused, and the examination adjourned to give time for further evidence and inquiries. I had requested the professional aid of Mr. Jeeves. To my surprise and dismay Mr. Jeeves begged me to excuse him. He said he was pre-engaged by Mr. Strahan to detect and prosecute the murderer of Sir P. Derval, and could not assist one accused of the murder. I gathered from the little he said that Strahan had already been to him that morning and told him of the missing manuscript — that Strahan had ceased to be my friend. I engaged another solicitor, a young man of ability, and who professed personal esteem for me. Mr. Stanton (such was the lawyer's name) believed in my innocence; but he warned me that appearances were grave, he implored me to be perfectly frank with him. "Had I held conversation with Sir Philip under the archway as reported by the witness? Had I used such or similar words? Had the deceased said, "I had a grudge against him?" Had I demanded the casket? Had I threatened Sir Philip that he would repent? And of what? His refusal?

"What was the reason of the grudge? What was

the nature of this casket, that I should so desire its possession?"

There, I became terribly embarrassed. What could I say to a keen, sensible, worldly man of law? Tell him of the powder and the fumes, of the scene in the museum, of Sir Philip's tale, of the implied identity of the youthful Margrave with the aged Grayle, of the elixir of life, and of magic arts? I—I tell such a romance! I the noted adversary of all pretended mysticism. I—I a sceptical practitioner of medicine! Had that manuscript of Sir Philip's been available—a substantial record of marvellous events by a man of repute for intellect and learning—I might, perhaps, have ventured to startle the solicitor of L—— with my revelations. But the sole proof that all which the solicitor urged me to confide was not a monstrous fiction or an insane delusion had disappeared; and its disappearance was a part of the terrible mystery that enveloped the whole. I answered, therefore, as composedly as I could, that "I could have no serious grudge against Sir Philip, whom I had never seen before that evening; that the words, which applied to my supposed grudge were lightly said by Sir Philip, in reference to a physiological dispute on matters connected with mesmerical phenomena; that the deceased had declared his casket, which he had shown me at the mayor's house, contained drugs of great potency in medicine; that I had asked permission to test those drugs myself; and that when I said he would repent of his refusal, I merely meant that he would repent of his reliance on drugs not warranted by the experiments of professional science.

My replies seemed to satisfy the lawyer so far, but "how could I account for the casket and the knife being found in my room?"

"In no way but this: the window of my study is a door-window opening on the lane, from which any one might enter the room. I was in the habit, not only of going out myself that way, but of admitting through that door any more familiar private acquaintance."

"Whom, for instance?"

I hesitated a moment, and then said, with a significance I could not forbear, "Mr. Margrave! He would know the *locale* perfectly; he would know that the door was rarely bolted from within during the daytime; he could enter at all hours; he could place, or instruct any one to deposit the knife and casket in my bureau, which he knew I never kept locked; it contained no secrets, no private correspondence — chiefly surgical implements, or such things as I might want for professional experiments."

"Mr. Margrave! But you cannot suspect him — a lively, charming young man, against whose character not a whisper was ever heard — of connivance with such a charge against you; a connivance that would implicate him in the murder itself, for if you are accused wrongfully, he who accuses you is either the criminal or the criminal's accomplice; his instigator or his tool."

"Mr. Stanton," I said firmly, after a moment's pause, "I do suspect Mr. Margrave of a hand in this crime. Sir Philip, on seeing him at the mayor's house, expressed a strong abhorrence of him, more than hinted at crimes he had committed; appointed me to come to Derval Court the day after that on which the murder was committed. Sir Philip had known something of this Margrave in the East — Margrave might dread exposure, revelations — of what I know not; but, strange as it may seem to you, it is my conviction that this young man, apparently so gay and so thoughtless, is the real criminal, and in some way, which I cannot conjecture, has employed this lying vagabond in the fabrication of a charge against myself. Reflect: of Mr. Margrave's antecedents we know nothing; of them nothing was known even by the young gentleman who first introduced him to the society of this town. If you would serve and save me, it is to that quarter that you will direct your vigilant and unrelaxing researches."

I had scarcely so said when I repented my candor, for I observed in the face of Mr. Stanton a sudden revulsion of feeling, an utter incredulity of the accusation I had thus hazarded, and for the first time a doubt of my own innocence. The fascination exercised by Margrave was universal; nor was it to be wondered at; for, besides the charm of his joyous presence, he seemed so singularly free from even the errors common enough with the young. So gay and boon a companion, yet a shunner of wine; so dazzling in aspect, so more than beautiful, so courted, so idolized by women, yet no tale of seduction, of profligacy, attached to his name! As to his antecedents, he had so frankly owned himself a natural son, a nobody, a traveller, an idler; his expenses, though lavish, were so unostentatious, so regularly defrayed. He was so wholly the reverse of the character assigned to criminals, that it seemed as absurd to bring a charge of homicide against a butterfly or a goldfinch as against this seemingly innocent and delightful favorite of humanity and nature.

However, Mr. Stanton said little or nothing, and shortly afterwards left me, with a dry expression of hope that my innocence would be cleared in spite of evidence that, he was bound to say, was of the most serious character.

I was exhausted. I fell into a profound sleep early that night; it might be a little after twelve when I woke, and woke as fully, as completely, as much restored to life and consciousness, as it was then my habit to be at the break of day. And, so waking, I saw, on the wall opposite my bed, the same luminous phantom I had seen in the wizard's study at Derval Court. I have read in Scandinavian legends of an apparition called the Scin-Læca, or shining corpse. It is supposed, in the northern superstition, sometimes to haunt sepulchres, sometimes to foretell doom. It is the spectre of a human body seen in a phosphoric light, and so exactly did this phantom correspond to the description of such an apparition in Scandinavian fable that I know not how to give it a better name than that of Scin-Læca — the shining corpse.

There it was before me, corpse-like, yet not dead; there, as in the haunted study of the wizard Forman! — the form and the face of Margrave. Constitutionally, my nerves are strong, and my temper hardy, and now I was resolved to battle against any impression which my senses might receive from my own deluding fancies. Things that witnessed for the first time daunt us, witnessed for the second time lose their terror. I rose from my bed with a bold aspect, I approached the phantom with a firm step; but when within two paces of it, and my hand outstretched to touch it, my arm became fixed in air, my feet locked to the ground. I did not experience fear; I felt that my heart beat regularly, but an invincible something opposed itself to me. I stood as if turned to stone, and then from the lips of this phantom there came a voice, but a voice which seemed borne from a great distance — very low, muffled, and yet distinct; I could not even be sure that my ear heard it, or whether the sound was not conveyed to me by an inner sense.

"I, and I alone, can save and deliver you," said the voice. "I will do so; and the conditions I ask, in return, are simple and easy."

"Fiend or spectre, or mere delusion of my own brain," cried I, "there can be no compact between thee and me. I despise thy malice, I reject thy services; I accept no conditions to escape from the one or to obtain the other."

"You may give a different answer when I ask again."

The Scin-Læca slowly waned, and, first fading into a pale shadow, then vanished. I rejoiced at the reply I had given. Two days elapsed before Mr. Stanton again came to me; in the interval the Scin-Læca did not reappear. I had mustered all my courage, all my common sense, noted down all the weak points of the false evidence against me, and felt calm and supported by the strength of my innocence.

The first few words of the solicitor dashed all my courage to the grouud. For I was anxious to hear news of Lilian, anxious to have some message from her that might cheer and strengthen me, and my first question was this:

"Mr. Stanton, you are aware that I am engaged in marriage to Miss Ashleigh. Your family are not unacquainted with her. What says, what thinks she of this monstrous charge against her betrothed?"

"I was for two hours at Mrs. Ashleigh's house last evening," replied the lawyer; "she was naturally anxious to see me as employed in your defence. Who do you think was there? Who, eager to defend you, to express his persuasion of your innocence, to declare his conviction that the real criminal would soon be discovered — who but that same Mr. Margrave, whom, pardon me my frankness, you so rashly and groundlessly suspected."

"Heavens! Do you say that he is received in that house? that he — *he* is familiarly admitted to *her* presence?"

"My good sir, why these unjust prepossessions against a true friend? It was as your friend that, as soon as the charge against you amazed and shocked the town of L——, Mr. Margrave called on Mrs. Ashleigh — presented to her by Miss Brabazon — and was so cheering and hopeful that ——"

"Enough!" I exclaimed — "enough!"

I paced the room in a state of excitement and rage, which the lawyer in vain endeavored to calm, until at length I halted abruptly; "Well — and you saw Miss Ashleigh? What message does she send to me — her betrothed?"

Mr. Stanton looked confused. "Message! Consider, sir — Miss Ashleigh's situation — the delicacy — and — and —"

"I understand! no message, no word, from a young lady so respectable to a man accused of murder."

Mr. Stanton was silent for some moments; and then said quietly, "Let us change this subject; let us think of what more immediately presses. I see you have been making notes; may I look at them?"

I composed myself and sat down. "This accuser! Have inquiries really been made as to himself, and his statement of his own proceedings? He comes, he says, from America — in what ship? At what port did he land? Is there any evidence to corroborate his story of the relations he tried to discover — of the inn at which he first put up, and to which he could not find his way?"

"Your suggestions are sensible, Dr. Fenwick. I have forestalled them. It is true that the man lodged at a small inn — the Rising Sun — true that he made inquiries about some relations of the name of Walls, who formerly resided at L——, and afterwards removed to a village ten miles distant — two brothers — tradesmen of small means but respectable character. He at first refused to say at what sea-port he landed, in what ship he sailed. I suspect that he has now told a falsehood as to these matters. I have sent my clerk to Southampton — for it is there he said that he was put on shore; we shall see — the man himself is detained in close custody. I hear that his manner is strange and excitable; but that he preserves silence as much as possible. It is generally believed that he is a bad character, perhaps a returned convict, and that this is the true reason why he so long delayed giving evidence, and has been since so reluctant to account for himself. But even if his testimony should be impugned, should break down, still we should have to account for the fact that the casket and the case-knife were found in your bureau. For, granting that a person could, in your absence, have entered your study and placed the articles in your bureau, it is clear that such a person must have been well acquainted with your house, and this stranger to L—— could not have possessed that knowledge."

"Of course not — Mr. Margrave did possess it!"

"Mr. Margrave again! — oh, sir."

I arose and moved away, with an impatient gesture. I could not trust myself to speak. That night I did not sleep; I watched impatiently, gazing on the opposite wall, for the gleam of the Scin-Læca. But the night passed away, and the spectre did not appear.

CHAPTER XLI.

The lawyer came the next day, and with something like a smile on his countenance. He brought me a few lines in pencil from Mrs. Ashleigh; they were kindly expressed, bade me be of good cheer; "she never for a moment believed in my guilt; Lilian bore up wonderfully under so terrible a trial; it was an unspeakable comfort to both to receive the visits of a friend so attached to me, and so confident of a triumphant refutation of the hideous calumny under which I now suffered, as Mr. Margrave!"

The lawyer had seen Margrave again — seen him in that house. Margrave seemed almost domiciled there!

I remained sullen and taciturn during this visit. I longed again for the night. Night came. I heard the distant clock strike twelve, when again the icy wind passed through my hair, and against the wall stood the Luminous shadow.

"Have you considered?" whispered the voice, still as from afar. "I repeat it — I alone can save you."

"Is it among the conditions which you ask, in return, that I shall resign to you the woman I love?"

"No."

"Is it one of the conditions that I should commit some crime — a crime perhaps heinous as that of which I am accused?"

"No."

"With such reservations, I accept the conditions you may name, provided I, in my turn, may demand one condition from yourself."

"Name it."

"I ask you to quit this town. I ask you, meanwhile, to cease your visits to the house that holds the woman betrothed to me."

"I will cease those visits. And before many days are over, I will quit this town."

"Now, then, say what you ask from me. I am prepared to concede it. And not from fear for myself, but because I fear for the pure and innocent being who is under the spell of your deadly fascination. This is your power over me. You command me through my love for another. Speak."

"My conditions are simple. You will pledge yourself to desist from all charges of insinuation against myself, of what nature soever. You will not, when you meet me in the flesh, refer to what you have known of my likeness in the Shadow. You will be invited to the house at which I may be also a guest; you will come; you will meet and converse with me as guest speaks with guest in the house of a host."

"Is that all?"

"It is all."

"Then I pledge you my faith; keep your own."

"Fear not; sleep secure in the certainty that you will soon be released from these walls."

The Shadow waned and faded. Darkness settled back, and a sleep, profound and calm, fell over me.

The next day Mr. Stanton again visited me. He had received that morning a note from Mr. Margrave, stating that he had left L—— to pursue, in person, an investigation which he had already commenced through another, affecting the man who had given evidence against me, and that, if his hope should prove well founded, he trusted to establish my innocence, and convict the real murderer of Sir Philip Derval. In the research he thus volunteered, he had asked for, and obtained, the assistance of the policeman Waby, who, grateful to me for saving the life of his sister, had expressed a strong desire to be employed in my service.

Meanwhile, my most cruel assailant was my old college friend, Richard Strahan. For Jeeves had spread abroad Strahan's charge of purloining the memoir which had been intrusted to me; and that accusation had done me great injury in public opinion, because it seemed to give probability to the only motive which ingenuity could ascribe to the foul deed imputed to me. That motive had been first suggested by Mr. Vigors. Cases are on record of men whose life had been previously blameless, who have committed a crime, which seemed to belie their nature, in the monomania of some intense desire. In Spain, a scholar reputed of austere morals, murdered and robbed a traveller for money in order to purchase books; books written, too, by Fathers of his Church! He was intent on solving some problem of theological casuistry. In France, an antiquary esteemed not more for his learning, than for amiable and gentle qualities, murdered his most intimate friend for the possession of a medal, without which his own collection was incomplete. These, and similar anecdotes, tending to prove how fatally any vehement desire, morbidly cherished, may suspend the normal operations of reason and conscience, were whispered about by Dr. Lloyd's vindictive partisan, and the inference drawn from them and applied to the assumption against myself, was the more credulously received, because of that over-refining speculation on motive and act which the shallow accept, in their eagerness to show how readily they understand the profound.

I was known to be fond of scientific, especially of chemical, experiments; to be eager in testing the truth of any novel invention. Strahan catching hold of the magistrate's fantastic hypothesis, went about repeating anecdotes of the absorbing passion for analysis and discovery which had characterized me in youth as a medical student, and to which, indeed, I owed the precocious reputation I had obtained.

Sir Philip Derval, according not only to report, but to the direct testimony of his servant, had acquired in the course of his travels many secrets in natural science, especially as connected with the healing art — his servant had deposed to the remarkable cures he had effected by the medicinals stored in the stolen casket — doubtless Sir Philip, in boasting of these medicinals in the course of our conversation, had excited my curiosity, inflamed my imagination, and thus, when I afterwards suddenly met him in a lone spot, a passionate impulse had acted on a brain heated into madness by curiosity and covetous desire.

All these suppositions, reduced into system, were corroborated by Strahan's charge that I had made away with the manuscript supposed to contain the explanations of the medical agencies employed by Sir Philip, and had sought to shelter my theft by a tale so improbable, that a man of my reputed talent could not have hazarded it if in his sound senses. I saw the web, that had thus been spread around me by hostile prepossessions and ignorant gossip; how could the arts of Margrave scatter that web to the winds? I know not, but I felt confidence in his promise and his power. Still, so great had been my alarm for Lilian, that the hope of clearing my own innocence was almost lost in my joy that Margrave, at least, was no longer in her presence, and that I had received his pledge to quit the town in which she lived.

Thus, hours rolled on hours, till, I think, on the third day from that night in which I had last beheld the mysterious Shadow, my door was hastily thrown open, a confused crowd presented itself at the threshold — the governor of the prison, the police superintendent, Mr. Stanton, and other familiar faces shut out from me since my imprisonment. I knew at the first glance that I was no longer an outlaw beyond the pale of human friendship. And proudly, sternly, as I had supported myself hitherto in solitude and suspense, when I felt warm hands grasping mine, heard joyous voices proffering congratulations, saw in the eyes of all that my innocence had been cleared, the revulsion of emotion was too strong for me — the room reeled on my sight — I fainted. I pass, as quickly as I can, over the explanations that crowded on me when I recovered, and that were publicly given in evidence in Court next morning. I had owed all to Margrave. It seems that he had construed to my favor the very supposition which had been bruited abroad to my prejudice. "For," said he, "it is conjectured that Fenwick committed the crime of which he is accused in the impulse of a disordered reason. That conjecture is based upon the probability that a madman alone could have committed a crime without adequate motive. But it seems quite clear that the accused is not mad; and I see cause to suspect that the accuser is." Grounding this assumption on the current reports of the witness's manner and bearing since he had been placed under official surveillance, Margrave had commissioned the policeman, Waby, to make inquiries in the village to which the accuser had asserted he had gone in quest of his relations, and Waby had there found persons who remembered to have heard that the two brothers named Walls lived less by the gains of the petty shop which they kept than by the proceeds of some property consigned to them as the nearest of kin to a lunatic who had once been tried for his life. Margrave had then examined the advertisements in the daily newspapers. One of them, warning the public against a dangerous maniac, who had effected his escape from an asylum in the west of England, caught his attention. To that asylum he had repaired.

There he learned that the patient advertised was one whose propensity was homicide, consigned for life to the asylum on account of a murder, for which he had been tried. The description of this person exactly tallied with that of the pretended American. The medical superintendent of the asylum hearing all particulars from Margrave, expressed a strong persuasion that the witness was his missing patient, and had himself committed the crime of which he had accused another. If so, the superintendent undertook to coax from him the full confession of all the circumstances. Like many other madmen, and not least those whose propensity is to crime, the fugitive maniac was exceedingly cunning, treacherous, secret, and habituated to trick and stratagem. More subtle than even the astute in possession of all their faculties, whether to achieve his purpose or to conceal it, and fabricate appearances against another. But while, in ordinary conversation, he seemed rational enough to those who were not accustomed to study him, he had one hallucination which, when humored, led him always, not only to betray himself, but to glory in any crime proposed or committed. He was under the belief that he had made a bargain with Satan, who, in return for implicit obedience, would bear him harmless through all the consequences of such submission, and finally raise him to great power and authority. It is no unfrequent illusion of homicidal maniacs to suppose they are under the influence of the Evil One, or possessed by a Demon. Murderers have assigned as the only reason they themselves could give for the crime, that "the Devil got into them," and urged the deed. But the insane have, perhaps, no attribute more in common than that of superweening self-esteem. The maniac who has been removed from a garret sticks straws in his hair and calls them a crown. So much does inordinate arrogance characterize mental aberration, that, in the course of my own practice, I have detected, in that infirmity, the certain symptom of insanity, long before the brain had made its disease manifest even to the most familiar kindred.

Morbid self-esteem accordingly pervaded the dreadful illusion by which the man I now speak of was possessed. He was proud to be the protected agent of the Fallen Angel. And if that self-esteem were artfully appealed to, he would exult superbly in the evil he held himself ordered to perform, as if a special prerogative, an official rank and privilege; then, he would be led on to boast gleefully of thoughts which the most cynical of criminals, in whom intelligence was not ruined, would shrink from owning. Then, he would reveal himself in all his deformity with as complacent and frank a self-glorying as some vain good man displays in parading his amiable sentiments and his beneficent deeds.

"If," said the superintendent, "this be the patient who has escaped from me, and if his propensity to homicide has been, in some way, directed towards the person who has been murdered, I shall not be with him a quarter of an hour before he will inform me how it happened, and detail the arts he employed in shifting his crime upon another—all will be told as minutely as a child tells the tale of some school-boy exploit, in which he counts on your sympathy, and feels sure of your applause."

Margrave brought this gentleman back to L——, took him to the mayor, who was one of my warmest supporters; the mayor had sufficient influence to dictate and arrange the rest. The superintendent was introduced to the room in which the pretended American was lodged. At his own desire a select number of witnesses were admitted with him—Margrave excused himself; he said candidly that he was too intimate a friend of mine to be an impartial listener to aught that concerned me so nearly.

The superintendent proved right in his suspicions,

and verified his promises. My false accuser was his missing patient; the man recognized Dr. * * * with no apparent terror, rather with an air of condescension, and in a very few minutes was led to tell his own tale, with a gloating complacency both at the agency by which he deemed himself exalted, and at the dexterous cunning with which he had acquitted himself of the task, that increased the horror of his narrative.

He spoke of the mode of his escape, which was extremely ingenious, but of which the details, long in themselves, did not interest me, and I understood them too imperfectly to repeat. He had encountered a seafaring traveller on the road, whom he had knocked down with a stone, and robbed of his glazed hat and pea-jacket, as well as of a small sum in coin, which last enabled him to pay his fare in a railway that conveyed him eighty miles away from the asylum. Some trifling remnant of this money still in his pocket, he then travelled on foot along the high road till he came to a town about twenty miles distant from L——; there he had stayed a day or two, and there he said "that the Devil had told him to buy a case-knife, which he did." "He knew by that order that the Devil meant him to do something great." "His Master," as he called the fiend, then directed him the road he should take. He came to L——, put up, as he had correctly stated before, at a small inn, wandered at night about the town, was surprised by the sudden storm, took shelter under the convent arch, overheard somewhat more of my conversation with Sir Philip than he had previously deposed — heard enough to excite his curiosity as to the casket: " While he listened his Master told him that he must get possession of that casket." Sir Philip had quitted the archway almost immediately after I had done so, and he would then have attacked him if he had not caught sight of a policeman going his rounds. He had followed Sir Philip to a house (Mr. Jeeves's). "His Master told him to wait and watch." He did so. When Sir Philip came forth, towards the dawn, he followed him, saw him enter a narrow street, came up to him, seized him by the arm, demanded all he had about him. Sir Philip tried to shake him off — struck at him. What follows, I spare the reader. The deed was done. He robbed the dead man, both of the casket and of the purse that he found in the pockets; had scarcely done so when he heard footsteps. He had just time to get behind the portico of a detached house at angles with the street, when I came up. He witnessed, from his hiding-place, the brief conference between myself and the policemen, and when they moved on, bearing the body, stole unobserved away. He was going back towards the inn, when it occurred to him that it would be safer if the casket and purse were not about his person; that he asked his master to direct him how to dispose of them; that his Master guided him to an open yard (a stone-mason's) at a very little distance from the inn; that in this yard there stood an old wych-elm tree, from the gnarled roots of which the earth was worn away, leaving chinks and hollows, in one of which he placed the casket and purse, taking from the latter only two sovereigns and some silver, and then heaping loose mould over the hiding place. That he then repaired to his inn, and left it late in the morning, on the pretence of seeking for his relations — persons, indeed, who really had been related to him, but of whose death years ago he was aware. He returned to L—— a few days afterwards, and, in the dead of the night, went to take up the casket and the money. He found the purse with its contents undisturbed; but the lid of the casket was unclosed. From the hasty glance he had taken of it before burying it, it had seemed to him firmly locked — he was alarmed, lest some one had been to the spot. But his Master whispered to him never to mind, told him that he might now take the casket, and would be guided what to do with it; that he did so, and, opening the lid, found the casket empty; that he took the rest of the money out of the purse, but that he did not take the purse itself, for it had a crest and initials on it, which might lead to the discovery of what had been done; that he therefore left it in the hollow amongst the roots, heaping the mould over it as before; that, in the course of the day, he heard the people at the inn talk of the murder, and that his own first impulse was to get out of the town immediately, but that his Master made him too wise for that, and bade him stay; that passing through the streets, he saw me come out of the sash-window door, go to the stable yard on the other side of the house, mount on horseback and ride away; that he observed the sash-door was left partially open; that he walked by it and saw the room empty; there was only a dead wall opposite; the place was solitary, unobserved; that his Master directed him to lift up the sash gently, enter the room, and deposit the knife and the casket in a large walnut-tree bureau which stood unlocked near the window. All that followed — his visit to Mr. Vigors, his accusation against myself — his whole tale — was, he said, dictated by his Master, who was highly pleased with him, and promised to bring him safely through. And here he turned round with a hideous smile, as if for approbation of his notable cleverness and respect for his high employ.

Mr. Jeeves had the curiosity to request the keeper to inquire how, in what form, or in what manner, the Fiend appeared to the narrator, or conveyed his infernal dictates. The man at first refused to say; but it was gradually drawn from him that the Demon had no certain and invariable form; sometimes it appeared to him in the form of a rat; sometimes even of a leaf; or a fragment of wood, or a rusty nail; but, that his Master's voice always came to him distinctly, whatever shape he appeared in; only, he said, with an air of great importance, his Master, this time, had graciously condescended, ever since he left the asylum, to communicate with him in a much more pleasing and imposing aspect than he had ever done before — in the form of a beautiful youth, or, rather, like a bright rose-colored shadow, in which the features of a young man were visible, and that he had heard the voice more distinctly than usual, though in a milder tone, and seeming to come to him from a great distance.

After these revelations the man became suddenly disturbed. He shook from limb to limb, he seemed convulsed with terror; he cried out that he had betrayed the secret of his Master, who had warned him not to describe his appearance and mode of communication, or he would surrender his servant to the tormentors. Then the maniac's terror gave way to fury; his more direful propensity made itself declared; he sprang into the midst of his frightened listeners, seized Mr. Vigors by the throat, and would have strangled him but for the prompt rush of the superintendent and his satellites. Foaming at the mouth, and horribly raving, he was then manacled, a strait-waistcoat thrust upon him, and the group so left him in charge of his captors. Inquiries were immediately directed towards such circumstantial evidence as might corroborate the details he so minutely set forth. The purse recognized as Sir Philip's, by the valet of the deceased, was found buried under the wych-elm. A policeman despatched, express, to the town in which the maniac declared the knife to have been purchased, brought back word that a cutler in the place remembered perfectly to have sold such a knife to a sea-faring man, and identified the instrument when it was shown to him. From the chink of a door ajar, in the wall opposite my sash-window, a maid-servant, watching for her sweetheart (a young journeyman carpenter, who habitually passed that way on going home to dine), had, though unobserved by the murderer, seen him come out of my window at a time that corresponded with the dates of his own story, though she had thought nothing of it at the moment. He might be a patient, or have called on business; she did not know that I was from home. The only point of importance not cleared up was that which related to the opening of the casket — the disappearance of the contents; the lock had been unquestionably forced. No one, however, could suppose that some third person had discovered the hiding-place and forced open the casket to abstract its contents and then rebury it. The only probable supposition was, that the man himself had forced it open, and, deeming the contents of no value, had thrown them away before he had hidden the casket and purse, and, in the chaos of his reason, had forgotten that he had so done. Who could expect that every link in a madman's tale would be found integral and perfect? In short, little importance was attached to this solitary doubt. Crowds accompanied me to my door, when I was set free, in open court, stainless! — it was a triumphant procession. The popularity I had previously enjoyed, superseded for a moment by so horrible a charge, came back to me ten-fold, as with the reaction of generous repentance for a momentary doubt. One man shared the public favor — the young man whose acuteness had delivered me from the peril, and cleared the truth from so awful a mystery; but Margrave had escaped from congratulation and compliment; he had gone on a visit to Strahan, at Derval Court.

Alone, at last, in the welcome sanctuary of my own home, what were my thoughts? Prominent amongst them all was that assertion of the madman, which had made me shudder when repeated to me: he had been guided to the murder and to all the subsequent proceedings by the luminous shadow of the beautiful youth — the Scin-Læca to which I had pledged myself. If Sir Philip Derval could be believed, Margrave was possessed of powers, derived from fragmentary recollections of a knowledge acquired in a former state of being, which would render his remorseless intelligence infinitely dire, and frustrate the endeavors of a reason, unassisted by similar powers, to thwart his designs or bring the law against his crimes. Had he then the arts that could thus influence the minds of others to serve his fell purposes, and achieve securely his own evil ends through agencies that could not be traced home to himself?

But for what conceivable purpose had I been subjected as a victim to influences as much beyond my control as the Fate or Demoniac Necessity of a Greek Myth? In the legends of the classic world some august sufferer is oppressed by powers more than mortal, but, with an ethical if gloomy vindication of his, chastisement, he pays the penalty of crime committed by his ancestors or himself, or he has braved, by arrogating equality with the gods, the mysterious calamity which the gods alone can inflict. But I, no descendant of Penelope, no Œdipus boastful of a wisdom which could interpret the enigmas of the Sphynx, while ignorant even of his own birth — what had I done to be singled out from the herd of men for trials and visitations from the Shadowland of ghosts and sorcerers? It would be ludicrously absurd to suppose that Dr. Lloyd's dying imprecation could have had a prophetic effect upon my destiny—to believe that the pretences of mesmerisers were specially favored by Providence, and that to question their assumptions was an offence of profanation to be punished by exposure to preternatural agencies. There was not even that congruity between cause and effect which fable seeks in excuse for its inventions. Of all men living, I, unimaginative disciple of austere science, should be the last to become the sport of that witchcraft which even imagination reluctantly allows to the machinery of poets, and science casts aside into the mouldy lumber-room of obsolete superstition.

Rousing my mind from enigmas impossible to solve— it was with intense and yet most melancholy satisfaction that I turned to the image of Lilian, rejoicing, though with a thrill of awe, that the promise so mysteriously conveyed to my senses had, here too, been already fulfilled — Margrave had left the town; Lilian was no longer subjected to his evil fascination. But an instinct told me that that fascination had already produced an effect adverse to all hope of happiness for me. Lilian's love for myself was gone. Impossible otherwise that she — in whose nature I had always admired that generous devotion which is more or less inseparable from the romance of youth — should have never conveyed to me one word of consolation in the hour of my agony and trial: that she who, till the last evening we had met, had ever been so docile, in the sweetness of a nature femininely submissive to my slightest wish, should have disregarded my solemn injunction, and admitted Margrave to acquaintance, nay, to familiar intimacy; at the very time, too, when to disobey my injunctions was to embitter my ordeal, and add her own contempt to the degradation imposed upon my honor! No, her heart must be wholly gone from me; her very nature wholly warped. An union between us had become impossible. My love for her remained unshattered — the more tender, perhaps, for a sentiment of compassion. But my pride was shocked, my heart was wounded. My love was not mean and servile. Enough for me to think that she would be at least saved from Margrave. *Her* life associated with his! — contemplation, horrible and ghastly! — from that fate she was saved. Later, she would recover the effect of an influence happily brief. She might form some new attachment — some new tie. But love once withdrawn is never to be restored — and her love was withdrawn from me. I had but to release her, with my own lips, from our engagement—she would welcome that release. Mournful but firm in these thoughts and these resolutions, I sought Mrs. Ashleigh's house.

CHAPTER XLII.

It was twilight when I entered, unannounced (as had been my wont in our familiar intercourse), the quiet sitting-room in which I expected to find mother and child. But Lilian was there alone, seated by the open window, her hands crossed and drooping on her knee, her eyes fixed upon the darkening summer skies, in which the evening star had just stolen forth, bright and steadfast, near the pale sickle of a half-moon that was dimly visible, but gave as yet no light.

Let any lover imagine the reception he would expect to meet from his betrothed, coming into her presence after he had passed triumphant through a terrible peril to life and fame—conceive what ice froze my blood, what anguish weighed down my heart, when Lilian, turning towards me, rose not, spoke not—gazed at me heedlessly as if at some indifferent stranger—and—and—— But no matter. I cannot bear to recall it even now, at the distance of years! I sat down beside her, and took her hand, without pressing it; it rested languidly, passively in mine — one moment; — I dropped it then, with a bitter sigh.

"Lilian," I said, quietly, "you love me no longer. Is it not so?"

She raised her eyes to mine, looked at me wistfully, and pressed her hand on her forehead, then said, in a strange voice, "Did I ever love you? What do you mean?"

"Lilian, Lilian, rouse yourself; are you not, while you speak, under some spell, some influence which you cannot describe nor account for?"

She paused a moment before she answered, calmly, "No! Again I ask what do you mean?"

"What do I mean? Do you forget that we are betrothed? Do you forget how often, and how recently, our vows of affection and constancy have been exchanged?"

"No, I do not forget; but I must have deceived you and myself ——"

"It is true, then, that you love me no more?"

"I suppose so."

"But, oh, Lilian, is it that your heart is only closed to me? or is it — oh, answer truthfully — is it given to another? — to him — to him — against whom I warned you, whom I implored you not to receive? Tell me, at least, that your love is not gone to Margrave ——"

"To him — love to him. Oh no — no ——"

"What, then, is your feeling towards him?"

Lilian's face grew visibly paler — even in that dim

light. "I know not," she said, almost in a whisper; "but it is partly awe — partly ——"

"What!"

"Abhorrence!" she said, almost fiercely, and rose to her feet, with a wild, defying start.

"If that be so," I said gently, "you would not grieve were you never again to see him ——"

"But I shall see him again," she murmured in a tone of weary sadness, and sunk back once more into her chair.

"I think not," said I, "and I hope not. And now hear me and heed me, Lilian. It is enough for me, no matter what your feelings towards another, to learn from yourself that the affection you once professed for me is gone. I release you from your troth. If folks ask why we two henceforth separate the lives we had agreed to join, you may say, if you please, that you could not give your hand to a man who had known the taint of a felon's prison, even on a false charge. If that seems to you an ungenerous reason, we will leave it to your mother to find a better. Farewell! For your own sake I can yet feel happiness — happiness to hear that you did not love the man against whom I warn you still more solemnly than before! Will you not give me your hand in parting — and have I not spoken your own wish?"

She turned away her face, and resigned her hand to me in silence. Silently I held it in mine, and my emotions nearly stifled me. One symptom of regret, of reluctance, on her part, and I should have fallen at her feet, and cried, "Do not let us break a tie which our vows should have made indissoluble; heed not my offers — wrung from a tortured heart! You cannot have ceased to love me!" But no such symptom of relenting showed itself in her, and with a groan I left the room.

CHAPTER XLIII.

I WAS just outside the garden-door, when I felt an arm thrown round me, my cheek kissed and wetted with tears. Could it be Lilian? Alas, no! It was her mother's voice, that, between laughing and crying, exclaimed hysterically: "This is joy, to see you again, and on these thresholds. I have just come from your house; I went there on purpose to congratulate you, and to talk to you about Lilian. But you have seen her?"

"Yes; I have but this moment left her. Come this way." I drew Mrs. Ashleigh back into the garden, along the winding walk, which the shrubs concealed from view of the house. We sat down on a rustic seat where I had often sat with Lilian, midway between the house and the Monks' Well. I told the mother what had passed between me and her daughter; I made no complaint of Lilian's coldness and change; I did not hint at its cause. "Girls of her age will change," said

I, "and all that now remains is for us two to agree on such a tale to our curious neighbors, as may rest the whole blame on me. Man's Name is of robust fibre; it could not push its way to a place in the world, if it could not bear, without sinking, the load idle tongues may lay on it. Not so Woman's Name — what is but gossip against Man, is scandal against Woman."

"Do not be rash, my dear Allen," said Mrs. Ashleigh, in great distress: "I feel for you, I understand you; in your case I might act as you do. I cannot blame you. Lilian is changed — changed unaccountably. Yet sure I am that the change is only on the surface, that her heart is really yours, as entirely and as faithfully as ever it was; and that later, when she recovers from the strange, dreamy kind of torpor which appears to have come over all her faculties and all her affections, she would awake with a despair which you cannot conjecture, to the knowledge that you had renounced her."

"I have not renounced her," said I, impatiently; "I did but restore her freedom of choice. But pass by this now, and explain to me more fully the change in your daughter, which I gather from your words is not confined to me."

"I wished to speak of it before you saw her, and for that reason came to your house. It was on the morning in which we left her aunt's to return hither that I first noticed something peculiar in her look and manner. She seemed absorbed and absent, so much so that I asked her several times to tell me what made her so grave, but I could only get from her that she had had a confused dream that she could not recall distinctly enough to relate, but that she was sure it boded evil. During the journey she became gradually more herself, and began to look forward with delight to the idea of seeing you again. Well, you came that evening. What passed between you and her you know best. You complained that she slighted your request to shun all acquaintance with Mr. Margrave. I was surprised that, whether your wish were reasonable or not, she could have hesitated to comply with it. I spoke to her about it after you had gone, and she wept bitterly at thinking she had displeased you."

"She wept! You amaze me. Yet the next day what a note she returned to mine!"

"The next day the change in her became very visible to me. She told me, in an excited manner, that she was convinced she ought not to marry you. Then came, the following day, the news of your committal. I heard of it, but dared not break it to her. I went to our friend the mayor, to consult with him what to say, what to do; and to learn more distinctly than I had done from terrified, incoherent servants, the rights of so dreadful a story. When I returned, I found, to my amazement, a young stranger in the drawing-room; it was Mr. Margrave — Miss Brabazon had brought him at his request. Lilian was in the room, too, and my astonishment was increased, when she said to me with a singular smile, vague but tranquil: 'I know all about

Allen Fenwick; Mr. Margrave has told me all. He is a friend of Allen's. He says there is no cause for fear.' Mr. Margrave then apologized to me for his intrusion in a caressing, kindly manner, as if one of the family. He said he was so intimate with you that he felt that he could best break to Miss Ashleigh an information she might receive elsewhere, for that he was the only man in the town who treated the charge with ridicule. You know the wonderful charm of this young man's manner. I cannot explain to you how it was, but in a few moments I was as much at home with him as if he had been your brother. To be brief, having once come, he came constantly. He had moved, two days before you went to Derval Court, from his hotel to apartments in Mr. ——'s house, just opposite. We could see him on his balcony from our terrace; he would smile to us and come across. I did wrong in slighting your injunction, and suffering Lilian to do so. I could not help it, he was such a comfort to me — to her, too — in her tribulation. He alone had no doleful words, wore no long face; he alone was invariably cheerful. 'Everything,' he said, 'would come right in a day or two.'"

"And Lilian could not but admire this young man, he is so beautiful."

"Beautiful? Well, perhaps. But if you have a jealous feeling, you were never more mistaken. Lilian, I am convinced, does more than dislike him; he has inspired her with repugnance, with terror. And much as *I* own *I like* him, in his wild, joyous, careless, harmless way, do not think I flatter you if I say that Mr. Margrave is not the man to make any girl untrue to you — untrue to a lover with infinitely less advantages than you may pretend to. He would be an universal favorite, I grant; but there is something in him, or a something wanting in him, which makes liking and admiration stop short of love. I know not why; perhaps, because, with all his good humor, he is so absorbed in himself, so intensely egotistical — so light; were he less clever, I should say so frivolous. He could not make love, he could not say in the serious tone of a man in earnest, 'I love you.' He owned as much to me, and owned, too, that he knew not even what love was. As to myself — Mr. Margrave appears rich; no whisper against his character or his honor ever reached me. Yet were you out of the question, and were there no stain on his birth, nay, were he as high in rank and wealth as he is favored by Nature in personal advantages, I confess I could never consent to trust him with my daughter's fate. A voice at my heart would cry, 'No!' It may be an unreasonable prejudice, but I could not bear to see him touch Lilian's hand!

"Did she never, then — never suffer him even to take her hand?"

"Never. Do not think so meanly of her as to suppose that she could be caught by a fair face, a graceful manner. Reflect: just before, she had refused, for your sake, Ashleigh Sumner, whom Lady Haughton said, 'no girl in her senses could refuse;' and this change in Lilian really began before we returned to L——; before she had even seen Mr. Margrave. I am convinced it is something in the reach of your skill as physician — it is on the nerves, the system. I will give you a proof of what I say, only do not betray me to her. It was during your imprisonment, the night before your release, that I was awakened by her coming to my bedside. She was sobbing as if her heart would break. 'O mother, mother!' she cried, pity me, help me — I am so wretched.' 'What is the matter, darling?' 'I have been so cruel to Allen, and I know I shall be so again. I cannot help it. Do not question me; only if we are separated, if he cast me off, or I reject him, tell him some day — perhaps when I am in my grave — not to believe appearances; and that I, in my heart of hearts, never ceased to love him!'"

"She said that! You are not deceiving me?"

"Oh no! how can you think so?"

"There is hope still," I murmured; and I bowed my head upon my hands, hot tears forcing their way through the clasped fingers.

"One word more," said I; "you tell me that Lilian has a repugnance to this Margrave, and yet that she found comfort in his visits — a comfort that could not be wholly ascribed to cheering words he might say about myself, since it is all but certain that I was not, at that time, uppermost in her mind. Can you explain this apparent contradiction?"

"I cannot otherwise than by a conjecture which you would ridicule."

"I can ridicule nothing now. What is your conjecture?"

"I know how much you disbelieve in the stories one hears of animal magnetism and electro-biology, otherwise ——"

"You think that Margrave exercises some power of that kind over Lilian? Has he spoken of such a power?"

"Not exactly; but he said that he was sure Lilian possessed a faculty that he called by some hard name, not clairvoyance, but a faculty which he said, when I asked him to explain, was akin to prevision — to second sight. Then he talked of the Priestesses who had administered the ancient oracles. Lilian, he said, reminded him of them, with her deep eyes and mysterious smile."

"And Lilian heard him? What said she?"

"Nothing; she seemed in fear while she listened."

"He did not offer to try any of those arts practised by professional mesmerists and other charlatans?"

"I thought he was about to do so, but I forestalled him; saying I never would consent to any experiment of that kind, either on myself or my daughter."

"And he replied ——?"

"With his gay laugh, 'that I was very foolish; that a person possessed of such a faculty as he attributed to Lilian, would, if the faculty were developed, be an invaluable adviser.' He would have said more, but I begged him to desist. Still I fancy at times — do not be angry — that he does somehow or other bewitch her, unconsciously to herself; for she always knows when he is coming. Indeed, I am not sure that he does not bewitch myself, for I by no means justify my conduct in admitting him to an intimacy so familiar, and in spite of your wish; I have reproached myself, resolved to shut my door on him, or to show by my manner that his visits were unwelcome; yet when Lilian has said, in the drowsy lethargic tone which has come into her voice (her voice naturally earnest and impressive, though always low), 'Mother, he will be here in two minutes — I wish to leave the room and cannot,' — I, too, have felt as if something constrained me against my will; as if, in short, I were under that influence which Mr. Vigors — whom I will never forgive for his conduct to you — would ascribe to mesmerism. But will you not come in and see Lilian again?"

"No, not to-night; but watch and heed her, and if you see aught to make you honestly believe that she regrets the rupture of the old tie from which I have released her — why, you know, Mrs. Ashleigh, that — that — " My voice failed — I wrung the good woman's hand, and went my way.

I had always till then considered Mrs. Ashleigh — if not as Mrs. Poyntz described her — "commonplace weak" — still of an intelligence somewhat below mediocrity. I now regarded her with respect as well as grateful tenderness; her plain sense had divined what all my boasted knowledge had failed to detect in my earlier intimacy with Margrave — viz. that in him there was a something present, or a something wanting, which forbade love and excited fear. Young, beautiful, wealthy, seemingly blameless in life as he was, she would not have given her daughter's hand to him!

CHAPTER XLIV.

THE next day my house was filled with visitors. I had no notion that I had so many friends. Mr. Vigors wrote me a generous and handsome letter, owning his prejudices against me on account of his sympathy with poor Dr. Lloyd, and begging my pardon for what he now felt to have been harshness, if not distorted justice. But what most moved me, was the entrance of Strahan, who rushed up to me with the heartiness of old college days. "Oh, my dear Allen, can you ever forgive me; that I should have disbelieved your word — should have suspected you of abstracting my poor cousin's memoir?"

"Is it found, then?"

"Oh, yes; you must thank Margrave. He, clever fellow, you know, came to me on a visit yesterday. He put me at once on the right scent. Only guess; but you never can! It was that wretched old housekeeper who purloined the manuscript. You remember she came into the room while you were looking at the memoir. She heard us talk about it; her curiosity was roused; she longed to know the history of her old master, under his own hand; she could not sleep; she heard me go up to bed; she thought you might leave the book on the table when you, too, went to rest. She stole down stairs, peeped through the keyhole of the library, saw you asleep, the book lying before you, entered, took away the book softly, meant to glance at its contents and to return it. You were sleeping so soundly she thought you would not wake for an hour; she carried it into the library, leaving the door open, and there began to pore over it; she stumbled first on one of the passages in Latin; she hoped to find some part in plain English, turned over the leaves, putting her candle close to them, for the old woman's eyes were dim, when she heard you make some sound in your sleep. Alarmed, she looked round; you were moving uneasily in your seat, and muttering to yourself. From watching you she was soon diverted by the consequence of her own confounded curiosity and folly. In moving, she had unconsciously brought the poor manuscript close to the candle; the leaves caught the flame; her own cap and hand burning first made her aware of the mischief done. She threw down the book; her sleeve was in flames; she had first to tear off the sleeve, which was, luckily for her, not sewn to her dress. By the time she recovered presence of mind to attend to the book, half its leaves were reduced to tinder. She did not dare then to replace what was left of the manuscript on your table; returned, with it, to her room, hid it, and resolved to keep her own secret. I should never have guessed it; I had never even spoken to her of the occurrence; but when I talked over the disappearance of the book to Margrave last night, and expressed my disbelief of your story, he said in his merry way: 'But do you think that Fenwick is the only person curious about your cousin's odd ways and strange history? Why, every servant in the household would have been equally curious. You have examined your servants of course?' 'No, I never thought of it.' 'Examine them now, then. Examine especially that old housekeeper. I observe a great change in her manner since I came here, weeks ago, to look over the house. She has something on her mind — I see it in her eyes.' Then it occurred to me, too, that the woman's manner had altered, and that she seemed always in a tremble and a fidget. I went at once to her room, and charged her with stealing the book. She fell on her knees, and told the whole story as I have told it to you, and as I shall take care to tell it to all to whom I have so foolishly blabbed my yet more foolish suspicions of yourself. But can you forgive me, old friend?"

"Heartily, heartily! And the book is burned?"

"See;" and he produced a mutilated manuscript. Strange, the part burned — reduced, indeed, to tinder — was the concluding part that related to Haroun — to

Grayle; no vestige of that part was left; the earlier portions were scorched and mutilated, though in some places still decipherable; but as my eye hastily ran over those places, I saw only mangled sentences of the experimental problems which the writer had so minutely elaborated.

"Will you keep the manuscript as it is, and as long as you like?" said Strahan.

"No, no; I will have nothing more to do with it. Consult some other man of science. And so this is the old woman's whole story? No accomplice — none? No one else shared her curiosity and her task?"

"No. Oddly enough, though, she made much the same excuse for her pitiful folly that the madman made for his terrible crime; she said, 'the Devil put it into her head.' Of course he did, as he puts everything wrong into one's head. That does not mend the matter."

"How! did she, too, say she saw a Shadow and heard a voice?"

"No; not such a liar as that, and not mad enough for such a lie. But she said that when she was in bed, thinking over the book, something irresistible urged her to get up and go down into the study; swore she felt something lead her by the hand; swore, too, that when she first discovered the manuscript was not in English, something whispered in her ear to turn over the leaves and approach them to the candle. But I had no patience to listen to all this rubbish. I sent her out of the house, bag and baggage. But, alas! is this to be the end of all my wise cousin's grand discoveries?"

True, of labors that aspired to bring into the chart of science new worlds, of which even the traditionary rumor was but a voice from the land of fable — nought left but broken vestiges of a daring footstep! The hope of a name imperishable amidst the loftiest hierarchy of Nature's secret temple, with all the pomp of recorded experiment, that applied to the mysteries of Egypt and Chaldæa the inductions of Bacon, the tests of Liebig — was there nothing left of this but what, here and there, some puzzled student might extract, garbled, mutilated, perhaps unintelligible, from shreds of sentences, wrecks of problems! O mind of man, can the works, on which thou wouldst found immortality below, be annulled into smoke and tinder by an inch of candle in the hand of an old woman!

When Strahan left me, I went out, but not yet to visit patients. I stole through by-paths into the fields; I needed solitude to bring my thoughts into shape and order. What was delusion, and what not? — was I right, or the Public? Was Margrave really the most innocent and serviceable of human beings, kindly affectionate, employing a wonderful acuteness for benignant ends? Was I, in truth, indebted to him for the greatest boon one man can bestow on another? For life rescued, for fair name justified? Or had he, by some demoniac sorcery, guided the hand of the murderer against the life of the person who alone could imperil his own? had he, by the same dark spells, urged the woman to the act that had destroyed the only record of the monstrous being — the only evidence that I was not the sport of an illusion in the horror with which he inspired me?

But if the latter supposition could be admissible, did he use his agents only to betray them afterwards to exposure, and that, without any possible clue to his own detection as the instigator? Then, there came over me confused recollections of tales of mediæval witchcraft, which I had read in boyhood. Were there not on judicial record, attestation and evidence, solemn and circumstantial, of powers analogous to those now exercised by Margrave? Of sorcerers instigating to sin through influences ascribed to Demons — making their apparitions glide through guarded walls, their voices heard from afar in the solitude of dungeons or monastic cells? subjugating victims to their will, by means which no vigilance could have detected, if the victims themselves had not confessed the witchcraft that had ensnared — courting a sure and infamous death in that confession — preferring such death to a life so haunted? Were stories so gravely set forth in the pomp of judicial evidence, and in the history of times comparatively recent, indeed, to be massed — pell-mell together, as a *moles indigesta* of senseless superstition — all the witnesses to be deemed liars? all the victims and tools of the sorcerers, lunatics? all the examiners or judges, with their solemn gradations — lay and clerical — from commissions of Inquiry to Courts of Appeal — to be despised for credulity, loathed for cruelty; or, amidst records so numerous, so imposingly attested — were there the fragments of a terrible truth? And had our ancestors been so unwise in those laws we now deem so savage, by which the world was rid of scourges more awful and more potent than the felon with his candid dagger? Fell instigators of the evil in men's secret hearts — shaping into action the vague, half-formed desire, and guiding with agencies, impalpable, unseen, their spell-bound instruments of calamity and death.

Such were the gloomy questions that I — by repute, the sternest advocate of common sense against fantastic errors — by profession, the searcher into flesh and blood, and tissue, and nerve, and sinew, for the causes of all that disease the mechanism of the universal human frame; — I, self-boasting physician, sceptic, philosopher, materialist — revolved, not amidst gloomy pines, under grim winter skies, but as I paced slow through laughing meadows, and by the banks of merry streams, in the ripeness of the golden August; the hum of insects in the fragrant grass, the flutter of birds amid the delicate green of boughs chequered by playful sunbeams and gentle shadows, and ever in sight of the resorts of busy work-day man. Walls, roof-tops, church-spires rising high. There, white and modern, the handwriting of our race, in this practical nineteenth century, on its square, plain masonry and Doric shafts, the Town-Hall, central in the animated market-place. And I — I — prying into long-neglected corners and dust-holes of memory for what my reason had flung there as worthless rubbish; reviving the jargon of French law, in the *procès verbal,* against a Gille de Retz, or an Urbain Grandier, and sifting the equity of sentences on witchcraft!

Bursting the links of this ghastly soliloquy with a laugh at my own folly, I struck into a narrow path that led back towards the city, by a quiet and rural suburb: the path wound on through a wide and solitary churchyard at the base of the Abbey-hill. Many of the former dwellers on that eminence now slept in the lowly burial-ground at its foot. And the place, mournfully decorated with the tombs which still mark distinctions of rank amidst the levelling democracy of the grave, was kept trim with the care which comes half from piety, and half from pride.

I seated myself on a bench, placed between the clipped yew-trees that bordered the path from the entrance to the church-porch; deeming vaguely that my own perplexing thoughts might imbibe a quiet from the quiet of the place.

"And oh," I murmured to myself, "oh that I had one bosom friend to whom I might freely confide all these torturing riddles which I cannot solve — one who could read my heart; light up its darkness; exorcise its spectres; one in whose wisdom I could welcome a guide through the Nature which now suddenly changes her aspect, opening out from the walls with which I had fenced and enclosed her as mine own formal garden — all her pathways, therein, trimmed to my footstep; all her blooms grouped and harmonized to my own taste in color; all her groves, all her caverns, but the soothing retreats of a Muse or a Science; opening out — opening out, desert on desert, into clueless and measureless space! Gone is the Garden? Were its confines too narrow for Nature? Be it so! The Desert replaces the garden, but where ends the Desert? Reft from my senses are the laws which gave order and place to their old, questionless realm. I stand lost and appalled amidst Chaos. Did my mind misconstrue the laws it deemed fixed and immutable? Be it so! But still Nature cannot be lawless; Creation is not a Chaos. If my senses deceive me in some things, they are still unerring in others; if thus, in some things, fallacious, still, in other things, truthful. Are there within me senses finer than those I have cultured, or without me vistas of knowledge which instincts, apart from my senses, divine? So long as I deal with the Finite alone, my senses suffice me; but when the Infinite is obtruded upon me, there are my senses faithless deserters? If so, is there aught else in my royal resources of Man

— whose ambition it is, from the first dawn of his glory as thinker, to invade, and to subjugate Nature — is there aught else to supply the place of those traitors, the senses, who report to my Reason, their judge and their sovereign, as truths, seen and heard, tales which my Reason forfeits her sceptre if she does not disdain as lies? Oh, for a friend! oh, for a guide!"

And as I so murmured, my eye fell upon the form of a kneeling child — at the farther end of the burial-ground, beside a grave with its new headstone gleaming white amidst the older moss-grown tombs, a female child, her head bowed, her hands clasped. I could see but the outline of her small form in its sable dress — an infant beside the dead.

My eye and my thoughts were turned from that silent figure, too absorbed in my own restless tumult of doubt and dread, for sympathy with the grief or the consolation of a kneeling child. And yet I should have remembered that tomb! Again I murmured with a fierce impatience, "Oh, for a friend! oh, for a guide!"

I heard steps on the walk under the yews. And an old man came in sight, slightly bent, with long, grey hair, but still with enough of vigor for years to come, in his tread, firm, though slow — in the unshrunken muscle of his limbs and the steady light of his clear, blue eye. I started. Was it possible? That countenance, marked, indeed, with the lines of laborious thought, but sweet in the mildness of humanity, and serene in the peace of conscience! I could not be mistaken. Julius Faber was before me. The profound pathologist, to whom my own proud self-esteem acknowledged inferiority, without humiliation; the generous benefactor to whom I owed my own smoothed entrance into the arduous road of fame and fortune. I had longed for a friend, a guide; what I sought stood suddenly at my side.

END OF VOLUME FIRST.

www.ingramcontent.com/pod-product-compliance
Lightning Source LLC
LaVergne TN
LVHW020117110826
845151LV00001B/189

* 9 7 8 1 4 2 5 5 4 2 1 5 3 *